# THE
# ESSENTIAL
# ENGLISHMAN

Lord Ribblesdale, painted by John Singer Sargent as
the epitome of the English gentleman.

# THE
# ESSENTIAL
# ENGLISHMAN

———— • ————

*compiled by*
*Nicolas Soames*
*and*
*Duncan Steen*

CASSELL

**Cassell Publishers Ltd**
Artillery House, Artillery Row
London SW1P 1RT

First published 1989

Distributed in the United States
by Sterling Publishing Co. Inc
387 Park Avenue South, New York, NY 10016–8810

Distributed in Australia by
Capricorn Link (Australia) Pty Ltd
PO Box 665, Lane Cove, NSW 2066

**British Library Cataloguing in Publication Data**
The essential Englishman.
1. English persons. National characteristics
I. Soames, Nicolas    II. Steen, Duncan
155.8'9'42

ISBN 0 304 31829 9

Designed by Vaughan Allen
Typeset in Linotype Cheltenham by Fakenham Photosetting Ltd,
Fakenham, Norfolk
Printed and bound in Great Britain by Richard Clay,
Bungay, Suffolk

# CONTENTS

The Englishman's home—in fantasy, at least—probably looks
very like Malvern Hall, painted amid a rural
arcadia by Constable.

# INTRODUCTION

There is no watertight excuse for this book. It strolls impertinently over ground that has been carefully mapped by the qualified authorities and elegantly appreciated by many devoted amateurs. Its purview is ludicrously broad—nothing less than an exhibition of the Englishman in his more characteristic manifestations through the ages. It is also based on an idea that might have seemed stale even 50 years ago, when, in the last days of a vast and tottering Empire, the national character was rather self-consciously gathering its forces, like the blind Samson, for its final self-destroying effort.

It is, wriggle out of it as we would, a hopelessly, damnably patriotic book. However, it is our opinion that the evils of nationalism, cultural hostility, race hatred and fear of social change are best countered by an open regard for the values of one's own society and a cheerful celebration of its virtues—and, on this basis, an honest recognition of its failures and weaknesses. Now that the British imperial bubble has been well and truly burst it is perhaps time to drop the adolescent posture of esteeming anyone except those who have made us and given us whatever freedoms we have. To pretend to appreciate another culture without appreciating one's own implies a psychological dislocation that is even more unhealthy than the doctrine of 'my country right or wrong'.

Pride may be a deadly sin, but unless the whole country should enjoy a sudden and totally unprecedented access of compassion, it will be found that pride, from time to time, can be made to serve a useful function, so that a proud people, conscious perhaps of some occasionally honourable showing in its long history, becomes simply ashamed to put up with poverty, squalor and injustice, with bigotry, cowardice and greed. And patriotism is certainly not dead. It is just that it now generally finds its expression on the sports pages, where we may still watch England going down with her colours nailed to the mast. 'I did my best, but that's cricket,' as Frank Bruno said after his attempt at the world heavyweight title.

The essential Englishman is not the eternal Englishman. In every century he will be found throwing his weight around in quite a different style. The common thread differs from the Russian 'soul', the German sense of destiny and the French *esprit*. It is instead perhaps the English 'character'—not as a fixed attitude, but as a sense of individualism. Someone once said that only in England would John Donne's proposition that 'No man is an island' be counted a paradox.

Like all things, however, the Englishman is impermanent. But, in the mess that dying cultures and empires leave behind, potent seeds are sometimes sown. For example, we can just glimpse, through the mists and forests of late-fifth-century England, after the legions had long gone, the last Roman Britons briefly holding back the tide of heathen barbarians in a hopeless struggle to maintain the vestiges of civilization. The chap in charge of those Britons used Roman cavalry tactics and probably thought of himself as, essentially, Roman. As King Arthur, however, he contributed to the essential Englishman some of his more honourable manifestations, and, as a mystical personification of the land itself, inspired an early national identity. Similarly patriotism—'Englishness'—is less important than the principles and individuals it has called forth . . . not to mention the qualities to inspire other peoples and the blunders to warn them.

It has been said that England is a country in the North Sea governed by Scotsmen. And many of our essential Englishmen are indeed Scots, Irish or Welsh. There is no way out of this. Indeed, a good many Englishmen nowadays can claim to be Caribbean, African or Pakistani. Racial purity is simply not English. So why is this book not called something like *The Essential Brit?* Because we don't want to subsume the essential individuality of the Scots, Irish and Welsh beneath the character of the dominant power.

Women are deliberately excluded, because to do them proper justice in a patriarchal society would require a deeper investigation than we have attempted. For the same sorts of reason certain everyday features of the English experience have been neglected or ignored completely, particularly work and domestic life. Donald Horne, in *God is an Englishman*, divides the English identity into two:

> In the 'Northern Metaphor' Britain is pragmatic, empirical, calculating, Puritan, bourgeois, enterprising, adventurous, scientific, serious, and believes in struggle. Its sinful excess is a ruthless avarice, rationalized in the belief that the prime impulse in all human beings is a rational, calculating, economic self-interest.
>
> In the 'Southern Metaphor' Britain is romantic, illogical, muddled, divinely lucky, Anglican, aristocratic, traditional, frivolous, and believes in order and tradition. Its sinful excess is a ruthless pride, rationalized in the belief that men are born to serve.

The 'northern metaphor' may be said to be British, and the 'southern metaphor' English. Both are essential and both are represented here: the Englishman is

The death of Harold, from the Bayeux tapestry. As the last ruler of
England to let in an invader, Harold lost honourably in the very last
stages of the match—a very English tradition. The episode was even
more English in that the sturdily traditional Saxon infantry tactics
were unsportingly defeated by the newfangled continental system
of armoured cavalry.

either a Roundhead or a Cavalier. But the 'southern metaphor' is the one with the
best tunes, and it is the one that dominates this book.

*The Essential Englishman* is a celebration and a distraction, rather than a
critique, and a tone of levity has been allowed to creep in even when treating
serious matters. How, for example, could the Englishman's equivocal conception of his liberty be more succinctly put than in this soliloquy, written by Marriott
Edgar, for Stanley Holloway?

*9*

> And it's through that there Magna Charter,
> As were signed by the Barons of old,
> That in England to-day we can do what we like,
> So long as we do what we're told.

Basically, we'll be happy if we can stiffen a few upper lips and insert a few spines where there were none before, and encourage the Englishman to take a more positive and responsible attitude towards his own patriotism—which is not about conquest and holding one's head up in the world's counting houses. As John Masefield wrote in *Sea Life in Nelson's Time*,

> It is not a song in the street, and a wreath on a column, and a flag flying from a window, and a pro-Boer under a pump. It is a thing very holy, and very terrible, like life itself. It is a burden to be borne: a thing to labour and to die for; a thing which gives no happiness and no pleasantness—but a hard life, an unknown grave, and the respect and bared heads of those who follow.

At the same time, it has not always been possible to dissociate ourselves from the sort of deplorable sentiments expressed in Michael Flanders' and Donald Swann's *Song of Patriotic Prejudice*:

> And all the world over each nation's the same—
> They've simply no notion of Playing the Game;
> They argue with Umpires, they cheer when they've won,
> And they practice beforehand, which spoils all the fun!
> The English, the English, the English are best!
> So up with the English and down with the rest!

In addition we have sounded an occasional note of querulous nostalgia:

> Say, is there Beauty yet to find?
> And Certainty? And Quiet kind?
> Deep meadows yet, for to forget
> The lies, and truths, and pain? . . . oh! yet
> Stands the Church clock at ten to three?
> And is there honey still for tea?

> Rupert Brooke, 'The Old Vicarage, Grantchester'

But this is a gentrified version of a pretty persistent attitude of griping melancholy that is inescapably English, from the doleful anxieties of Anglo-Saxon seafarers right up to the present day.

Finally, we would prefer in general to sidestep the great matter of the English *gentleman*, mainly because he himself rebuffs any attempt at classification—perhaps his most essentially English aspect. We certainly hold no particular brief for him. Rupert Brooke's winning fantasy, in *The Life and Death of John*

*Rump*, of the English gentleman who looks upon the face of God and is unimpressed is a pleasing balance to the poet's celebrated sonnet:

GOD John Rump, of Balham, Leeds, and Canterbury,
Why are you wearing hideous black clothes?
RUMP Because I am an English Gentleman.
GOD John Rump, we gave you life and all its wonder.
What splendid tidings have you got to tell?
RUMP God, I have been an English Gentleman.
GOD Infinite splendour has been in your power;
John Rump, what have you got to show for life?
RUMP God, I have been an English Gentleman.
GOD (*rising angrily*) Was it for this we sent you to the world,
And gave you life and knowledge, made you man,
Crowned you with glory? You could have worked and laughed,
Sung, loved, and kissed, made all the world a dream,
Found infinite beauty in a leaf or word . . .
. . . Perish eternally, you and your hat!
RUMP (*not wincing*) You long haired aesthetes, get you out of heaven!
I, John Rump, I, an English Gentleman,
Do not believe in you and all your gushing.
I am John Rump, this is my hat, and this
My umbrella. I stand here for sense,
Invincible, inviolable, eternal,
For safety, regulations, paving-stones,
Street lamps, police, and bijou-residences
Semi-detached. I stand for sanity,
Comfort, content, prosperity, top-hats,
Alcohol, collars, meat. Tariff Reform
Means higher wages and more work for all.

(As he speaks, GOD and the seraphic multitude grow faint, mistier and mistier, become ineffectually waving shadows, and vanish. The floor of Heaven rocks . . . the thrones and the glassy sea . . . all has vanished. JOHN RUMP remains, still and expressionless, leaning on his umbrella, growing larger and larger, infinitely menacing, filling the universe, blotting out the stars . . .)

Oliver Twist asks for more. Illustration by George Cruikshank. In
nineteenth century England the education of children was a hit or
miss affair — usually miss, unless you were the hero of a Dickens
novel. Meanwhile, Palmerston was enthralling the House of Commons
with a vision of England as the hope of the 'desperate and forlorn'
throughout the world.

———— • ————

# CHAPTER ONE

# THE ENGLISHMAN'S SALAD DAYS

Generations of cunning and vicious school-children have learnt, a little late in the day, that

> . . . trailing clouds of glory do we come
>     From God, who is our home:
> Heaven lies about us in our infancy!
> Shades of the prison-house begin to close
>     Upon the growing Boy
> But he beholds the light, and whence it flows,
>     He sees it in his joy;
> The Youth, who daily farther from the east
>     Must travel, still is Nature's Priest,
>     And by the vision splendid
>     Is on his way attended . . .
>
> Wordsworth, 'Intimations of Immortality'

In fact, this 'vision splendid' is not encouraged to linger in the consciousness of a growing English boy. All too soon he is uniformed, tying knots, rubbing sticks together, getting badges for hiking, and generally taking a less priestly and more resourceful interest in Nature. With the famous two-fingered salute of the Cub scouts, he firmly declares 'We'll do our best!' or, more enigmatically, 'Dyb, dyb, dyb; dob, dob, dob.'

Nevertheless, parental slushiness cannot be helped. Hartley Coleridge is known to posterity as the prattling child of Wordsworth's friend Coleridge:

> Sunday—Dec. 21, 1799, Hartley said—When I'm a man, I'll get a Ladder, & get up to the Sky, & pick out the Stars, & give them to Anny Sealy—I'll pick 'em out with a knife—
>
> Coleridge, *The Notebooks*

Hartley Coleridge was fortunate that his father was not inspired to set his captivating chatter to verse and accompany it with enchanting illustrations, as did the father of Christopher Robin Milne:

> Hush! Hush! Whisper who dares!
> Christopher Robin is saying his prayers.

A. A. Milne, Now We Are Six, 1927

# AWAY TO SCHOOL

Eventually boys refuse to say they believe in fairies, and are unmoved by the imminent demise of Tinker-Bell. And the paternal Englishman, having tenderly admired his son go 'hoppity, hoppity, hoppity, hoppity, hoppity, hoppity *hop*', is visited with the atavistic urge to send him away to be flogged and brutalized for a decade or so. It is hard to appreciate that this is for the boy's own good. A Venetian diplomat observed in 1497:

> The want of affection in the English is strongly manifested towards their children . . . they put them out, both males and females, to hard service in the houses of other people . . . And these are called apprentices, and during that time they perform all the most menial offices; and few are born who are exempted from this fate, for every one, however rich he may be, sends away his children into the houses of others, whilst he, in return, receives those of strangers into his own. And on inquiring their reason for this severity, they answered that they did it in order that their children might learn better manners.

Andrea Trevisano, Italian Relation of England

Sometimes even Englishmen are obtuse enough to complain:

> Suddenly . . . they are whisked off to places of dreary internment, where the most extraordinary tribal values and standards prevail . . . until such time as their characters have been formed in the same hard, dense and unpleasant mould as that of those who teach them.

Osbert Sitwell, 'On Private Schools', 1935

Of course, Sitwell is here speaking about the very best schools. More modest establishments could not be expected to match their standards. Dotheboys Hall, where the eponymous hero of Dickens's novel *Nicholas Nickleby* (1838–9) is employed by Wackford Squeers and his lady wife, does not attempt to. More than ample in its provision of brutality and 'brimstone and treacle', its pupils nevertheless do not emerge, if they emerge at all, with the éclat that a really good school confers. And there were many places like Dotheboys Hall, run, as

Dickens remarked in his Preface to the novel, by 'ignorant, sordid, brutal men, to whom few considerate persons would have entrusted the board and lodging of a horse or a dog'.

Expensive schools, run by scholars and gentlemen, are not the same at all, notwithstanding the sort of judgment Stephen Spender passes on his old preparatory school: 'It would have surprised my parents to have known that they might just as well have had me educated at a brothel for flagellants as at the school referred to . . .'

So intrinsic to the Englishman's education is a good beating that in medieval times a master of grammar at Cambridge, on being presented with the insignia of his office, a psalter and a birch, was obliged to demonstrate his aptitude for his vocation by beating a boy on the spot—the boy getting fourpence for his pains.

Any repugnance a schoolmaster might feel for his sad duty would soon wear off. In his *The Compleat Gentleman* (1622) Henry Peacham confides, 'I knew one, who in Winter would ordinarily in a cold morning, whip his Boyes over for no other purpose than to get himselfe a heat.'

There was little incentive to develop more imaginative teaching methods, because few Englishmen looked back on 'a cruel and capricious pedagogue' (Gibbon) with much rancour. Coleridge, when he heard that his vicious old headmaster was on his death-bed, prayed:

> . . . may all his faults be forgiven; and may he be wafted to bliss by little cherub boys, all head and wings, with no *bottoms* to reproach his sublunary infirmities.
>
> Charles Lamb, 'Christ's Hospital Five and Thirty Years Ago',
> from *The Essays of Elia*, 1823

By contrast, in his *Reminiscences and Recollections 1810–1860*, Captain Rees Howell Gronow records the case of a naval man who had been given the command of a frigate and who was unable to resist the opportunity for delayed revenge offered by his jurisdiction. He invited his old teacher, Dr Busby, headmaster of Westminster School during the reign of Charles II, aboard for dinner. Instead of dinner, the pedagogue was treated to two dozen lashes. A pleasing tale, but it is significant that the schoolmaster walked straight into the trap, never considering for a moment that his former pupils might regard him with anything other than fond affection.

The great and much loved Dr John Keate (1773–1852), headmaster of Eton in the early part of the nineteenth century, flogged an average of ten boys a day—except Sundays, when he took a rest. By this time wholesale beating was a public business, appreciated by one and all as a golden thread in the rich tapestry of school life. Over the years a certain ceremony inevitably developed.

With exquisite civility a boy would be invited to submit to discipline. After a regulated number of strokes he would rise from his posture of humiliation and state of undress, and offer thanks for his correction. And his chastiser, rather than admit that the pleasure was all his, would attempt to give the impression that the whole procedure had been as distressing to him as it must have been for his victim. The moral balance restored, they would shake hands. There is evidence to suggest that it was commonly a refreshing and stimulating experience for both parties.

Many Old Boys naturally felt something missing in their lives ever afterwards. The dignified ritual of a flogging at a good public school left some communicants with a sense of having participated at some high and holy rite:

> From the moment the accolade has been laid—not across your shoulders —you are a member of a sort of strange order of Chivalry . . . To have been flogged, in accordance with traditions laid down from our antiquity . . . was to receive an indelible hallmark . . .

Leslie Stephen, 'Thoughts of an Outsider: Public Schools', 1873

# A LESSON IN SURVIVAL

The English are a kindly people. But, in order to get on and make their mark, they need also to be very insensitive. After all, their hegemony among the trading nations of the world was accomplished through the ruin of countless children's lives. It is the business of a good school to inure a boy to not only his own pain but also that of others. In this, as in other respects, the English resemble the Japanese.

'Now, when *I* was a boy . . .' is the oft-heard preamble to reminiscences of unlikely privations and unpleasant tribal initiations. The implication is always: 'Well, it didn't do *me* any harm.' In his *Essay on Education* (1802) the Reverend William Barrow records approvingly the peppery predication of an eighteenth-century naval officer: 'Were it not . . . for the dormitory at Westminster and the quarter-deck of a man of war, we should soon be a nation of macaronies.'

The Englishman wears his childhood like a campaign medal. Some childhoods carry more honour than others. The zinc tub on the hearth, bread and dripping (if you were quick and lucky), heartless landlords and pawnbrokers, gritty laconic repartee, scrubbed doorsteps and steep cobbled streets, the crowds of anxious womenfolk at the pit-head, the hard-won scholarship to the local grammar, the confrontation with the sneering son of the mill-owner—this is the sort of upbringing which, in recollection, gives a man an assurance equal to that of any public-school Old Boy, for it carries the essential stamp of the ideal English education. It is purgatorial and character-forming. It is about survival.

Public schools offered training in psychological survival and in the government of primitive societies. However, this could never be made quite as practical as the education in sheer physical survival received by the victims of England's precocious urbanization:

> Such was the nameless one of whom we speak. We cannot say he thrived; but he would not die. So, at two years of age, his mother being lost sight of, and the weekly payment having ceased, he was sent out in the street to 'play', in order to be run over. Even this expedient failed . . . They gave him no food: he foraged for himself, and shared with the dogs the garbage of the streets. But he still lived; stunted and pale, he defied even the fatal fever which was the only inhabitant of his cellar that never quitted it.

This early life of an orphan, as described by Benjamin Disraeli in his novel of the 'Two Nations' (the rich and the poor), *Sybil* (1845), exhibits just the sort of pluck that expensive schools were expected to draw out of their charges.

In Thomas Hughes's *Tom Brown's Schooldays* (1857) we find that, on his first day at school, Tom took part in the great school-house football match. In the early nineteenth century this was a manly and straightforward battle between two armies, each mustering a hundred or two.

> And here they are amongst us. Meet them like Englishmen, you School-house boys, and charge them home. Now is the time to show what mettle is in you—and there shall be a warm seat by the hall fire, and honour, and lots of bottled-beer to-night, for him who does his duty in the next half-hour . . .

The gentlest of controversialists may recall the real satisfaction of carrying a dispute to the noble level of fisticuffs. The Rev. J. Matthews was marked for life during a fight he had with another boy at Shrewsbury School over the merits of Dr Samuel Butler's edition of Aeschylus. And Thomas Hughes blustered in *Tom Brown's Schooldays* (1857) that 'After all, what would life be without fighting, I should like to know? Every one who is worth his salt has his enemies . . . who will not let him live his life in quiet till he has thrashed them.'

Public-school life during the nineteenth century was a matter of barbaric splendour, replete with cruel tyranny and abject slavery, tribal loyalties, arcane and savage rituals, high chivalry, rebellion, battle and drunken carousing. At an English public school the slavery and the tyranny were real: there was no one to say: 'It doesn't matter. It's only a game.'

The whole system of prefects wielding absolute authority over lesser mortals began—naturally enough for the English—as a measure to cut costs. 'Nobody could have guessed' wrote Leslie Stephen in his essay on public schools, 'that an ideal education would be provided by bringing together a few hundred lads and requesting them to govern themselves.'

The unlikely truth was that, as Talleyrand admitted, '*La meilleure éducation, c'est l'education Publique Anglaise; et c'est détestable.*' Detestable because it was not theoretical: it was a practical education, hung on a very slender academic framework. For example, Tom Brown's father did not ask much of his son's school: 'If he'll only turn out a brave, helpful, truth-telling Englishman, and a gentleman, and a Christian, that's all I want.' As a realist, he did not expect an attempt to be made to train his son's mind.

The Normans prided themselves on their ignorance. In his book *The English* (1984) Christopher Hibbert cites an unidentified gentleman at a medieval banquet: 'I swear by God's body I'd rather my sons should hang than study letters. For it becomes the sons of gentlemen to blow the horn sweetly, to hunt cunningly, and elegantly carry and train a hawk. But the study of letters should be left to the sons of rustics.'

Roger Ascham, in 'The Scholemaster' (1570), noted the same values operating in his own century: 'It is pitie, that commonlie more care is had, yea and that emonges verie wise men, to find out rather a cunnynge man for their horse than a cunnynge man for their children.' And these principles still apply in the twentieth century, if the cheery prediction that follows the unfortunate hero of Evelyn Waugh's *Decline and Fall* out of Oxford is anything to go by: 'I expect you'll be becoming a schoolmaster, sir. That's what most of the gentlemen does, sir, that gets sent down for indecent behaviour.'

## SCHOOL VICES AND VALUES

The vigorous tradition of pederasty in English schools goes back at least as far as the early sixteenth century, when the headmaster of Eton, Nicholas Udall, was imprisoned for buggery. He was later appointed headmaster of Westminster. Just as surprising is the fact that, while public schools were notorious for being 'nurseries of all vice and immorality', as Henry Fielding summed them up in *Joseph Andrews* (1742), they somehow garnered a reputation as a forcing house for stout, honest, God-fearing Englishmen. Two putative reasons for this mental aberration come to mind. First, a public school was meant to offer a trial run at life: if one was going to be *sans peur et sans reproche* in later life, one probably needed to spend a few years being dastardly. As hinted by the title of Henry Drummond's uplifting tale for boys, 'Baxter's Second Innings' (1892), a public-school man got a second chance. 'Life is simply a cricket match—with Temptation a bowler. He's the fellow who takes nearly every boy's wicket some time or other.' Second, though the English give the impression of upholding standards of behaviour unaltered since first thrashed out around the table at Camelot, this is simply not the case.

A revealing feature of life at Eton, illustrating the extraordinary lengths to which the English will go to preserve traditional structures while trying to move with the times, was the practice of 'shirking'. To obviate the necessity of altering the time-honoured rule of the school which banned boys making excursions 'out of bounds', masters simply acted as if they did not see the boys who broke the rule, as long as the boys themselves 'shirked' the masters—that is, made some formal attempt to scuttle out of view. Boys could thus be flogged not for being 'out of bounds' but for failing to 'shirk' a master.

Always the most striking victory of formal appearances over content seems to occur in the religious context. John Chandos, in *Boys Together*, records some extraordinary performances from school chaplains amidst near-mayhem from the juvenile congregations:

> The fastest of several fast clerical performers in Thomas Trollope's time at Winchester was known as the 'diver'. It was his practice in conducting a service to continue intoning rapidly without pause to the limit of his capacity, then while he recharged himself with air, he continued to read silently so that when he 'reappeared'—on the surface—he was several lines further down the page . . .
>
> Goodford was a boy at school with Gladstone. Later, when as Provost he read prayers, only one word, Wuffaw (wherefore), was generally intelligible. Whenever in the conduct of a service, Wuffaw was heard more than once, an audible groan went up, for it meant that he had strayed back to the beginning of the prayer . . .
>
> Plumptre used to begin his discourse with a roar emitted from one side of his mouth, which moved in declining sound to finish in a whisper from the opposite side of his mouth, pursued with earnest fidelity by his squint . . .

In 1861 Harriet Martineau (in *Health, Husbandry and Handicraft*) was 'amazed and shocked' at the 'sensual cast of mind of the boys in a great Public School' revealed in *Tom Brown's Schooldays*, particularizing the 'eagerness and passion of sausages' evinced by the juniors after the football match. The shocking thing is that a lubricious appetite for sausages was not the worst of it. Thomas Hughes mentions but one or two of the English gentleman's traditional pursuits to which a boy is normally introduced at school. Violence, intimidation, extortion, vandalism, drunkenness, gross indecency, blasphemy, poaching, gambling and whoring—all were eminently respectable vices. Boys were expected to practise them and to be flogged for them. Even expulsion did not endanger one's career prospects.

There was no noticeable difference in behaviour between those boys who were to end up commanding irregular cavalry on the North-West Frontier and those whose ultimate destiny was a village rectory or a bishopric. Before the Victorian era it was perfectly common for a boy intended for holy orders to leave school without having received any religious instruction whatsoever. Dr John Keate at Eton dealt with religious enthusiasm as he dealt with any other vice that came to his notice: 'I'll flog him. It's all conceit. That boy, if he is a bigot now, will sicken of religion and become an infidel when he leaves school.'

Gradually, a furrow of earnest Christian zeal was ploughed across the

*The Fight Interrupted.* Painting by William Mulready. William Hazlitt
had it that 'the English . . . fight as they box, not out of malice, but to
show pluck and manhood. Fair play and Old England for ever!' The
reality of English school life was often brutality and bullying.

previously untroubled brow of the English schoolboy. The steady ooze of
Christian principles that had always oiled an Englishman's moral articulation
threatened to become a flood of righteousness and guilt. Games — once played in
a cavalier, idle spirit — came to be honoured with a spirit of duty and even
Calvinist zeal. Games, cold showers, prayer and more games were supposed to
ward off the spectre of masturbation and the terrifying mental and physical decay
it brought with it. Honest contemporary accounts of the natural tendencies of
young males when vigilantly secluded from the company of females are
obviously scarce. John Addington Symonds (1840–1893), however, in his only
recently published memoirs, opens the door for us on a dormitory at Harrow in

the 1850s, underlining H. H. Munro's arch maxim from half a century later: 'You can't expect a boy to be depraved till he has been to a good school.'

> Every boy of good looks had a female name and was recognized either as a public prostitute or as some bigger fellow's bitch . . . The talk in the studies and dormitories was incredibly obscene. One could not avoid seeing acts of onanism, mutual masturbation and the sport of naked boys in bed together. There was no refinement, no sentiment, no passion, nothing but animal lust in these occurrences.

So unlike the school-life of Tom Brown, which was being conjured up at about this same time.

Education in the modern sense was quite foreign to the ethos of the old public schools:

> Thought would destroy their paradise.
> No more;—where ignorance is bliss,
> 'Tis folly to be wise.

> Thomas Gray, 'Ode on a Distant Prospect of Eton College'

Traditionally, the English gentleman was taught to compose verses in Latin and Greek. As this is an accomplishment beyond the capacity of any but a special few with a peculiar gift in this direction, the English gentleman was effectively taught nothing at all—except the profane values of classical authors and the lewd example of their amoral gods. Dr Keate's enigmatic embargo—'I'll have no folios carried about; if I catch a boy with a folio, I'll flog him'—refers to what might be an emblem for the distinctive tone of the public schools; for, according to W. E. Gladstone, strong drink was commonly carried about within the sober covers of a *Princeps*—an early Virgil, apparently.

For a long time English society was run by public-school men on the grounds that they could be relied on not for their intelligence but for their loyalty. Kim Philby's great sin was his betrayal not of his country but of its governing classes. Whereas in continental Europe the practice of 'sneaking' (called '*prenez la marque*' in France, because the only way a boy could avoid continued punishment was to report the transgression of someone else, thus passing on '*la marque*') was built into the educational system, the English favoured the development of a strong fraternity over mere good behaviour. This pagan system of ethics was threatened by the introduction of religious education. Religion was only the thin end of the wedge: in its radical forms, it meant democracy. Qualifications would be needed: science, mathematics and foreign languages would have to be looked into.

Up until then, Puritans had been careful to avoid sending their sons to a public school. Instead, the Puritans had since the seventeenth century offered an all-round education, eschewing the heathen classics, at their 'Dissenting Academies'. The working classes were not forgotten: 'Charity Schools' were established 'to inculcate a love of industry and a fear of God in the poor'. And in Gloucester during the eighteenth century, Robert Raikes, appalled at the bad language he heard from children employed in pin-making on their one day off in the week, clapped them into 'Sunday School'.

## COLD SHOWERS AND OTHER HARDSHIPS

Whatever the other privations of being at public school, one of the major miseries has always been the regular chore of writing home. Here is the effort of an eighteenth-century Eton schoolboy:

> My dear Mama,
> I wright to tell you I am very retched, and my chilblains is worse agen. I have not made any progress and I do not think I shall. i am very sorry to be such expense to you, but i do not think this schule is very good. One of the fellows has taken the crown of my new hat for a target, he has burrowed my watch to make wheal, with the works, but it won't act—me and him have tried to put the works back, but we think some wheels are missing as they won't fit. I hope Matilda's cold is better i am glad she is not at a schule. I think I have got the consumption the boys at the place are not gentlemen but of course you did not know that when you sent me hear, i will try not to get bad habits.
> The trousers have worn out at the knee, i think the tailor must have cheated you, the buttons have come off, and they are loos at the back i don't think the food is good but I should not mind if I was stronger. The peace of meet i sent you is off the beef we had on Sunday but on other days it is more stringey. There are black beetles in the kitchen and sometimes they cook them in the dinner which can't be wholesome when you are not strong. Dear mama I hope you and papa are well and dont mind my being uncomfortable because i dont think i shall last long please send me some more money as i owe 8d if you think you can't spare it i can burrow it of a boy who is going to leave at the half-quarter and then he won't ask for it again but perhaps you wd not like me to be obliged to his parents as they are trades people and I think you deal at their shop i did not mention it or i dare say they would have put it down in the bill.

> Your loving but retched son

The public schools originally served to mitigate, devalue and punish the weaknesses—vanity, arrogance and self-indulgence—of those born to privilege. Over the years, however, they have served this function less and less, becoming instead 'private academies for the education of young gentlemen'. In a letter to *The Times* for 6 January 1858 we find that at least one 'old boy' was already complaining about modern hothouse education:

Sir,—I belong to the School of Muscular Christianity, and, if I take up my pen to write about Public Schools, you will know at once that I am not about to complain of the deficiency of education in these institutions, but rather of its increase since I was at Public School myself. So far from wishing that my children now about to follow my steps at the same school should be instructed in Political Economy and Chymistry, that they should have all the -ologies, -actics and -graphies at their fingers' ends, I only wish them to be taught Greek and Latin in the old way; nay, I will be content if they are only taught Latin, for to my mind the way to teach a child anything is to teach him *one* thing well; when he has mastered that he can and will teach himself anything; but if you try to teach him everything you will teach him nothing, and when his education is over you will have a weed instead of a flower in your house . . .

I regret to observe the invasion of what may be called the flannel-waistcoat and comforter element, and I grieve that with regard to sports, which really are half Public School education, a course is pursued which resolves itself into a fear lest the boys should take cold. I may be a very hard-hearted parent, but I own I think that a Westminster boy ought to take the water like a duck, and that it does not much matter whether a weak boy or two is removed to what we are taught to consider a better and happier place . . . And now, having eased my soul and gone back to 'old ways', after trying many new fangled notions, allow me to sign myself,

ONCE A BOY

This uncomplicated philosophy of education does not seem quite so bracing however, when it is extended to the unprivileged classes, as Dickens showed in *Oliver Twist*. As a ward of the parish, Oliver was elected by his fellow orphans in the workhouse to ask for more gruel:

Child as he was, he was desperate with hunger, and reckless with misery. He rose from the table; and advancing to the master, basin and spoon in hand, said, somewhat alarmed at his own temerity:

'Please, sir, I want some more.'

The master was a fat, healthy man; but he turned very pale. He gazed in stupefied astonishment on the small rebel for some seconds, and then clung for support to the copper. The assistants were paralysed with wonder; the boys with fear.

'What!' said the master at length, in a faint voice.

'Please, sir,' replied Oliver, 'I want some more.'

The master aimed a blow at Oliver's head with the ladle; pinioned him in his arms; and shrieked aloud for the beadle.

The board were sitting in solemn conclave, when Mr Bumble rushed into the room in great excitement, and addressing the gentleman in the high chair, said,

'Mr Limbkins, I beg your pardon, sir! Oliver Twist has asked for more!'

There was a general start. Horror was depicted on every countenance.

'For *more?*' said Mr Limbkins. 'Compose yourself, Bumble, and answer me distinctly. Do I understand that he asked for more, after he had eaten the supper allotted by the dietary?'

'He did, sir,' replied Bumble.

'That boy will be hung,' said the gentleman in the white waistcoat. 'I know that boy will be hung.'

Nobody controverted the prophetic gentleman's opinion.

The workhouse board consider putting Oliver out to work as an apprentice to Mr Gamfield, a chimney sweep:

'It's a nasty trade,' said Mr Limbkins, when Gamfield had again stated his wish.

'Young boys have been smothered in chimneys before now,' said another gentleman.

'That's acause they damped the straw afore they lit it in the chimbley to make 'em come down agin,' said Gamfield; 'that's all smoke, and no blaze; vereas smoke ain't o' no use at all in making a boy come down, for it only sinds him to sleep, and that's wot he likes. Boys is wery obstinit, and wery lazy, gen'lmen, and there's nothink like a good hot blaze to make 'em come down vith a run. It's humane too, gen'lmen, acause, even if they've stuck in the chimbley, roasting their feet makes 'em struggle to hextricate theirselves.'

# STUDENT DAYS

For the student, some kind of cultivation of the intellect becomes unavoidable. Plunged into a more or less cerebral environment, he cannot help picking up a lot of useless mental clutter—clutter that has to be shaken off before the Englishman can start to feel like himself again. John Aubrey remembered Sir Henry Blount inveighing against the universities—'The learning that they learned there they were to unlearne againe, as a man that is button'd or laced too hard, must unbutton before he can be at his ease.'

More highly valued than a ready familiarity with the current state of one's discipline is the diplomatic aplomb with which one carries one's ignorance. In *A Frenchman in England* (1784) de la Rochefoucauld mentions the case of the Reverend Langford of Great Massingham, who was awarded his doctorate for his cunning reply to the tricky question as to 'whether the sun turns round the earth or the earth round the sun'. Quite unflustered, he said, 'Sometimes the one, sometimes the other.' And A. J. P. Taylor claimed in *A Personal History* (1983) that 'G. N. Clark became the first professor of economic history at Oxford by the simple device of pleading that he knew nothing of economic history, and was anxious to learn'.

The essential thing an Englishman picks up at one of the two ancient universities is what is usually called a 'manner'. The Oxford or Cambridge 'manner' includes a deprecating awareness of the student's regrettable superior-

Young lords of creation: undergraduate members of the Oxford and
Cambridge athletics team during the 1870s.

ity to the rest of creation. It is otherwise indefinable, although one can identify a
certain abstracted assurance and an intellectual circumspection; these, taken
together with a gentle and fastidious irony, are supposed to mark the Oxford or
Cambridge man as unmistakably as college blazers, ties and scarves mark the
alumni of 'other places'.

## THE YOUTHFUL VISION

It is all too easy for an Englishman to plug into his childhood. As a toddler he has
as his representative Winnie the Pooh, the bear with 'little brain' and touchingly
simple needs. (For reasons unknown, Pooh is widely regarded in North America
as a sort of mystic sage.) Rupert, another bear, is timeless in a quite different way.
There seems to be no end or meaning to his adventures. A mesmerizingly
unimaginative creation, Rupert owes his survival to the typical English regard for
terrible old things.

The Harrow football eleven of 1867. Harrow was founded in 1615 to
educate the poor boys of the parish. Two hundred and fifty years on it
was, with other public schools, churning out a regulation issue
English Gentleman.

The quintessential English animals, though, are found in Kenneth
Grahame's *The Wind in the Willows* (1908), in which an air-headed aristocrat
(Toad) and a feral proletariat (the stoats and weasels) are brought to heel by the
solid, home-loving bourgeoisie (Badger, Ratty and Mole).

In adventure stories for boys, the essential Englishman stands out with
almost alarming simplicity, for in many respects that is where he comes from.
Among cheeky but loyal cockneys, frightful bounders, irredeemable Europeans
and utterly fiendish Orientals he remembers the old school and stands up for the

underdog. In a world of dastardly and untrustworthy foreigners and other chaps who haven't been to a decent school, he can be relied on to keep a straight bat where women are concerned. Moreover, he has a chum, with whom he enjoys a close but entirely manly relationship. And behind every Biggles there is also old Alma Mater.

The English schoolboy novel is a genre unparalleled in any other literature, from the unctuous soul-searching of F. W. Farrar's *Eric, or Little by Little* (1858) to the farcical adventures of Billy Bunter, the 'Owl of the Remove'. For many years the demand for rehashes of the old formula was insatiable, almost like that for Mills and Boon romances. The common ingredients were the playing fields (and the hero's triumphs thereon), the chapel (and the vows to be pure he makes therein), the bully to whom he gives a thrashing (and who years later thanks him brokenly for putting him straight), the young 'un to whom he lends a helping hand, the unjust punishment he accepts rather than give someone else away, and the frank chat with his wise mentor—plus, with Billy Bunter, the misappropriation of 'tuck' and the laying on of a fives bat: 'Yarooh! Leggo, you beasts!'

The reality could be very different—an inglorious season with the second eleven, a sensible exercise of discretion with regard to the school bully, well merited punishments for puerile and unkind japes, and neurotic, possibly mad schoolmasters. But then schooldays do not have the importance that they once had, at least for public schoolboys, who no longer have an empire to administer or a country to govern. The spirit of the old schools of England haunts instead the modern monster comprehensives, for it is in these places that the future of England lies. Tom Brown has given way to the equally sterling Adrian Mole.

The Englishman's youth is ideally not so much an individual as a collective experience, like that of men who have been through a great war together, with a similar regard for rank attained, battle honours, and casualties. The school song is both a celebration and a lament for a lost idyll. Derek Jameson remembers his old school song as more defiant than nostalgic:

> Detmold Road forever,
> It's standing firmly still;
> The years go past, we grow up fast,
> But Detmold can, and will,
> Carry on the burning torch,
> Through times both good and ill . . .

By contrast, the famous Eton Boating Song, written by the classical scholar William Cory Johnson (1823–1892), shows no consciousness of impending threat. Detmold Road School may have disappeared from the face of Upper Clapton, but the sweet surge and glide of the Eton Boating Song goes on forever.

*Albuhera. "Steady the Drums and Fifes"*. Painting by Lady Butler. It is
the role of infantry to occupy ground and absorb as much punishment
as the enemy cares to inflict. For those regiments that chose virtual
annihilation at Albuhera in 1811 rather than fail in that role, this
ghastly victory remains one of a handful of the most precious battle
honours that any regiment may lay claim to.

# CHAPTER TWO

— • —

# THE ENGLISHMAN
# AT ARMS

It is said that on the eve of 14 October 1066 the Normans were up all night praying while the English got drunk. If the English felt under the weather the next day, or the Normans any love for their fellow men, it did not show. The Normans were surprised that King Harold's 'house-carles', wielding great battle-axes and on foot, were not intimidated by cavalry. The English were bewildered, on being lured down from Senlac Ridge by an enemy in retreat, to find they had been duped: it was not 'a stand-up gentleman-like battle' (as, centuries later, Sir Harry Smith called the battle of Aliwal, 1846). The English did not break, however. They retreated in good order, punishing the Norman attempts to rout them. Harold and the 'house-carles' fell where they stood.

We may pass over the Romans and the Celts: the business-like legions, the ruthless Iceni under Boudicca, the fey and fantastic Round Table. It was among the Anglo-Saxons, from Alfred the Great to their last spitting defiance, from the marshlands of Ely, of the Conqueror's 'cold heart and bloody hand', that the lineaments of the Englishman-at-arms begin to appear—'staunch and tenacious in adversity, kind and gentle in victory', as Montgomery once described the British soldier.

The cry of Byrhtwold in 991, in the hour of defeat at the battle of Maldon, according to the poem of that name, already expressed the discipline of the English with their backs to the wall:

> Mind must be firmer, heart the fiercer,
> Courage greater, even as our strength fails.

It is a spirit that English commanders have always been able to call on when ruses and manoeuvrings have proved vain. The authentic Anglo-Saxon battle cry was heard again at the terrible battle of Albuhera in 1811, where Colonel Inglis, lying riddled with grapeshot, called to the men of the 57th Foot behind him: 'Die hard 57th! Die hard!' Which they proceeded to do. Only a third of the men survived, and their officers were virtually extinguished.

King Alfred, in the ninth century, was already practising Charles Napier's nineteenth-century recipe for imperial rule: 'a good thrashing first, and great kindness afterwards'. Sellar and Yeatman's account in *1066 and All That* (1930) of Alfred's magnanimity in victory is not altogether inaccurate:

> The English resisted the Danes heroically under Alfred, never fighting except against heavy odds, till at the memorable Peace of Wedmore Alfred compelled the Danes, who were now (of course) beaten, to stop being Danes and become English and therefore C. of E. and get properly married.

The Anglo-Saxon dough merely required the leavening of Norman savoir-faire and swank to start making its presence felt over the Channel. The Normans were basically Norsemen with a French veneer. They liked invading and plundering. The new English kings returned home as often as they could, to bully their stay-at-home relatives—at Crécy, Poitiers and Agincourt—and to claim their inheritance, or at least some pocket-money.

In considering the motivation of the English soldier, we should not forget the unapologetic desire for gain, the spoils of war, which carried poorly paid troops 'into the breach once more' with more interest than a fine speech could usually summon up. But nor should we forget the sheer excitement of it: when Nelson, at the battle of Copenhagen, splinters and shot flying all around, remarked that it was 'warm work' but that he 'would not be elsewhere for thousands', he was talking not about duty but about the pleasures of war. And, of course, there is also the perennial opportunity that war provides to 'cut a dash': as Mr Pickwick commented, 'We know, Mr Weller—we, who are men of the world—that a good uniform must work its way with women, sooner or later.'

In their military excursions the English commonly found themselves very heavily outnumbered but, far from home, hungry and tired, they fashioned an unglamorous strategy that left the glory-hunting chivalry of France lying in great heaps on the battlefield. At Crécy, in 1346, the French knights charged the English lines some 15 times, only to have their horses shot from under them or stumble into unsportingly dug holes. As they floundered in the mud, many of the French nobility were unceremoniously despatched by English yeomen armed with long knives. In 1415, before the battle of Agincourt, the well breakfasted French could be heard gaily calling out to each other by the English archers, waiting hungrily for their prey. The French men-at-arms advanced in such numbers that they fell over one another, and the English bowmen went about their unchivalrous business with brutal efficiency. A pattern of success was being set: a small, integrated force could worst an uncoordinated army, however large. In fact, the size of the British army became something of a standing joke on the continent: Bismarck, on being asked what he would do if the British army were to invade, said that he would call out the constabulary and have it arrested.

The prediction which, according to Shakespeare, Henry V made before Agincourt, that

> ... gentlemen in England, now a-bed,
> Shall think themselves accurs'd they were not here,

is a fine fallacy. 'Gentlemen in England, now a-bed' generally think themselves well out of it. The military success of the English has come about largely because they are an unmilitaristic people, for whom war is a necessary evil and whose general attitude is that soldiers should be kept in their place. According to the Earl of Stanhope's *Notes of Conversations with Wellington* (1888), the Iron Duke once observed of Napoleon that

> he could do whatever he pleased; and no man ever lost more armies than he did. Now with me the loss of every man told. I could not risk so much; I knew that if I ever lost five hundred men without the clearest necessity, I should be brought upon my knees to the bar of the House of Commons.

The English Civil War was remarkable among seriously contested political revolutions for the restraint and good manners that generally accompanied the vigour and ineptitude with which it was prosecuted. When John Hampden, the fairest and most decent of Roundheads, was mortally wounded at Chalgrove, King Charles offered to send his personal physician to look after him. And friendships were not necessarily affected. Sir William Waller wrote to his opponent in the Southwest, Sir Ralph Hopton: 'My affections for you are so unchangeable that hostility itself cannot violate my friendship, but I must be true to the cause which I serve.' Hopton defeated Waller at Roundway Down in 1643 and then, in the following year, Waller bested Hopton at Alresford. But, according to Waller, it was nothing personal: 'We are both upon the stage, and we must act the parts that are assigned us in this tragedy. Let us do it in a way of honour, and without personal animosities.'

We may note here that this same ability of the common English soldier to 'play the game' without the emotional investment of the true fanatic was observed in 1804 by Robert Jackson, Inspector-General of Army Hospitals (*A View of the Formation, Discipline and Economy of Armies*):

> An Englishman is accustomed from early youth to enter the lists of combat without ... passion or (personal) enmity. This practice ... is almost peculiar to the people of England; and to this, perhaps, may be ascribed that good sense and self-command which gives up a contest in the more serious conflicts of war, without feeling or manifesting such vexation and despair as create confusion and lead to total rout.

One wonders, however, if some of the Cavaliers took the business of war seriously enough. Time and time again, the Royalist cavalry would ignore golden

MILITARY EDUCATION.—*General.* " Mr. de Bridoon, what is the general use of cavalry in modern warfare?" *Mr. de Bridoon.* " Well, I suppose to give tone to what would otherwise be a mere vulgar brawl!"

The traditional view of cavalry from Mr Punch.

opportunities to follow up an irresistible charge, instead racing each other to the Roundhead baggage-train to see what they could find in the way of loot.

Conversely, there can be no doubting the seriousness with which the Parliamentarians played the game. Primed with some pre-battle Bible-bashing, Cromwell's God-fearing Eastern Association Horse were not going to sell the battle for the pick of the booty: first the battle, *then* the booty. Moreover, Cromwell did not like indiscipline: at the Royalist surrender of Winchester, when six Roundhead troopers broke the terms of surrender by looting, Cromwell had one of them executed and sent the other five to the Royalists for punishment. Needless to say, the gesture was appreciated and the troopers were returned unharmed.

Even the Puritans were human, though. Their official policy required that the images and stained glass of Winchester Cathedral be smashed, yet in this instance (among others) religious convictions could not displace more fundamental loyalties: a Roundhead stood with drawn sword at the entrance to the tomb of William of Wykeham to protect the remains of the founder of Winchester College from the general desecration.

In the Civil War each side appears to have played their roles to the hilt. The Cavaliers ('Wrong but Wromantic', according to Sellar and Yeatman) were led by the almost impossibly dashing Prince Rupert, with his dog 'Boy' (said by the Puritans to be his diabolical advisor), the hard-drinking and unscrupulous but brilliant cavalry commander, Lord George Goring, and the languid, versifying Duke of Newcastle, who had difficulty getting up for a battle if it started much before midday. The Roundheads ('Right but Repulsive') had an almost equally appropriate line-up, from sensible Sir Thomas (Black Tom) Fairfax and the dour Presbyterian, Lord Leven, to old 'Ironsides' himself, the pious and brutal Oliver Cromwell. Looking at it now, we can see that there could never have been any other outcome.

## WHEN SHALL THEIR GLORY FADE?

In the seventeenth century the cavalry ruled the battlefield. At the outset of the Civil War the Royalists had a clear advantage in this department, as Cromwell himself remarked to his cousin, John Hampden:

> Your troops ... are most of them old decayed serving men, tapsters, and such kind of fellows; do you think that the spirits of such base, mean fellows will ever be able to encounter gentlemen that have honour, and courage, and resolution in them? You must get men of a spirit that is likely to go as far as gentlemen will go, or you will be beaten still.

Cromwell found the troopers he needed among the free and independent characters of the eastern counties.

Portrait of Oliver Cromwell by Samuel Cooper. The English forerunner
of Napoleon, Lenin, Hitler and other Men of Destiny, the Lord
Protector was never taken for more than he always was, an odd
mixture of religious zealot and plain-speaking English gent.

That difference was observed shortly from the beginning of the war: that
though the King's troops prevailed in the charge, and routed those they
charged, they never rallied themselves in order, nor could be brought to
make a second charge again the same day, whereas Cromwell's troops if they
prevailed, or though they were beaten and routed, presently rallied again,
and stood in good order till they received new orders.

Edward, Earl of Clarendon,
*History of the Rebellion*, 1702–4

The typical British military values of staunchness and tenacity favour the soldier who has both feet on the ground. Cavalry, on the other hand, are almost essentially dashing; Wellington thought that it was due to the superior quality of British horses that British cavalry inevitably reverted to their sabre-flashing, swaggering ways. At Waterloo they got out of control, and at the battle of Talavera (1809) the 23rd Light Dragoons raced each other into a concealed ditch, breaking a lot of bones and leaving the German Hussars, with whom they were supposed to be advancing, to finish the job without them.

After the Napoleonic Wars, the couturiers got to work on cavalry uniforms, as if they knew that the British cavalry was heading for its apotheosis on 25 October 1854 and were making sure that the spectacle would be as gorgeous and glittering a display of aristocratic bravado as the world would ever see. Captain Gronow, in his *Recollections and Reminiscences, 1810–1860*, recorded the opinion of the French Marshal Excelmann:

> Your horses are the finest in the world, and your men ride better than any continental soldiers . . . The great deficiency is in your officers, who have nothing to recommend them but their dash and sitting well in their saddles . . . The British cavalry officer seems to be impressed with the conviction that he can dash and ride over everything; as if the art of war were precisely the same as that of fox-hunting . . .
>
> Permit me . . . to point out a gross error as regards the dress of your cavalry. I have seen prisoners so tightly habited that it was impossible for them to use their sabres with facility.

At Balaclava, the heroic charge of the Heavy Brigade, uphill, to rout a body of cavalry twice its strength, was but a prelude to the action which, in its spectacular absurdity, immediately displaced all other images of cavalry for the Englishman. The Charge of the Light Brigade appears inexplicable in terms of mere incompetence, the blunder unrolling before us with the seeming inevitability of tragedy. Thus Captain Nolan reins in beside Lord Lucan, reaches from his saddle to hand over the written order, points at the Russian battery ahead and says: 'There is the enemy, and there are the guns, sir, before them. It is your duty to take them.' The order is passed to the certifiable Lord Cardigan. Lord George Paget lights up a cheroot, which will still be between his teeth when he and the wreckage of the Light Brigade are through the Russian guns. The Russians were aghast to discover that the survivors they captured were stone-cold sober.

Of course, the media blew the whole thing up out of proportion. Battles are a confusing business at the best of times. Lord George Paget's main gripe later was that someone had blundered in the design of the campaign medals. 'They look like decanter labels,' he complained.

# THE SCUM OF THE EARTH

> We few, we happy few, we band of brothers;
> For he today that sheds his blood with me,
> Shall be my brother; be he ne'er so vile,
> This day shall gentle his condition.

Shakespeare's evocation of the spirit that carried the English army to victory at Agincourt is a romanticized Elizabethan one, but Henry V must have known what Froissart had observed after Crécy in the previous century: 'The might of the realm most standeth upon archers which are not rich men.' However, until the middle classes found themselves in the front line in the Great War, soldiers were a despised breed of men. Shakespeare's Falstaff expresses a more realistic Elizabethan disgust with their pressed professional levies:

> If I be not ashamed of my soldiers, I am a soused gurnet . . . a mad fellow met me on the way, and told me I had unloaded all the gibbets, and pressed the dead bodies. No eye hath seen such scarecrows. I'll not march through Coventry with them, that's flat:—nay, and the villains march wide between the legs, as if they had gyves [shackles] on; for indeed, I had the most of them out of prison. There's not a shirt and a half in all my company: and the half shirt is two napkins, tacked together . . . and the shirt to say the truth, stolen from my host at St Albans . . .

One eighteenth-century cavalry officer, Captain Pope of Schomberg's Horse, complained of his recruits: 'Such a set of ruffians and imbeciles you never beheld . . . None of them have sat a horse, and when they get their swords I fear they will cut their horses' heads off rather than the enemy's.' Wellington was no less critical: 'The French system of conscription brings together a fair sample of all classes; ours is composed of the mere scum of the earth.' And he was realistic about their motivation: 'People talk of their enlisting for their fine military feeling—all stuff—no such thing. Some of our men enlist for having got bastard children—some for minor offences—many more for drink . . .' Wellington had seen the atrocities of which his troops were capable at the sack of Badajoz (1812). He resisted the abolition of the cat o' nine tails until his dying day. Even the humane Charles Napier had to admit: 'There are always some ruffians who may be flogged with satisfaction.' The dreadful instrument did not become a museum piece until 1881, some 100 years after its abolition elsewhere in Europe.

However, just as Wellington earned his men's grudging respect as 'the long-nosed bugger that licks the French', so they in turn earned his trust for their skill and courage once schooled in battle. From a conversation which he had with Creevey just after Waterloo one gets some idea of just how much Wellington knew his victory had depended on the exceptional showing by British troops:

> 'It has been a damned nice thing—the nearest run thing you ever saw in your
> life' . . . Then, as he walked about, he praised greatly those Guards who kept
> the farm (meaning Hugomont) against the repeated attacks of the French;
> and then he praised all our troops, uttering repeated expressions of astonish-
> ment at our men's courage. He repeated so often its being so nice a thing—so
> nearly run a thing, that I asked him if the French had fought better than he had
> ever seen them do before.—'No', he said, 'they have always fought the same
> since I first saw them at Vimeiro.'

Not universally respected for their intelligence or sense of initiative, British
soldiers were trained to maintain a sense of self-possession. Wellington was
equally scathing of troops who gave way to the intoxication of pursuit as of those
who gave way to panic. Robert Jackson, from the same period, wrote:

> The English soldier is not impetuous to the same extent as the soldiers of
> some countries; . . . he ordinarily retains command of himself . . . He
> performs his duties with correctness; but he performs them as duties which
> are not to exceed a certain limit; there is in fact something like discretion—a
> bargain with himself in all his acts . . . He thus, even as a soldier, retains the
> base of the national character, namely, a spirit of independence . . .

*A View of the Formation, Discipline and Economy of Armies*, 1804

## OFFICERS AND GENTLEMEN

James II, who saw some action in foreign service while in exile on the continent,
remarked:

> 'Tis observed that of all nations the English stick the closest to their officers,
> and it's hardly seen that our common Soldiers will turn their backs, if they
> who commanded them do not first show them the bad example, or leave
> them unofficer'd by being kill'd themselves upon the place.

We are beginning to approach the secret of British 'morale', which seems to be
rooted in a combination of the clear distinction and close rapport between
officers and men. As early as 1727 it was laid down, by Lieutenant-Colonel
Humphrey Bland of His Majesty's Own Regiment of Horse, that 'in order . . . to
dissipate their [the soldiers'] fears, and fortify their courage, the officers should
assume a serene and cheerful air; and in delivering their orders, and in their
common discourse with the men, they should address themselves in an affable
and affectionate manner.'

It was important not to make a fuss in the heat of battle. Hence the almost
absurdly laconic exchange reported between Wellington and Lord Uxbridge at
Waterloo when the latter's knee was shattered by grapeshot: 'By God, sir, I've lost
my leg!' 'By God, sir, so you have!'

However desperate the situation (and Wellington could recall that at the

The Duke of Wellington by Sir Thomas Lawrence. Wellington
embodied the English ideal of practical improvisation and making do
beneath a mask of phlegmatic hauteur. Of his French opponents he
said, 'They plan their campaigns just as you might make a splendid
piece of harness. It looks very well; and answers very well; until it gets
broken; and then you are done for. Now I made my campaigns of
ropes. If anything went wrong, I tied a knot; and went on.'

battle of Vimeiro, in 1808, there was a messenger bearing such fearful news that his hair literally stood on end), the Iron Duke maintained his sang-froid. Before Waterloo, when Captain Gronow observed the Duke and his staff looking 'as gay and unconcerned as if they were riding to meet the hounds in some quiet English county', he knew that this was how they *meant* to look. Indeed, Wellington was ready to follow the hounds at the drop of a hat:

> Salamanca, 22 July 1812
>     Marmont came down upon us the first night with a thundering cannonade, and placed his army en masse on the plain before us, almost within gunshot. I was told that, while Lord Wellington was riding along the line, under a fire of artillery, and accompanied by a numerous staff, a brace of greyhounds in pursuit of a hare passed close to him. He was at the moment in earnest conversation with General Castanos; but the instant he observed them he gave the view hallo and went after them at full speed, to the utter astonishment of his foreign accompaniments. Nor did he stop until he saw the hare killed; when he returned and resumed with the commander-in-chief as if nothing had happened.
>
> Sir John Kincaid, *Adventures in the Rifle Brigade*, 1830

The business of British officers was not to cover themselves in glory but simply to do their duty, uphold the honour of the regiment, play the game, and not let the side down. While a whiff of heroism may sometimes have been unavoidable in discharging one's duty and generally doing the decent thing, it was improper to be anything but apologetic about it. Thus, on being treated to Belgian adulation after Waterloo, Wellington responded when asked if he were pleased to be the hero of the hour: 'Not in the least; if I had failed, they would have shot me.'

Wellington's austere conception of duty was perhaps extreme, but it was also influential. On being given a somewhat demeaning command at Hastings in 1806 he summed it up: 'I am "nimmukwallah", as we say in the East; that is, I have eaten of the King's salt, and therefore I conceive it to be my duty to serve with unhesitating zeal and cheerfulness, when and wherever the King or his Government may think proper to employ me.'

Tennyson offered the bays of honour quite rightly to the plodder:

> Not once or twice in our rough island-story
> The path of duty was the way to glory.
>
> 'Ode on the Death of the Duke of Wellington'

The ethos of the British army is very much a product of an aristocratic code. This pride communicates itself through the ranks: experienced soldiers scorn to duck or flinch when under fire. Wellington again: 'The British Army is what it is because it is officered by gentlemen . . . men who would scorn to do a dishonourable thing and who have something more at stake than a reputation for military smartness.' However, Wellington was also capable of looking down his long nose at the lack of professionalism amongst his officers. Not only he; the Adjutant-General noted at the start of the Peninsular War that 21 out of the 41 regiments were commanded 'literally by boys or idiots; I have had the curiosity to count them over.' And even the long-suffering Wellington felt entitled to deprecate the appointment to his staff of Sir William Erskine: 'I have always understood him to be a madman.' But the Military Secretary in London was unabashed by this objection: 'No doubt he is a little mad at times, but in his lucid intervals he is an uncommonly clever fellow, though I must say he looked a little mad as he embarked.'

The best of Wellington's officers were easy-going fellows, who seemed unable to exert themselves except when on the battlefield: 'There is not much difficulty in posting a British army for a general action, or in getting the officers and men to do their duty in the action. The difficulty consists in bringing them to the point where the action can be fought.'

Eventually, reform came to the privileged world of officers and gentlemen. Lord Cardigan had been able to buy his immortal command of the Light Brigade for £30,000, but the end of such practices was heralded in *Punch* in 1871. Under the heading 'A Notice to Gallant but Stupid Young Gentlemen' the magazine informed them that they could purchase their commissions in the army 'up to the 31st day of October. After that you will be driven to the cruel necessity of deserving them.'

## CITIZEN ARMIES

For hundreds of years Englishmen have periodically oiled ancient weapons and dusted off old uniforms to parade together and prepare to defend their 'sceptr'd isle' against threats of heavily armed invasion. The complacency of the militia was apparent even in Elizabethan times. Sir John Norreys, in charge of the defence of the realm as the Spanish Armada approached, said: 'I wonder that I can see no man in the kingdom affeared but myself.' And the Home Guard in 1940 was evidently just as sanguine:

> Every day that passes brings nearer the time when the enemy will attempt invasion and when that time comes . . . we must be prepared to give a good account of ourselves . . . We must all strive to qualify ourselves to give Jerry a perfectly appalling time should he have the temerity to land in this country.
>
> Lieut.-Col. D. C. Crombie, Order of the Day to the 5th Battalion, Bideford, Devon Home Guard, 31 December 1941

The brilliant recruitment drive of the Great War exploited the various extraordinary social groupings of England with the formation of 'Pals' battalions, creating an immediate if at times bizarre *esprit de corps*. The 'Sportsmen's Battalion' was open to those 'used to shooting, hunting and outdoor sport . . . upper and middle classes only'; then there were 'Public Works' battalions, 'Football' battalions and even the 'Bantams', for short men.

By 1914 the games-playing ethos had become enshrined in official policy. According to a War Office booklet, if an officer 'induces his platoon to be determined to produce the best football teams in the battalion, he will have done a great deal to make it the best platoon in every way.' And in a famous but not unique incident on 1 July 1916, that terrible first day of the battle of the Somme, Captain Nevill of the 8th East Surreys literally 'kicked off' against the Germans. Two footballs sailed across no-man's-land as the East Surreys went over the top. On one was printed: 'The Great European Cup-Tie Finals. East Surreys *v.* Bavarians. Kick off at zero.' On the other appeared: 'No Referee.' Captain Nevill offered a prize for the first platoon to kick a ball into the German trenches. No one claimed the prize. Nevill was mown down along with most of his team.

By this time the army no longer consisted of the dregs of society led by its froth. With their hour of dubious glory on the Somme, the middle classes had arrived. The CO of the 56th Division in Burma noted in 1944 that 'the British soldier must be driven to dig in as soon as he occupies an area, and not to waste time in sight-seeing, souvenir-hunting and brewing tea'.

The cat o' nine tails might no longer seem appropriate as a corrective for his various vices, but the tradition continued that the British soldier should be made to feel like the scum of the earth. NCOs are famous for the floridity of their critical opinions: 'If you don't swing that arm laddie, I'll tear it off, stick it up your arse, and have you for a lollipop!' Their superiors are usually less graphic, but can be equally wounding. Field-Marshall Slim is reported once to have remarked, on inspecting his motorcycle escort: 'When I looked at your uniforms I thought that you'd been cleaning your motorcycles with them. Now that I've looked at your motorcycles, I see that I was wrong.'

> The parade sergeant-major was addressing the King's Squad of the Royal Marines:
> 'On the 26th June, 1926, you will be marching into the arena at Olympia. Seated in the Royal box will be 'er Majesty, Queen Mary. 'Er 'usband, King George V, our Colonel-in-Chief, will not be present as 'e is sick-a-bed at Buckingham Palace . . .
> 'You will go through your stuff, and when you 'ave done, 'er Majesty will get into 'er carriage and drive back to Buckingham Palace . . . She will say: "I've bin to Olympia, George", and 'e will say: "Oh, 'ave you, Mary, and 'ow was those young Marines of mine?" and she will say: "Well, excuse me, George, but they was bloody awful" – AND SO YOU ARE!'
>
> Bruce Lockhart, *The Marines Were There*, 1950

Always on the look-out for new military resources, it seems that the Germans published a manual between the wars on how to instil a sense of humour in their troops. John Laffin described it in *Tommy Atkins* (1966):

> The methodical Germans . . . after the defeat of 1914–1918 . . . considered at length the matter of morale and came to the conclusion that much of the English soldier's steadiness was due to his sense of humour . . . In a manual about sense of humour the Germans published one of Bruce Bairnsfather's famous drawings of 'Old Bill', sitting in a wrecked building with a great shell-hole in the wall. A rookie asks, 'What made that hole?' 'Mice,' replies 'Old Bill'. The Germans added a footnote: 'It was not mice; it was a shell'.

## AGAINST THE ODDS

Relying as much as they do on sea power, the English are not in general militaristic. As a result of this, and of their serene self-confidence, they are used to being caught with their trousers down. The army has thus a lot of experience in defence, in making do, in desperate retreats and evacuations – Corunna in 1811, Mons in 1914, Dunkirk in 1940, and so on. In their imperial wars the pattern was the same: initial outrage, a massacre or disastrous underestimation of the enemy would be followed by a heroic rearguard action; then, finally, people pulled themselves together and delivered a sharp rap on the knuckles.

Of course, eventual victory makes a satisfactory conclusion. But it is not in victory that we find the English with their heads held high but in the hour of defeat. For it is only then that they can show 'character'.

The archetypal British infantry action was fought, between catastrophe and victory, in the Zulu war of 1877, when 100 or so men of the 24th Foot, led by two stolid but inexperienced officers, held Rorke's Drift against 4,000 Zulus. It should have been a massacre, but their luck, their nerve, and their ammunition held out. It was a small triumph of discipline and character over fearsome and reckless courage, and can be taken as representative of the great strength of the British: to weather the storm. This is not to say that the British themselves are not likewise capable of recklessness on occasion. A case in point came at Chilianwala in 1849, when the same regiment, the 24th Foot, advanced overenthusiastically against the Sikh guns and suffered 50 per cent casualties. The colonel of the 61st Foot remarked with rueful pride of his own men during this engagement: 'Fine fellows. Fine fellows. Couldn't stop 'em. Saw game ahead and I couldn't hold them in.' But the 'butcher's bill' for this style of fighting was generally unacceptable.

A characteristic display of cool nerve against overwhelming odds was evident at Crécy, when the French opened hostilities with their Genoese cross-bowmen. According to Froissart's *Chronicles*:

> When the Genoese began to approach, they made a great leap and cry to abash the Englishmen. But they stood still and stirred not for all that. Then the Genoese again the second time made another leap and a fell cry and stept forward a little, and the English removed not one foot. Thirdly again they leapt and cried and went forward till they came within shot; then they shot fiercely with their crossbows. Then the English archers stept forth one pace and let fly their arrows so wholly together and so thick that it seemed snow.

Concentrated fire-power became the chief weapon of the British army in the formation known as 'the thin red line'. This sometimes required a good deal of self-possession. At Balaclava Sir Colin Campbell reminded the 93rd Highlanders as they faced the Russian cavalry, 'There is no retreat. You must die where you stand.' In the event, the Russians were too unnerved by the obvious discipline of Campbell's troops to attempt to break through.

Just how unnerving it could be to charge a British line becomes clear from this account from a French general, Marshal Bugeaud, of what it was like in the Peninsular War:

> . . . cries of 'Vive l'Empereur! En avant à la Baionette!' broke from our mass. Some men hoisted their shakos on their musket, the quick-step became a run: the ranks began to be mixed up: the men's agitation became tumultuous, many soldiers began to fire as they ran. And all the while the red English line, still silent and motionless, even when we were only 300 yards away, seemed to take no notice of the storm which was about to break upon it . . . At this moment of painful expectation the English line would make a quarter-turn—the muskets were going up to the 'ready'. An indefinable sensation nailed to the spot many of our men, who halted and began to open a wavering fire. The enemy's return, a volley of simultaneous precision and deadly effect, crashed upon us like a thunderbolt. Decimated by it we reeled together . . . Then three formidable 'Hurrahs' terminated the long silence of our adversaries. With the third they were down upon us, pressing us into a disorderly retreat . . .

This British view of the clash of French *audace* with British phlegm comes from an anonymous diarist of the 71st of the battle of Fuentes de Orono, in May 1811:

> How different the duty of the French officers from ours. They, stimulating the men by their example, the men vociferating, each chaffing each until they appear in a fury, shouting, to the points of our bayonets. After the first huzza the British officers, restraining their men, still as death. 'Steady lads, steady,' is all you hear, and that in an undertone.

On his first and last outing against the British at Waterloo, Napoleon naturally expected the thin red lines of British musketry to give way before the hammer-blows of his column assaults, and the regimental squares to break when he sent his cavalry in wave after wave against them. According to Captain Gronow, when the Little Corporal saw the British prepared for battle he exulted: '*Je les tiens donc ces Anglais!*' It was in vain that General Foy warned him: '*Sire, l'infanterie anglaise en duel c'est le diable.*'

Wellington, on receiving a message from General Halkett that 'his brigade, which had lost two-thirds, should be relieved', sent this reply: 'Tell him what he asks is impossible: he and I, and every Englishman on the field must die on the spot we now occupy.' This was not a case of Wellington succumbing, for once, to theatrical heroics: by 1815 such self-sacrifice was a reasonable expectation.

After the awesome performance of British regiments at Albuhera in 1811 the French Marshal Soult admitted: 'There is no beating these troops, in spite of their generals . . . I always thought they were bad soldiers; now I am sure of it. I had turned their right, pierced their centre, and everywhere victory was mine, but they did not know how to run.'

In *The Face of Battle* (1976) the military historian John Keegan reinforced the idea that the battle of Waterloo was won on the playing fields of Eton:

> Hence, in a way, it is that the most perceptive of all the comments about Waterloo is the best known and apparently the most banal; that it was 'won on the playing-fields of Eton'. The Duke, who was an Etonian, knew very well that few of his officers were schoolfellows and that football bears little relation to war. But he was not speaking of himself, nor was he suggesting that Waterloo had been a game. He was proposing a much more subtle idea: that the French had been beaten not by wiser generalship or better tactics or superior patriotism but by the coolness and endurance, the pursuit of excellence and of intangible objectives for their own sake which are learnt in game-playing—that game-playing which was already becoming the most important activity of the English gentleman's life. Napoleon had sent forward each of his formations in turn. They had been well led; many of the British speak with admiration of the French officers' bravery. But they had not been able to carry their men with them the final step. Each formation in turn had swung about and gone back down the hill. When at last there were no more formations to come forward, the British still stood on the line Wellington had marked out for them, planted fast by the hold officers had over themselves and so over their men. Honour, in a very peculiar sense, had triumphed.

On occasions, though, British regimental squares did break. One such instance occurred in 1885 at Abu Klea, when the Sudanese attacked a force going to the relief of Gordon at Khartoum. In his patronizing way, Kipling honoured the achievement in 'Fuzzy-Wuzzy':

> We've fought with many men acrost the seas,
>     An' some of 'em was brave an' some was not:
> The Paythan an' the Zulu an' Burmese;
>     But the Fuzzy was the finest o' the lot.
> We never got a ha'porth's change of 'im:

'E squatted in the scrub an' 'ocked our 'orses,
'E cut our sentries up at Sua*kim*,
   An' 'e played the cat an' banjo with our forces.
      So 'ere's *to* you, Fuzzy-Wuzzy, at your 'ome in the Soudan;
      You're a pore benighted 'eathen but a first-class fightin' man;
      We gives you your certificate, an' if you want it signed
      We'll come an' 'ave a romp with you whenever you're inclined.

We took our chanst among the Kyber 'ills,
   The Boers knocked us silly at a mile,
The Burman give us Irriwaddy chills,
   An' a Zulu *impi* dished us up in style:
But all we ever got from such as they
   Was pop to what the Fuzzy made us swaller;
We 'eld our bloomin' own, the papers say,
   But man for man the Fuzzy knocked us 'oller.
      Then 'ere's *to* you, Fuzzy-Wuzzy, an' the missis and the kid;
      Our orders was to break you, an' of course we went an' did.
      We sloshed you with Martinis, an' it wasn't 'ardly fair;
      But for all the odds agin' you, Fuzzy-Wuzzy, you broke the
         square.

In general, though, what the enemy had to contend with was not so much the morale of the British army as a whole but that of the individual regiment. In his early autobiography, *Goodbye to All That* (1929), Robert Graves reveals the profound mortification of the regiment that broke at Abu Klea, as well as trumpeting the glory of his own:

> I will try to recall my war-time feelings about the Royal Welch Fusiliers. I used to congratulate myself on having chosen, quite blindly, this of all regiments. 'Good God!' I used to think, 'suppose that when the war broke out I had been living in Cheshire and had applied for a commission in the Cheshire Regiment.' I thought how ashamed I should have been to find in the history of that regiment (which was the old Twenty-second Foot, just senior in the line to the Royal Welch, which was the Twenty-third) that it had been deprived of its old title 'The Royal Cheshires' as a punishment for losing a battle. Or how lucky not to have joined the Bedfords. Though the Bedfords had made a name for themselves in this war, they were still called 'The Peacemakers.' For they only had four battle-honours on their colours and none of these more recent than the year 1711; it was a sneer that their regimental motto was: 'Thou shalt not kill.' Even the Black Watch, the best of the Highland regiments, had a stain on its record; and everyone knew about it. If a Tommy of another regiment went into a public bar where men of the Black Watch were drinking, and felt brave enough to start a fight, he would ask the barmaid not for 'pig's ear', which is rhyming-slang for beer, but for a pint of 'broken square'. Then belts would be unbuckled.

The Royal Welch record was beyond reproach. There were twenty-nine battle-honours on its colours, a number only equalled by two other two-battalion regiments. And the Royal Welch had the advantage of these since they were not single regiments, but recent combinations of two regiments each with its separate history. The First Battalion of the Royal Welch Fusiliers had twenty-six battle-honours of its own, the remaining three having been won by the Second Battalion in its short and interrupted existence. They were all good bloody battle-honours, none of them like that battle of the Argyll and Sutherland Highlanders into which, it was said, they had gone with nine hundred men and from which they had come out with nine hundred and one — no casualties, and a band-boy come of age and promoted a private. For many hard battles, such as The Boyne and Aughrim and the capture of Lille, the Royal Welch had never been honoured. The regiment had fought in each of the four hardest fought victories of the British army, as listed by Sir John Fortescue. My regimental history is rusty, but I believe that they were The Boyne, Malplaquet, Albuhera and Inkerman. That is three out of four. It may have been Salamanca or Waterloo instead of The Boyne. It was also one of the six Minden [1759] regiments and one of the front-line regiments at that. They performed the unprecedented feat of charging a body of cavalry many times their own strength and driving it off the field. The surrender at York Town in the American War of Independence was the regiment's single disaster, but even that was not a disgrace. It was accorded the full honours of war. Its conduct in the hard fighting at Lexington, at Guildford Court House, and in its suicidal advance up Bunker's Hill, had earned it them.

No wonder it was felt as an affront when British troops cracked. In his *Journals* William St Leger, who was killed in 1918, recorded the collapse of raw British troops at Cambrai on 30 November 1917:

> We marched down the road passing men without arms and equipment walking back towards the village. They were the 12th Division, we found afterwards, who had broken and given way before the Hun attack. 'Look at them, sir!' said Drill Sergeant Brittain. 'Soldiers, sir! SOLDIERS! 'Ardly CREDITABLE, sir! To think that British soldiers could do a thing like that, sir!' We passed our Brigadier standing by the side of the road smoking a cigarette, notebook in hand. We found afterwards that he was taking the names of everyone of the 12th Division going back and heard that he had put 1,500 under arrest.

# STOKING THE BOILERS WITH THE GRAND PIANO

After the fall of France in June 1940 Hitler remarked: 'The British have lost the war, but they don't know it.' But at this quite hopeless time, the moral force that keeps the Englishman at his post, that almost absurd sense of being inext-inguishable ('How dare you say, sir, of her Majesty's troops, that they are *ever* at their last gasp' was Sir Colin Campbell's rebuke to an over-realistic colleague during the Indian Mutiny), that knowledge of being right and that understanding of what has to be done—that *spirit* was carefully and calculatingly nurtured in the British people by Winston Churchill. As Margery Allingham pointed out in a letter she wrote to American friends in 1940, Churchill could do this because he knew the spirit was there:

> Mr Churchill is the unchanging bulldog, the epitome of British aggressive-ness and the living incarnation of the true Briton in fighting, not standing any damned nonsense, stoking the boilers with the grand piano and enjoying-it mood. Also he never lets go. He is so designed that he cannot breathe if he does. At the end of the fight he will come crawling in, unrecognisable, covered with blood and delighted, with the enemy's heart between his teeth. Moreover, he always has been like this as far as anybody remembers, and his family before him. After half a century the country has got into the true with him, but it is its fighting not its normal angle. In handing over his own precious bit and bridle to Mr Churchill the British horse gave himself the master whom he knew to be far more ruthless in a British way than anything possible to be produced elsewhere in Europe. Mr Churchill would ride his horse to the death and die with it as a matter of course, and be sublimely confident of its thanks as they trudged off to join the shades together . . .

In May 1940 the British Army found itself in a familiar situation—in full retreat. While crack regiments fought a sacrificial rearguard action, a unique operation, peculiarly English—an amateur, half-baked, d.i.y., makeshift enterprise—was taking place. The most untidy armada ever assembled—pleasure steamers, fishing boats, smart racing yachts and boats for messing about on the river, even an old imperial gunboat that had last seen active service on the Yangtse River—an armada nearly a thousand strong, manned by businessmen and fishermen, pensioners and playboys, was being led off by the old Isle of Wight car ferry, the *Wootton*, across the Channel towards the beaches of Dunkerque. Over several days they would help to evacuate 338,226 men under furious bombardment.

'Bloody marvellous!' trumpeted a banner headline in the *Daily Mirror*, as the last boats limped home. To the Luftwaffe, as they prepared to do battle with what one German Fighter Commander called 'the Lords', the British must have seemed unnervingly cheerful, even rather braced, at having their entire army driven ignominiously into the sea. With victories in Poland, Belgium and France behind them, the German pilots stationed at Wissant for the Battle of Britain were warned against complacency by Oberst 'Onkel Theo' Osterkamp—'Now we're going to fight "the Lords", and that's something else again'.

His class-conscious view was not an inappropriate one. In the 1930s the R.A.F. had been known as the best flying club in Europe. And as the Battle of Britain began, fully a third of British fighter pilots came from the 'Auxiliary Air Force', composed of weekend fliers, aristocrats and millionaires. The A.A.F. was organized into locally based squadrons that were really more like exclusive clubs, whose members sported fancy scarves and silk-lined flying jackets in the dandified daredevil tradition of the English aristocracy. The Battle of Britain was the last and finest hour of the fox-hunting man – indeed 'Tally Ho! was the universally accepted code in Fighter Command for signalling 'enemy sighted'.

Even supplemented by another body of enthusiastic amateurs, the Royal Air Force Volunteer Reserve (for which one did not have to qualify as a gentleman), Fighter Command was outnumbered three or four to one. Their job was to survive until late September – the end of the season – as an effective check to the possibility of an invasion. That they snatched a cliff-hanger victory was owing to a number of factors.

Firstly, ranged against the charismatic figure of Hermann 'Der Dicke' Göring was the dry and charmless Hugh 'Stuffy' Dowding, who fought his three-month battle with traditional British parsimony.

Secondly, 'Stuffy' was backed by a despotic Minister of Aircraft, Lord Beaverbrook, who terrorized the munitions industry into producing enough new and repaired fighters to keep the Luftwaffe tripping over a couple of squadrons of Spitfires on every raid.

The British also had the advantage of a Scots boffin called Watson-Watt, who cobbled together a workable radar system – which the Germans never quite appreciated, if we are to believe the report of one shot-down British P.O.W. who was plaintively asked by his interrogator, 'Why are you always there when we come over?'

The Battle of Britain was a very British victory. Unspectacular, an artful exercise in husbanding the hastily drummed-up technological, political and military resources of a nation of shopkeepers, it was also a victory of stubborn pride. In early June Churchill's trumpet call sounded across the land:

> Even though large tracts of Europe and many old and famous States have fallen or may fall into the grip of the Gestapo and all the odious apparatus of Nazi rule, we shall not flag or fail. We shall go on to the end. We shall fight in France, we shall fight on the seas and oceans, we shall fight with growing confidence and growing strength in the air, we shall defend our island, whatever the cost may be. We shall fight on the beaches, we shall fight on the landing grounds, we shall fight in the fields and in the streets, we shall fight in the hills; we shall never surrender . . .

This decision was accepted quite literally, even by mandarins at Whitehall. As the first onslaught of the Luftwaffe was awaited, Sir Alexander Cadogan of the Foreign Office noted in his diary for 29th June, with a tetchy submission to his duty as an Englishman:

> Everything is as gloomy as can be. Probability is that Hitler will attempt invasion in the next fortnight. As far as I can see, we are, after years of leisurely preparation, completely unprepared. We have simply got to die at our posts—a far better fate than capitulating to Hitler as these damned Frogs have done. But uncomfortable.

One further advantage the British possessed was that they were for once playing at home. There was a certain chivalric innocence and simplicity about the long hot immortal summer of 1940 that is lacking in any other battle of the twentieth century, and as the British pilots engaged in their honourable combat with the gentlemen of the Luftwaffe they had beneath them a spectacular panorama of what they were fighting for. Their 'thin red line' stretched this time from Tangmere, guarding the approaches to Southampton, to Hawkinge and Manston in Kent—over the downs of the southern counties of England, over rolling country lanes, hopfields, cricket pitches and the rearing white cliffs of Dover.

By early September however, Fighter Command had, to all intents and purposes, lost. Most of its front-line airfields were out of action, and in two weeks it had lost a quarter of its pilots. At this point, the Luftwaffe let the R.A.F. off the hook. On 7th September the Germans stopped bombing the vital air bases of Fighter Command and started bombing London instead. Not realizing their mistake they set one last all-out attack on the capital for 15th September to lure up and destroy the last of their elusive enemy. On this day all Fighter Command's reserves were finally committed to battle. A less stuffy Hugh Dowding would have cried 'Up Guards and at 'em!' The German pilots returned with the news that the R.A.F. had not left the field for an early bath after all. There had been a cock-up somewhere. Hitler postponed the invasion of England indefinitely.

Churchill insisted 'Never in the history of human conflict has so much been owed by so many to so few'. The survivors of 'the few' agreed that he must have been talking about their mess bill.

*The Battle of Trafalgar.* Painting by J. M. W. Turner. Nelson's death during the battle
was not as calamitous as Wellington's would have been. As Admiral Villeneuve said after
the battle, 'To any other nation the loss of a Nelson would have been irreparable,
but in the British fleet off Cadiz, every Captain was a Nelson.'

————— • —————

# CHAPTER THREE

# THE ENGLISH MAN-O'-WAR

I t is perhaps difficult to appreciate now the mystique the English once had, the aura of invincibility that surrounded this sparse, mongrel people and dis-armed or demoralized its enemies. It derived from a natural and cheerful presumption of superiority: without being overbearing or offensive in any way—indeed, always trying to be kindly and encouraging towards less happy breeds—the English sincerely believed that to be bred an Englishman was to be stamped 'best quality'.

They were able to develop an authority that was almost occult because it was based on their mastery of the sea. Charles Napier suggested something of this when he said: 'An English admiral is difficult to reckon up. He may be wise, or he may be otherwise, no man knows, for he dwells not upon the hearth, but away upon the waters: however, all men know that he has a strength of cannon at his back.'

When Admiral Bridport allayed fears of French invasion in 1798—'they might come as they could, [but] for his own part, he could only say that they should not come by water', according to *Naval and Military Anecdotes* (1823)—he was expressing the assurance of English sea-power, based as it was on technique, experience and morale rather than on numerical superiority. Napoleon acknowledged that the English seemed to be a sort of latent force within the sea itself: 'If it had not been for you English, I would have been Emperor of the East; but wherever there is water to float a ship, we are sure to find you in our way.'

King Alfred, the legendary founder of the English navy, was so far from ruling the waves that in his first engagement against the Danes his fleet ran aground at Poole. And, if the Saxons launched the navy ingloriously, the Normans appear to have fought at sea like cartoon characters: naval bombard-ment at the time was a matter of hurling large rocks to damage the enemy's ship while infesting his decks with a mixture of soft soap and triangular iron spikes to discommode the crew. In 1191, however, Richard the Lion-Heart seems to have made a breakthrough. In a naval encounter off the Holy Land he realized that the bow of the low-slung galley from which he was making futile attempts to board a Saracen galleon was sharp and iron-tipped—almost as if it had been designed specifically to ram ruinous holes in enemy hulls. Actually, that was exactly what the bow had been designed to do: shipwrights had been following traditional patterns since Roman times. Anyway, Richard's Christians decided to give it a try, and were delighted to see the Saracen ship go down with all hands.

It is doubtful if Edward III and his son, the Black Prince, expected such satisfyingly dramatic results when they adopted the same ploy at the battle of 'Les Espagnols sur Mer' in 1350. The sailing cogs in which they attempted to ram the enemy ships split on impact and, even as the English boarded and captured the Spaniards, were sinking fast.

However, a style was already being set, of attack and be damned. With gradual refinements it was to be the predominant English naval tactic right up until the battle of Jutland in 1916. Indeed, after the example made in 1756 of Captain Byng, who was court-martialled and shot for not doing his utmost to engage the enemy, admirals found themselves strongly encouraged not to depart from this policy. In *Candide* Voltaire commented on the event with dry admiration: '*Dans ce pays-ci il est bon de tuer de temps en temps un amiral pour encourager les autres.*'

Nelson, through his friend and mentor Captain Locker, inherited the tactic of Admiral Hawke, under whom Locker had fought at Quiberon Bay in 1759: 'Always lay the Frenchmen close, and you will beat him.' And Nelson took this policy of unhesitating assault to a breathtaking extreme. The battle of Cape St Vincent was 1797's version of the 'Battle of Britain'. England stood alone, when Sir John Jervis (later to be ennobled as Lord St Vincent), with 15 ships, attacked 27 Spanish ships of the line as they were on their way to join French and Dutch fleets in preparation for the invasion of England. During the battle Nelson flouted the contemporary conventions of naval warfare by breaking out of line with his single ship, the *Captain*, to take on seven of the enemy. Then, the *Captain* being shot to pieces, Commodore Nelson personally led a boarding party to appropriate the ship nearest to him—and in an astonishing act of audacity he kept on going, as it were, to board the ship on the other side, a 'first rate' of 100 guns. This coup was ever afterwards known as 'Nelson's Patent Bridge for Boarding First Rates'.

In the following year, at Aboukir Bay on the Nile, Nelson—in command this time—committed the entire fleet to a scheme of attack so apparently crackbrained that the French, totally unprepared, were quite annihilated. Nelson's verdict was: 'Victory is not a name strong enough for such a scene.' False modesty was not his style.

Almost always outnumbered, the great English admirals did not bother to reckon up the odds too carefully. Inevitably, though, this dare-devil moral confidence was eroded, even as the navy continued to bask in its unchallengeable splendour. Towards the end of the nineteenth century there were commanders who were loath to practise their gunnery for fear of blistering their paintwork, while Admiral Sir Arthur Wilson deplored submarines and torpedoes as 'underhand, unfair, and un-English'. At the battle of Jutland in 1916 Admiral Jellicoe, the 1st Earl Jellicoe and, it was said, the only man who could lose the war in an afternoon, settled for at least *not* losing it. Even his swashbuckling deputy, Admiral David Beatty, was reduced to querulousness as a second English battleship went down: 'There seems to be something wrong with our ships today.'

## FREEBOOTERS AND GUNBOATS

Since the Middle Ages official government policy has been to safeguard England's 'wooden walls'. In 1436, the *Libelle [Booklet] of Englyshe Polycye* was counselling

> Keep then the sea
> That is the wall of England,

a policy that 400 years later had become, thanks to Thomas Campbell's 'Ye Mariners of England' (1801) an anthem:

> Britannia needs no bulwarks,
> No towers along the steep;
> Her march is o'er the mountain waves
> Her home is on the deep.

Despite the posture of cocky resolution that the English public invariably adopted whenever the current conquerers of Europe—whether Spanish, French or German—had decided that England was next on their list, an optimistic piece of information was brought to the attention of Philip II of Spain by the Jesuit, Father Parsons: 'Sixteen times England has been invaded. Twice only the native race have repelled the attacking force.' Well, tell it not in Gath.

The navy that harried the Spanish Armada to its catastrophe was not, however, conceived by some sensible monarch and nursed by a government department. Rather it was the unexpectedly respectable child of the pirates and slavers who thrived at a time when the tight-fisted Virgin Queen had her head turned by the easy money and the braggartry of Francis Drake.

Drake came from a long tradition of larger-than-life plundering folk. Chaucer included a representative of the buccaneering business in *The Canterbury Tales*: the 'Shipman' is a sinister figure, perhaps because Chaucer was

himself a customs officer and thus professionally unsympathetic. But the great fifteenth-century English pirates, like John Jolly and Harry Paye, seem to have been popular rumbustious characters, whose tales of chase and capture, washed down with boat-loads of claret and brandy, made them as famous in their home towns as they were infamous to the authorities on the continent.

By 1567 the boisterous English piratical tradition had developed a harder edge. John Hawkins and Francis Drake, on an innocent slave-trading expedition in the Caribbean, were lying at anchor in the harbour of San Juan de Ullua when they were joined by a Spanish treasure fleet. Agreements were signed that the two fleets should share their anchorage in peace. After two days, Hawkins suddenly smelt a rat, but it was too late for the Englishmen ashore. Both Drake in the *Judith* and Hawkins in the *Minion* got out of the harbour alive, but from that nightmare in San Juan de Ullua sprang their will to break the Spaniard at sea.

For nearly 30 years, from 1567, when the sense of justice and fair play of the Devon men was first aroused, until 1595, when the two national heroes set off for the Spanish Main on their last sad but overblown adventure—both lost their lives—English sea-dogs were the plague of Spanish shipping. The Spaniards feared more than any other '*El Draque*', 'the Dragon'. He harried them with a playful deft boldness and a good-humoured magnanimity, born of total confidence. Though the story may be apocryphal, the character of the man is certainly caught in the image of the stocky sea-captain refusing to be diverted from his game of bowls by the first sighting of the Spanish Armada—which was so vast, it was said, that the very sea seemed to groan beneath the weight of it.

Elizabeth found it rewarding to encourage these depredations but at the same time politic to confine them to a strictly 'sporting' level, so that she could put off openly declared war for as long as possible. A careful team manager, she offered her protection to those court gallants and desperadoes who played the game by certain unspecified rules—basically, maximum profit with minimum violence.

The piratical interest in 'prizes' remained the inspiration of the navy well into the nineteenth century. As James Stephen observed in *War in Disguise* (1805), 'the nautical character is peculiarly of a kind to be influenced by such dazzling but precarious prospects'.

In Drake, however, there was a sterner purpose. As relations with Spain foundered, in 1587 he 'singed the King of Spain's beard' in Cadiz harbour. In a letter written during this expedition, the proletarian captain tutored his queen in words which Montgomery, nearly 400 years later, pinned up in his caravan in the desert: 'There must be a beginning of any great matter, but the continuing unto

*Left:* Portrait of Sir Francis Drake c1580–5. Ruddy, proud, greedy, Drake poses in his padded breeches like a ruffled rooster. He glows with physical vitality rather than with power in the political or purely dominating sense.

the end until it be thoroughly finished yields the true glory.' Montgomery passed on Drake's message in his own style: 'The important thing to remember is that we are going to finish with this chap Rommel once and for all.' Nelson likewise had an instinctive understanding of Drake's insight: at the battle of Copenhagen, when ordered to 'leave off action' by his C.-in-C., Admiral Hyde Parker, he flatly refused to leave the business half-finished, saying: 'Leave off action? Now damn me if I do!' He then played shamelessly to the gallery of posterity by putting his telescope to his blind eye, and announcing: 'I really do not see the signal.'

Both Drake and Nelson had immense vanity. But they were impelled throughout their prodigious careers by something else: a code of duty and an idea of fair and decent behaviour which they shared with their more common-place compatriots, and which tyrants defied at their peril. The battle of Copenhagen was fought against the Danes. Nelson prepared for it with his usual care and fought it with his usual panache, but there was, as Southey noted in his biography of Nelson (1813), something missing—'that indignation against the enemy, and that impression of retributive justice which at the Nile had given a sterner temper to his mind'. Nelson said himself, 'It is annihilation that the Country wants . . . to bring Bonaparte to his marrow-bones.'

After Trafalgar (1805) the Royal Navy gradually developed absolute control over the oceans of the world, but generally it used its power with such a sense of tact and justice, particularly in allowing free trade, as effectively to disarm other European powers. A particularly high moral line was taken against pirates and slavers. Drake would probably have puzzled over this, as he had been both; but perhaps he would have appreciated the scope for individual initiative to be exercised, and for an assured moral overview to be acted upon, by the commanders of English gunboats all over the world. As in his time, there were certain rules. Thus in 1840 Commander Denman was able to send in his marines to clear out an enormous Spanish slaving enterprise in Sierra Leone only because of the involvement of a British subject, a black woman who had been kidnapped by one of the main suppliers of slaves to the Spaniards.

Drake would have been delighted with the action taken by Captain the Hon. Henry Keppel. A British subject had been jailed by the Portuguese in Macao for failing to take his hat off during a procession on the feast of Corpus Christi. Popish dogs! A formal protest proved futile; Keppel, at the head of a band of sailors and marines, took a more direct tack, swiftly releasing the prisoner by the use of force. The official British response was a typical diplomatic balancing act: as Keppel put it in his *A Sailor's Life Under Four Sovereigns* (1899), 'For this I was reprimanded by the Admiralty, and thanked by Lord Palmerston.'

Injured diplomatic relations could sometimes be healed on site. In 1903, when the British Consul in Tonga had been insulted, the sloop *Pylades* was called in to enforce an apology, which it did. Then, the British flag having been hoisted and honoured with a 21-gun salute, a rugby team from the *Pylades* played the Tongans and lost. According to one account, 'the home team won the match as they were naked and covered with grease, so they were quite uncollarable'.

The character of the imperial naval Englishman is perhaps most vividly represented by Captain Pakenham. In his spotless white naval uniform, surrounded by a mob of angry brigands and accompanied only by a Turkish interpreter and a solitary midshipman aide, he was not at all perturbed by the company he found himself in and the reports of the atrocities they were supposed to have committed. He flipped open his gold cigarette case and said to his interpreter: 'Tell these ugly bastards that I am not going to tolerate any more of their bestial behaviour.'

# MORALE

The strength of the navy has always been the loyalty and sense of community within it. On the quarterdeck there has ever been a mix between the privileged and/or aristocratic and those who had to work hard for their rank. Drake was one of those who had to come up the hard way, but he got on well with his Commander-in-Chief, Lord Howard, who had (virtually) inherited his naval rank. In a letter to Lord Walsingham Howard wrote: 'Sir, I must not omit to let you know how lovingly and kindly Sir Francis Drake beareth himself.'

After the battle of the Nile Nelson said, 'I had the happiness to command a band of brothers.' The famous 'Nelson touch' was largely a product of the trust he reposed in his fellow officers. This faith was extended to all His Majesty's sailors. It was notably expressed in his signal before the battle of Trafalgar, which he intended to read: 'England confides that every man will do his duty.' However, the word 'confides' being unavailable in the limited vocabulary of naval signals, the message was changed to 'England expects this day that every man will do his duty.' 'These words,' Lady Maria Callcott solemnly suggested to the young readers of her *Little Arthur's History of England* (1835), 'should never be forgotten by any Englishman.'

Some seamen bridled a little at the message, crying, 'Do our duty! Of course we'll do our duty!' And Admiral Lord Collingwood was somewhat impatient at the seemingly endless signals that were being run up: 'I wish Nelson would stop signalling. We all know what to do.' Still, as Lieutenant Ellis of HMS *Ajax* wrote, 'the men cheered vociferously—more, I believe, from love and admiration of their Admiral and leader than from a full appreciation of this . . . signal.'

Considering the cruel and arbitrary recruitment procedures in force for much of the Royal Navy's history, when press-gangs were the order of the day, the evident high morale of the common sailors at Trafalgar constitutes a tribute to Englishmen's ability to settle down and revel in the most adverse material circumstances . . . just so long as they are part of a glorious tradition.

Dr Johnson could not understand this: 'No man will be a sailor who has contrivance enough to get himself into a jail; for being in a ship is being in a jail with the chance of being drowned . . . a man in jail has more room, better food, and commonly better company.' And his argument is unanswerable. Sailors had to put up with the stench of the bilges and the slowly decomposing provisions, the efforts of the ship's cook, to whom 'the composing of a minced pie is metaphysics', ship's biscuits, or 'hard tack', which had to be eaten in the dark if one was squeamish about eating live weavils (officers generally had theirs baked again — 'a few hard taps on the table brought out the little browned carcases') . . . But there was one consolation.

Churchill declared once that 'the Royal Navy has for long been founded on Nelson, rum, buggery and the lash, and so founded it shall continue'. While the last two of this grand quartet may not be prized traditions, the rigmarole surrounding drinking at sea is a typical example of the Englishman's effortless ability to produce meaningless rituals as a way of cementing group loyalties. Thus naval men should never stand for the 'loyal toast'; on Saturdays the toast is always a maudlin 'sweethearts and wives' (followed by the hoary quip, 'and may they never meet'); on Thursdays it is 'bloody war, and a sickly season' (thus quick promotion). Between 1740 and 1970, rum was watered down strictly according to the original prescription of Admiral Vernon, 'Old Grogram' to his seamen, on account of the grogram cape he wore (hence the term 'grog'): half a pint of rum and a quart of water 'to be mixed in a scuttled butt kept for that purpose, and to be done upon deck'. Extra grog would be issued on special occasions. On board the *Revenge*, after a particularly hot day's work in 1805, 'Orders were given to fetch the dead bodies . . . and throw them overboard . . . the next call was "all hands to splice the mainbrace"' (J. Nastyface, *Nautical Economy*, 1836).

There was an extravagance about these men who were the essential teeth of the nation: in their legendary physical strength and courage, and also in their open-hearted pleasure in music and dancing — at least one assumes it was usually open-hearted, despite this mind-boggling entry from the log of Captain William Bligh (later to suffer a mutiny): 'Two men discovered to be shirking their dancing had their grog stopped . . . for risking their health.'

There has also been a long tradition of amateur dramatics: even while Shakespeare was still at work in London, his plays were being performed on board ship. And in 1848, on board HMS *Plover*, 40 or 50 local Esquimaux were treated to a recherché entertainment entitled 'How to Settle Accounts with your Laundress'.

Sailors also had an eye for the elegant lines of a ship, and for the moods and caprices of the sea, that made them more than just fighting machines. And from this crowded and comfortable island, a glimpse of the sea always brought the wide-eyed devil out of the solid English citizen. The great men-o'-war had a

*The Middle Watch of the 'Hector'* by Rowlandson shows a jolly party of sailors
and their guests aboard a man-o'-war in Portsmouth harbour.
In battle this was one of the main gun decks and vividly conveys the cramped conditions
between decks on a Royal Navy ship of the line.

power and grace that pierced the heart of even the most commercial and pacific
Englishman, for whom the sea was a bottomless source of riches and a bound-
less sphere of adventure and glory. Thus, when Admiral St Vincent, who in
retirement always wore his Star of the Order of the Bath, was asked by a boy
where he had found it, the great man replied, 'I found it upon the sea, and if you
become a sailor, and search diligently, you may find just such another.'

Accustomed to coolly manning the guns while the blood and brains of his
friends splatter around him, Jack Tar has always been honoured for his careless
courage. The exiled James II, watching his French invasion fleet being drubbed
off Barfleur, remarked wistfully, 'None but my brave English tars could have done
so gallant a deed.' An Official Medical Report in the Crimea, where seamen
fought alongside soldiers, complained:

> There is no class of men so regardless of their lives as the thoroughbred
> seamen of Her Majesty's Navy; and it is difficult to make them believe that
> there is not something discreditable in crouching behind stone walls in the
> presence of the enemy . . .

They were a terrible foe. In *A Sailor's Life* (1899), Admiral Sir Henry Keppel recalled an attack on imperial war junks near Canton: 'At this moment there arose from the boats as if every man took it up at the same instant, one of those British cheers so full of meaning that I knew at once it was all up with John Chinaman.'

In 1942, English command of the sea through the great men-o'-war was brought to an end, when Japanese aircraft sank the *Renown* and the *Prince of Wales* off Malaya. Nevertheless, it was clear to an airman flying over the sinking ships that the stuffing was in no way being knocked out of Jack Tar:

> During that hour I had seen many men in dire danger waving, cheering and joking as if they were holiday-makers at Brighton . . . It shook me, for here was something above human nature. I take my hat off to them, for in them I saw the spirit that wins wars.

## THE NELSON TRADITION

Horatio Nelson, an operatic figure, a young romantic, one-eyed, his empty sleeve pinned to his bemedalled breast, was loved in his own person (even by the man he cuckolded) as no Englishman has been loved before or since. At Portsmouth in 1805, when he was on his way to Trafalgar, people fell on their knees as he passed. Dying in the hour of total victory, his last words express the man: his vanity ('Don't throw me overboard'), his passion ('Take care of my dear Lady Hamilton'), his unashamed affection for his friends ('Kiss me, Hardy'—no true Englishman will ever believe the modern revisionist nonsense that the old sea-dog should have been talking about something as fanciful as Kismet) and finally his joy at having performed his task ('Thank God I have done my duty').

John Masefield wrote in *Sea Life in Nelson's Time* (1905), 'If all the outward and visible signs of our greatness should pass away, we would still leave behind us a durable monument of what we were in the sayings and doings of the English admirals.'

Nelson's successor in supreme command was Lord Collingwood: a 'taut hand', to whom is ascribed the warning, 'I'll make you touch your hats to a midshipman's coat if it's only hung out on a broomstick to dry.' Collingwood lacked Nelson's charm, although he was clearly devoted to his dog, Bounce, who always accompanied him at sea. In one of his letters, he projected his vanity in his new rank onto his pet:

> The consequential airs he gives himself since he became a right honourable dog are insufferable. He considers it beneath his dignity to play with commoners' dogs, and truly thinks that he does them grace when he condescends to lift up his leg against them. This I think is carrying the insolence of rank too far.

In a letter home to his wife, he revealed the melancholy of the English sea-man—usually masked by discipline, dangerous seas or grog—and perhaps something of what he fights for: 'Tell me, how do the trees that I planted thrive? Is there shade under the three oaks for a considerable summer seat? Do the poplars grow at the walk and does the wall of the terrace stand firm?'

His conduct at Trafalgar was noted by more than one eye-witness:

> . . . descending to the quarterdeck, he visited the men there, enjoining them not to fire a shot in waste, looking himself along the guns to see that they were properly pointed, and commending the sailors, particularly a black man, who was afterwards killed, but who, while he stood beside him, fired ten times directly into the port-holes of the *Santa Ana*.
>
> . . . the Admiral spoke to me about the middle of the action, and again for five minutes immediately after its close: and on neither occasion could I observe the slightest change from his ordinary manner . . . I wondered how a person whose mind was occupied by such a variety of most important concerns could, with the utmost ease and equanimity, inquire kindly after my welfare, and talk of common matters as if nothing of consequence was taking place.

During his circumnavigation of the world in 1577–80, Francis Drake established once and for all a new rule of the sea: an English sea-captain is virtually a law unto himself. He did this by putting on trial and executing his obstreperous companion Thomas Doughty. Such was the skill with which Drake communicated the necessity for this that he took communion and had a last dinner with his old friend before sending him to the block. Afterwards, he spoke to the ship's company:

> My masters, I am a very bad orator, for my bringing up hath not been in learning . . . Here is such controversy between the sailors and the gentlemen and such stomaching between the gentlemen and the sailors, that it doth even make me mad to hear it. But, my masters, I must have it left. For I must have the gentlemen to haul and draw with the mariner, and the mariner with the gentleman. What! Let us show ourselves all to be of a company, and let us not give occasion to the enemy to rejoice at our decay and overthrow . . . To say you come to serve me I will not give you thanks, for it is only Her Majesty that you serve.

A Spanish grandee, Francisco de Zarate, captured with his ship by the *Golden Hind*, described his captor in a letter to the Viceroy Enriquez:

> He is . . . one of the greatest sailors living, both from his skill, and power of commanding. He ordered me to sit next to him and began giving me food from his own plate, telling me not to grieve, that my life and property were

safe . . . When our ship was sacked, no man dared take anything without his orders. He shows them great favour, but punishes the least fault . . . He treats them with affection and they him with respect.

In the late nineteenth century, captains of the Royal Navy were still made of the same stuff. T. T. Jeans, in *Reminiscences of a Naval Surgeon* (1927), described Captain Edward Chichester of the *Immortalité* thus:

> Fierce, truculent and hot-tempered, he was as warm-hearted, single-minded, obstinate and unreasonable as a child. Every characteristic of him, good and bad, was big, and the biggest things about him were his love of England and of his own West country . . .

The commitment to his profession that is required of an English naval officer tends to preclude complete mastery of the finer social graces. Nelson's finesse at sea unfortunately did not extend to his on-shore affairs, but the English public were generous in the allowances they made for sailors. Jane Austen's fatuously vain Sir Walter Elliot, as he tells this story, was exceptional:

> I was to give place to Lord St Ives, and a certain Admiral Baldwin, the most deplorable-looking personage you can imagine; his face the colour of mahogany, rough and rugged to the last degree; all lines and wrinkles, nine grey hairs of a side, and nothing but a dab of powder at top. 'In the name of heaven, who is that old fellow?' said I to a friend of mine who was standing near (Sir Basil Morley). 'Old fellow!' cried Sir Basil. 'It is Admiral Baldwin. What do you take his age to be?' 'Sixty,' said I, 'or perhaps sixty-two.' 'Forty,' replied Sir Basil, 'forty, and no more.' Picture to yourselves my amazement: I shall not easily forget Admiral Baldwin. I never saw quite so wretched an example of what a sea-faring life can do; but to a degree, I know it is the same with them all: they are all knocked about, and exposed to every climate, and every weather, till they are not fit to be seen. It is a pity they are not knocked on the head at once, before they reach Admiral Baldwin's age.

> *Persuasion*, 1818

It may seem odd that, since 1758, members of the Royal family have been regularly introduced into this brutalizing world. But it is certainly the kind of eccentric tradition that has ensured the survival of the monarchy. Indeed, when William IV came to the throne he was more naval officer than king, with a sea dog's social polish. And towards the end of the nineteenth century the Khedive of Egypt was astonished, on inspecting one of Her Majesty's ships at Alexandria, to find one of Her Majesty's own grandsons loading it with coal.

Determined efforts have been made to make gentlemen out of naval officers,

Admiral Lord Nelson, portrait by Beechey. Of the many portraits of
Nelson, this one suggests a shock-headed feral genius, enabling him
to express the implacable hatred of the French that he took in with his
mother's milk. Oddly enough, wherever he went, people would bring
their children to touch him as if he were a saint.

but something about naval life hinders the process. Captain Marryat demonstrated the difficulty in the character of 'Gentleman Chucks':

> He attempted to be very polite, even when addressing the common seamen, and, certainly, he always commenced his observations to them in a very gracious manner, but, as he continued, he became less choice in his phraseology. . . . ' Allow me to observe, my dear man, in the most delicate way in the world, that you are spilling that tar upon the deck – a deck, sir, if I may venture to make the observation, I had the duty of seeing holystoned this morning. You understand me, sir, you have defiled his Majesty's forecastle. I must do my duty, sir, if you neglect yours: so take that – and that – and that – (thrashing the man with his rattan) – you d – d hay-making son of a sea-cook – do it again, d – n your eyes, and I'll cut your liver out.'
>
> *Peter Simple*, 1834

# THE ENGLISH MUSE AT SEA

Sir Richard Grenville was evidently slightly mad – 'he was a man very unquiet in his mind', according to the Dutch account of his 'single-handed' attack on the Spanish Armada on 13 September 1591. The vulgar grandiloquence he displayed is an inescapable strain in the English sea-captain; however, suicidal bravado such as his could only boost the legend of the English sea-devil.

> And the stately Spanish men to their flagship bore him then,
> Where they laid him by the mast, old Sir Richard caught at last,
> And they praised him to his face with their courtly foreign grace;
> But he rose upon their decks, and he cried:
> 'I have fought for Queen and Faith like a valiant man and true;
> I have only done my duty as a man is bound to do:
> With a joyful spirit I Sir Richard Grenville die!'
> And he fell upon their decks, and he died.
>
> And they stared at the dead that had been so valiant and true,
> And had holden the power and glory of Spain so cheap
> That he dared her with one little ship and his English few;
> Was he devil or man? He was devil for aught they knew,
> But they sank his body with honour down into the deep.
>
> Tennyson, 'The Last Fight of the Revenge'

It is difficult to estimate the power of the past. In 'Drake's Drum', Henry Newbolt suggested that the West Country spirit of at least one of England's great preservers was ready to do the job again:

> Drake he's in his hammock an' a thousand mile away,
>     (Capten, art tha sleepin' there below?),
> Slung atween the round shot in Nombre Dios Bay,

An' dreamin' arl the time o' Plymouth Hoe.
Yarnder lumes the Island, yarnder lie the ships,
  Wi' sailor lads a-dancin' heel-an'-toe,
An' the shore-lights flashin', an' the night-tide dashin',
  He sees et arl so plainly as he saw et long ago.

Drake he was a Devon man, an' ruled the Devon seas,
  (Capten, art tha sleepin' there below?),
Rovin' tho' his death fell, he went wi' heart at ease.
  An' dreamin' arl the time o' Plymouth Hoe.
'Take my drum to England, hang et by the shore,
  Strike et when your powder's runnin' low;
If the Dons sight Devon, I'll quit the port o' Heaven,
  An' drum them up the Channel as we drummed them
    long ago.'

Drake he's in his hammock till the great Armadas come,
  (Capten, art tha sleepin' there below?),
Slung atween the round shot, listenin' for the drum,
  An' dreamin' arl the time o' Plymouth Hoe.
Call him on the deep sea, call him up the Sound,
  Call him when ye sail to meet the foe;
Where the old trade's plyin' an' the old flag flyin'
  They shall find him ware an' wakin', as they found him
    long ago!

It was with the battle of Quiberon Bay, in 1759, that the English Navy finally wrested predominance from the French and Spanish. 'Rule Britannia' appeared for the first time in this year, as did 'Heart of Oak', composed by David Garrick and William Boyce. Such was the latter's popularity that it became customary for sailors to be summoned to their quarters for battle by the beating of a drum to its rhythm.

Come cheer up, my lads, 'tis to glory we steer,
To add something more to this wonderful year:
To honour we call you, not press you like slaves,
For who are so free as the sons of the waves?
  Heart of oak are our ships, heart of oak are our men;
  We always are ready, steady boys, steady,
  We'll fight, and we'll conquer again and again.

We ne'er see our foes, but we wish them to stay;
They never see us, but they wish us away;
If they run, why we follow, and run them ashore;
For, if they won't fight us, we cannot do more.
  Heart of oak, etc.

They swear they'll invade us, these terrible foes;
They frighten our women, our children, and beaus;
But, should their flat-bottoms in darkness get o'er,
Still Britons they'll find, to receive them on shore.
    Heart of oak, etc.

We'll still make 'em run, and we'll still make 'em sweat,
In spite of the Devil, and Brussel's gazette;
Then cheer up, my lads, with one heart let us sing,
Our soldiers, our sailors, our statesmen and King.
    Heart of oak, etc.

The groggy glory of the Royal Navy as it sailed slowly, grandly, into relative insignificance, was captured in 'West Indian Cruise', reproduced from Sydney Greenwood's *Stoker Greenwood's Navy* (1983):

Drinking for the Empire, boozing for the Raj,
Sozzling for the honour of the Flag,
After quarts of Planters Punch,
And a very special lunch,
No wonder that our knees begin to sag.
But we stagger back at Sunset to put on our Mess Undress,
And bloody but unbowed go racing back,
To have a little snorter,
With the Governor's lovely daughter,
For the honour of the dear old Union Jack.

Drinking for the Empire, boozing for the Crown,
Sozzling for the good old Union Jack,
We never make a fuss,
Cause' they're all alike to us,
Whether white, or nearly white, or merely black.
They come aboard in thousands every time we enter port,
No wonder that our wine bills are so large,
From shoving tots of Coatses,
Down a thousand thirsty throatses,
For the prestige of the glorious British Raj.

Drinking for the Empire, boozing for the Flag,
Boozing for Britannia Rules the Waves,
We display the well known verve,
Of the Fleet in Which we Serve,
And show them how an Englishman behaves.
Though the party may be bloody, we keep stiff the upper lip,
And never let the locals get us down,
Crying Dulce et Decorum,
We must drain another jorum,
To the never dying credit of the Crown.

Drinking for the Empire, boozing for the Queen,
Sozzling for the country of the free,
When the Social Sec. compels,
We all land at seven bells,
For cocktails, bridge and dancing with HE.
Though the body's feeling jaded, and the tongue is somewhat furred,
And a peaceful night aboard would be just grand,
Our weary limbs we gird on,
Assume the white man's burden,
For the honour of the dear old Motherland.

Drinking for the Empire, boozing for the Flag,
Soaking for the balance of World Power.
They are many, we are few,
But we know what each must do,
And men shall say 'This was their finest hour'.
We will sozzle in the ballroom, and sozzle on the beach,
We will sozzle on the hillside, we will sozzle on the street,
But we never will surrender,
Being guardians of the splendour,
Of a Nation that has never known defeat.

Portrait of John Plampin by Thomas Gainsborough. The English
invented the 'gentleman farmer'. John Plampin would not be getting
mud on his beautiful coat, but implicitly associates himself with the
natural and authentic life of the countryside rather than the artifice
and corruption of courts and cities.

# CHAPTER FOUR

—————— • ——————

# THE RURAL ENGLISHMAN

Turn into the churchyard in any sleepy untroubled corner of England, and there, among yew trees or in the cool, musty church, you will find memorials to explorers, warriors and statesmen, individuals who, wherever their duty or ambition took them, however large and bloody the canvas on which they painted, whatever the honours they received from a grateful nation, always knew that they belonged here, in this quiet place.

Wide-ranging and pugnacious, the English are soft and homely where it comes to their own land: 'England may not unfitly be compared to a house, not very great, but convenient, and the several shires may properly be resembled to the rooms thereof . . .', as Thomas Fuller began his survey, *The Worthies of England* (1662).

England was made to seem homogeneous and secure as early as the eleventh century. The Domesday Book laboriously accounted for every single settlement in the land, and for everything of marketable value in it. Since then innumerable surveys, less painstaking and usually more readable, have followed — by antiquaries, poets and journalists. Over a period of time, the English came to feel that they knew what they spoke of when they pronounced the name 'England'.

Together with their delight in all her intimate details, the English were quick to gather all these myriad facts into an idea, even a myth. This myth of England was developed particularly by those men who spent their lives abroad in her service. They were sustained by an idea of England which took on a feminine, rural form, a mammarial ideal to set against the weird and exotic reality in which they spent their lives.

The ideal was established by the end of the reign of Elizabeth I. Shakespeare expressed it in *Richard II*:

> This other Eden, demi paradise . . .
> This blessed plot, this earth, this realm, this England . . .'

John Milton, in *Paradise Lost,* summed up the Garden of Eden as if it might be any English gentleman's country estate:

> Thus was this place
> A happy rural seat of various view.

Ben Jonson had earlier, in 1612, praised the country house of Robert Sidney as almost literally paradisiacal:

> The painted partridge lies in every field,
> And, for thy mess, is willing to be killed . . .
> Thou hast thy ponds that pay thee tribute fish,
> Fat aged carps, that run into thy net . . .

(Later on the English gentry would insist, in the same vein, that foxes enjoyed a good run quite as much as did their pursuers.)

And, though England's rural charms, under the pressure of her ever-increasing progeny, might in parts become less voluptuous, the protestations of devotion became ever more misty-eyed and extravagant. It was with an almost religious fervour that W. E. Henley asked himself, in 'Pro Rege Nostro' (1900):

> What have I done for you,
> England, my England?

Despite clear evidence of the brutal facts of rural life, its boredom, its deprivation, even its starvation—particularly as capitalist agriculture got into its stride—rural England became a source of enchantment and 'rootedness' for an increasingly city-pent and insecure populace, even into the twentieth century. P. G. Wodehouse and Agatha Christie reassured us that there was a seemingly eternal Garden of Eden, within easy reach of Paddington station, where serpents and snakes in the grass might raise their ugly heads, but would surely be baffled and beaten in the end. At a slightly higher level of brow, however, novelists were introducing sex into Eden, and affirming the natural innocence of sex by association with the natural rhythms of the country. In the famous opening chapter of *The Rainbow*, D. H. Lawrence's ploughmen enjoy a dark symbolic intercourse with the earth '. . . feeling the pulse and body of the soil, that opened to the furrow for the grain and became smooth and supple after their ploughing, and clung to their feet with a weight that pulled like desire'.

However, the type of rural Englishman most easily identified, and for this reason much imitated abroad, is the English country gentleman. All you need to set yourself up as one is a bit of land, a large house, a few horses, a collection of assorted dogs and servants, clothes of indeterminate age, shape or colour, a hip flask, a gun and an air of breezy assurance.

# *AN INHABITED LANDSCAPE*

The English landscape is an inhabited one, and John Keats liked it that way:

> . . . give me a long brown plain for my money, so that I may meet with some of Edmund Ironside's descendants; give me a barren mould, so I may meet with some shadowing of Alfred in the shape of a gypsy, a huntsman, or a shepherd. Scenery is fine, but human nature is finer . . .

Kipling, in 'Puck's Song' (from *Puck of Pook's Hill*, 1906), read an ancient and terrible record beneath the unassuming exterior of the English countryside:

> See you the ferny ride that steals
> Into the oak-woods far?
> O that was whence they hewed the keels
> That rolled to Trafalgar. . . .
>
> See you the dimpled track that runs
> All hollow through the wheat?
> O that was where they hauled the guns
> That smote King Philip's fleet. . . .
>
> See you our stilly woods of oak,
> And the dread ditch beside?
> O that was where the Saxons broke
> On the day that Harold died. . . .

G. K. Chesterton took his history from an even less reliable source: the 'rolling English road' was seen through a benevolent drunken haze:

> Before the Roman came to Rye or out to Severn strode,
> The rolling English drunkard made the rolling English road.
> A reeling road, a rolling road, that rambles round the shire,
> And after him the parson ran, the sexton and the squire;
> A merry road, a mazy road, and such as we did tread
> The night we went to Birmingham by way of Beachy Head.
>
> I knew no harm of Bonaparte and plenty of the Squire,
> And for to fight the Frenchman I did not much desire;
> But I did bash their baggonets because they came arrayed
> To straighten out the crooked road an English drunkard made,
> Where you and I went down the lane with ale-mugs in our hands,
> The night we went to Glastonbury by way of Goodwin Sands.

According to a contemporary, Thomas Bewick, the celebrated early-nineteenth-century wood-engraver from Northumberland's '. . . manners were somewhat rustic . . . but he was shrewd and disdained to ape the gentleman'. In his *Memoir* (1830), Bewick recalled the characters who lived on the Commons near his childhood home—people shortly to be dispossessed by the Enclosure Acts:

> . . . one of these 'Will Bewick' . . . was the first person from whom I gathered a kind of general knowledge of Astronomy and of the Magnitude of the universe—He had, the Year through noticed the appearances of the stars and the Planets and would discourse largely on the subject.
>
> I think I see him yet, sitting on a mound or seat, by the Hedge of his Garden, regardless of the cold and intent upon viewing the heavenly bodies, pointing to them with his large hands and eagerly imparting his knowledge to me, with a strong voice, such a one as one seldom hears—I remember well with being much struck with his appearance—his stern-looking brows—high cheek-bones—quick eye and longish visage, and at his resolution (upon another occasion) when he determined upon risking his own life to save that of another man.—This Man, in the employ of my father, while at work as a Pitman, had lost his way, in the coal Workings and was a wanting, for perhaps a day or two (my father being from home) when our old neighbour, just described, who was also a Pitman & knew the workings, equipt himself with every thing he thought necessary for so hazardous an undertaking, and when he was about to go down the Pit shaft, I felt much distressed at seeing my Mother trembling in great agitation of mind, for the safety of both him & his lost associate—After travelling and traversing through the old workings of the colliery, for a long time—so long that it was feared he had also lost himself—he however having found the Man alive at last—when with his well known thundering voice, from the bottom of the Shaft, he called 'Alls Well'—to the inexpressible joy of all who now crowded the Pit heap or surrounded its mouth.

In *A Song for Every Season* (1971), Bob Copper told of another archetypal 'English countryman':

> John, then, if ever there was, could be regarded as a typical downland shepherd. His crook and his dog were his constant companions and he had developed that mode of walking peculiar to men who are used to covering long distances alone and often in bad weather. He strode forward from the hips, thrusting his heavy-booted feet over the ground in long raking strides which carried him along at surprising speed with little apparent effort. He was above average height, broad-shouldered, but the thing I remember above all else was the aura of calm that surrounded him. His actions, speech and thought were all geared down in speed and proclaimed an inner peace that made his presence as soothing and reassuring as the slow, quiet ticking of a grandfather clock. He had a fund of tales and experiences which he loved to narrate with his short-stemmed briar pipe held rigidly in position by one strong, isolated off-white upper incisor. His anecdotes were often protracted and included long repetitions of dialogue literally punctuated with 'he sez t' me and so I sez t' 'im'. As the humour of a remembered

*The Harvest Moon* by Samuel Palmer. The English view of the countryside alternates
between the earthy and the exalted. Palmer was definitely of the latter tendency.
His visions of a Kentish Arcadia show images, like this one, of timeless
fruitfulness to set against the horrors of Victorian industrial society.

situation reclaimed him his eyes would twinkle through lids that gave the
impression of closing upwards like a pigeon's and his words came through a
grin that widened as the story unfolded. His voice would gradually climb
higher and higher in pitch until he became almost, if not quite, unintelligible.
But so infectious was his mood that, although the theme had been lost,
everyone ended up laughing as merrily as he.

'I slept in a goose coop, one night, over St John's,' he said, opening a story
that at once appeared to have Chaucerian potentialities. 'We used to set off
from Rott'n'dean three days before a sale t'give us plentys of time on the road
so as not to tire th' ship out too much and allow us one day for pitching 'em
out into the various lots. On the road, the same as when we got there, we used
to doss down wherever we could, y'see. Wal, we was sleeping rough in a barn
there and that ol' heap o' straw we wuz laying in was just alive wid rats. Rats?
I've never known so many rats in m' life. They wuz swarming about like ants
on a ant heap, my boy, and kept runnin' all over us. I'm jiggered if I could

sleep no how. Presen'ly I sees this ol' goose coop over in the corner so I crawls inside and shuts the door. That kept 'em off all right and I sleeps like a top.' Here his voice started to soar. 'Nex' mornin' I'm damned if t'other cheps could find me anywheres. They looked all over th' place. Then drackly they sees me fast asleep in this 'ere coop. "C'mon," they 'ollers, "look lively, John, you'll hatch out if y' lays in there any longer."'

William Cobbett's view was that, as the gentry grew prosperous, the labouring classes suffered: it was a case of 'rich land and poor labourers'. When the labourers rose up, however, as in the 'Bread or Blood' and 'Captain Swing' revolts of the early nineteenth century, the objects of their wrath were not the gentry but the farmers or yeomen.

> . . . a yeoman is a commoner, one undignified with any title of gentility. A condition of people almost peculiar to England, seeing in France, Italy and Spain . . . no medium between gentlemen and peasants. Whereas amongst us the yeomen . . . are in effect the basis of all the nation, formerly most mounting the subsidy book in peace with their purses, and the muster roll in war with their persons.
>
> Thomas Fuller, *The Worthies of England*, 1662

In the seventeenth century, in the famous portrait of Mr Hastings by Anthony Cooper, First Earl of Shaftesbury, we are presented with the English country gentleman in his raw and unrefined condition. The basic ingredients are all there, though: the slovenliness, the animals under your feet and occupying the chairs, the chapel used as a sort of pantry, the rough and easy intimacy with the servants . . .

> Mr Hastings was an original in our age, or rather the copy of our nobility in ancient days, in hunting and not warlike times. He was low, very strong, and very active, of a reddish flaxen hair, his clothes always green cloth, and never all worth when new five pounds. His house was perfectly of the old fashion, in the midst of a large park well stocked with deer, and near the house rabbits to serve his kitchen, many fish-ponds and great store of wood and timber; a bowling green in it, long but narrow, full of high ridges, it being never levelled since it was ploughed; they used round sand balls and it had a banqueting-house like stand, a large one built in a tree. He kept all manner of sport-hounds that ran buck, fox, hare, otter and badger, and hawks long and short winged; he had a walk in the New Forest and the manor of Christ Church. This last supplied him with red deer, sea and river fish; and indeed all his neighbours' grounds and royalties were open to him, who bestowed all his time in such sports, but what he borrowed to caress his neighbours' wives and daughters, there being not a woman in all his walks of the degree of a yeoman's wife or under, and under the age of forty, but it was extremely her fault if he were not intimately acquainted with her. This made him very popular, always speaking kindly to the husband, brother or father, who was

to boot very welcome to his house whenever he came; there he found beef pudding and small beer in great plenty, a house not so neatly kept as to shame him and his dirty shoes, the great hall strewed with marrow bones, full of hawks' perches, hounds, spaniels and terriers, the upper sides of the hall hung with the fox-skins of this and the last year's skinning, here and there a polecat intermixed, guns and keepers' and huntsmen's poles in abundance. The parlour was a large long room as properly furnished; in a great hearth paved with brick lay some terriers and the choicest hounds and spaniels; seldom but two of the great chairs had litters of young cats in them, which were not to be disturbed, he having always three or four attending him at dinner, and a little white round stick of fourteen inches long lying by his trencher that he might defend such meat as he had no mind to part with to them. The windows which were very large, served for places to lay his arrows, crossbows, stonebows and other such like accoutrements; the corners of the room full of the best chose hunting and hawking poles; an oyster table at the lower end, which was of constant use twice a day all the year round, for he never failed to eat oysters before dinner and supper through all seasons . . . On one side of this end of the room was the door of a closet, wherein stood the strong beer and the wine, which never came thence but in single glasses, that being the rule of the house, exactly observed for he never exceeded in drink or permitted it. On the other side was a door into an old chapel, not used for devotion; the pulpit, as the safest place, was never wanting of a cold chine of beef, pasty of venison, gammon of bacon, or great apple pie with thick crust extremely baked.

He was well-natured, but soon angry, calling his servants bastard and cuckoldy knaves, in one of which he often spoke the truth to his own knowledge, and sometimes in both, though of the same man. He lived to a hundred, never lost his eyesight, but always writ and read without spectacles and got to horse without help. Until past fourscore he rode to the death of a stag as well as any.

This manner of country life offered itself as a butt for the urbane Englishman's wit:

> 'Yet Sir, (said I) there are many people who are content to live in the country.'
> JOHNSON: 'Sir . . . they who are content to live in the country are fit for the country.'

In a letter of 1768 to George Montagu, Horace Walpole expressed a similar disgust:

> Mr Chute tells me you have taken a new house in Squireland, and have given yourself up for two years more to port and parsons. I am very angry, and resign you to the works of the devil or the Church, I don't care which. You will get the gout, turn Methodist, and expect to ride to Heaven upon your own great toe . . . Will you end like a fat farmer, repeating annually the price of oats and discussing stale newspapers?

Later, in the nineteenth century, in *Crotchet Castle* (1831), Thomas Love Peacock had offered an equally scathing but rather more sinister picture of a country squire, for a more brutal age:

> Sir Simon Steeltrap of Steeltrap Lodge, Member for Crouching-Curtown, Justice of the Peace for the county, and Lord of the United Manors of Spring-gun-and-Treadmill; a great preserver of game and public morals. By administering the laws which he assists in making, he disposes, at his pleasure, of the land and its live stock, including all the two-legged variety, with and without feathers, in a circumference of several miles round Steeltrap Lodge. He has enclosed commons and woodlands; abolished cottage gardens; taken the village cricket-ground into his own park, out of pure regard to the sanctity of Sunday; shut up footpaths and alehouses (all but those which belong to his electioneering friend, Mr Quassia, the brewer); put down fairs and fiddlers; committed many poachers; shot a few; convicted one-third of the peasantry; suspected the rest; and passed nearly the whole of them through a wholesome course of prison discipline which finished their education at the expense of the county.

Characters such as this had a redoubtable opponent in the figure of William Cobbett:

> I saw great Cobbett riding,
> The horseman of the shires;
> And his face was red with judgement
> And a light of Luddite fires:
> And south to Sussex and the sea the lights leapt up for liberty
> The trumpet of the yeomanry, the hammer of the squires.
>
> G. K. Chesterton, 'The Old Song'

It was at Birmingham (in 1829 clearly a more rural place than it has become) that Cobbett heard the siren song of a peaceful country life drawing him away from his political mission. He described the scene in *Rural Rides*:

> As we advanced on the way, the snow became deeper on the fields, and I really longed to be out in it and thought much more, for the time, about the tracking of hares than about the making of speeches. I could not help reflecting, and mentioning to my daughter, how strangely I had been by degrees pulled along, during my whole life, away from those pursuits and scenes which were most congenial to my mind. Being at Botley, I was disentangling myself from London by degrees. I had got very nearly to the smock-frock and I was inculcating in the minds of my children, as they grew up, a love of country life. I hated London, and saw it as seldom as possible. Just at this time venomous Gibbs laid hold on me and, having heard that it was the intention of the Government to crush me, my resentment urged me on to combat. My natural taste, my unsubduable bias for the country has

*Harvest Scene. Afternoon* by G. R. Lewis, 1815. This is the classic
rural English idyll, soon to be irretrievably damaged by falling wheat prices
and the monstrous magic of industrialization.

never been, and can never be overcome as long as I have life. But to yield, to
prostrate myself, to suffer myself to be subdued or humbled by *such men* was
what my soul recoiled at.

# THE VIEW FROM THE CITY

Logan Pearsall Smith followed the Oscar Wilde school of thought ('Nature is so
uncomfortable') in his disdain for the great outdoors: 'Thank God the sun has
gone in and I don't have to go out and enjoy it.' However, he retained a rose-tinted
view of rural life from his armchair:

> The fields and old farms, the little river, the village church among its elms,
> the formal gates of the park with the roofs of the great house beyond, all
> made, in the level sun, a dream-like picture. I was strangely happy; and how
> familiar to my long-acquainted eyes was every detail of the scene before me!
> There were the trout-streams I had fished in, the meadows I had galloped
> over—through how many countless, quiet English years had I not lived in this
> very landscape, and loved and hunted, courting innumerable vicars'

daughters from cover to cover of all the countless, mild, old-fashioned novels of English country life which I have dreamed away my own life in reading?

'Paradise Regained', from *More Trivia*, 1921

English townspeople are prepared to meet Nature halfway, in the form of picnics, to be religiously endured at Glyndebourne, Goodwood and point-to-point meetings, and whenever the weather looks as if it might hold, almost as if they were placating some antique rural deity. Pepys was witness to an apparently successful and enjoyable seventeenth-century picnic (though our impression of enjoyment may come from the evident pleasure with which Pepys ogled the ladies):

> I away to my boat, and up with it as far as Barne Elmes. . . I walked the length of the Elmes, and with great pleasure saw some gallant ladies and people come with their bottles, and basket, and chairs, and form, to sup under the tree by the waterside, which was mighty pleasant.

In 1770 Horace Walpole was invited to a picnic supper given by Lord and Lady Temple for Princess Amelia. He recalled:

> The idea was really pretty, but as my feelings have lost something of their romantic sensibility, I did not quite enjoy such an entertainment 'al fresco' quite as much as I should have done 20 years ago . . . I could not help laughing as I surveyed our troop, which instead of tripping lightly to such an Arcadian entertainment, were hobbling down by the balustrades, wrapped up in coats and great-coats, for fear of catching cold.

By the nineteenth century, the picnic was dropping its pretence of being an Arcadian idyll, and was approaching its final form, as a kind of outward-bound survival course. As Surtees remarked in *Plain or Ringlets*, 'a picnic should entail a little of the trouble and enterprise of life, gathering sticks, lighting the fire, boiling the pot, buying or stealing the potatoes'.

## *THE RUSTIC SPIRIT*

It may be said that the English have turned patriotism into a fine art. It is not always a brassy trumpet call. Often it is uncertain, searching out the elusive but long-matured spirit of a people, deep-rooted as an oak, in the quiet places of England:

> He is English as this gate, these flowers, this mire.
> And when, at eight years old, Lob-lie-by-the-fire
> Came in my books, this was the man I saw.
> He has been in England as long as dove and daw,

Calling the wild cherry tree the merry tree,
The rose campion Bridget-in-her-bravery;
And in a tender mood he, as I guess,
Christened one flower Love-in-Idleness;
And, while he walked from Exeter to Leeds
One April, called all cuckoo-flowers Milkmaids.
For reasons of his own, to him the wren
Is Jenny Pooter. Before all other men
'Twas he first called the Hog's Back the Hog's Back.
That Mother Dunch's Buttocks should not lack
Their name was his care. He too could explain
Totteridge and Totterdown and Juggler's Lane;
He knows if any one. Why Tumbling Bay
Inland in Kent is called so he might say.

Edward Thomas, 'Lob'

A. E. Housman showed us the rural Englishman as a lost child, in an anxious and unhappy present:

Into my heart an air that kills,
From yon far country blows.
What are those blue remembered hills,
What spires, what farms are those?

That is the land of lost content,
I see it shining plain,
The happy highways where I went,
And cannot come again.

'A Shropshire Lad'

Finally, Gerard Manley Hopkins captured, within the brackets of his Roman Catholic belief, a spirit of individuality, independence — eccentricity even — that in England seems programmed into the very fall of the light:

Glory be to God for dappled things —
For skies of couple-colour as a brinded cow;
For rose-moles all in stipple upon trout that swim;
Fresh-firecoal chestnut-falls; finches' wings;
Landscape plotted and pieced — fold, fallow and plough;
And all trades, their gear and tackle and trim.

All things counter, original, spare, strange;
Whatever is fickle, freckled (who knows how?)
With swift, slow; sweet, sour; adazzle, dim;
He fathers-forth, whose beauty is past change:
              Praise him.

'Pied Beauty'

*Young Man Among Roses* by Nicholas Hilliard. The jewelled
narcissism of this miniature perfectly conveys the lovesick plaints of
the Elizabethan sonneteers. Andrea Trevisano had observed in 1497,
'The English are great lovers of themselves, and of everything
belonging to them. They think that there are no other men than
themselves and no other world than England, and whenever they see a
handsome foreigner they say that "he looks like an Englishman".'

# CHAPTER FIVE

·

# THE AMOROUS ENGLISHMAN

T here's nothing half so sweet in life
As love's young dream

warbled one of the most popular of Romantic poets, Thomas Moore, in one of his
*Irish Melodies*. In fact, for the average Englishman who is not himself under the
ether, there is nothing half so wearisome or embarrassing as love's young dream.
When he is transfixed by the Laughing Love God, he tends to find himself out of
his depth, as P. G. Wodehouse observed on Bertie Wooster's behalf:

> I am a man who can read faces, and Chuffy's had seemed to me highly
> suggestive. Not only had its expression, as he spoke of Pauline, been that of a
> stuffed frog with a touch of the Soul's Awakening about it, but it had also
> turned a fairly deepish crimson in colour. The tip of the nose had wiggled,
> and there had been embarrassment in the manner. The result being that I had
> become firmly convinced that the old schoolmate had copped it properly
> and was in love.
>
> *Thank-you Jeeves*, 1934

This sort of confusion arises from the Englishman's refusal to take seriously
anything which is clearly outside the realms of common sense. And much of his
literature is an attempt by the Laughing Love God to explain himself at the court
of common sense: 'Yes, I know it's silly, but ...' Shakespeare admitted, 'My
mistress' eyes are nothing like the sun', and in 'The Triple Fool' John Donne said
suavely:

> I am two fools, I know,
> For loving, and for saying so
> In whining Poetry.

There is also a darker side to the Englishman's bashfulness. Not only is love silly,
it is also wicked, fearful and nasty. Chaucer sighed, 'Allas, allas, that ever love

was sinne.' Milton went into more detail in *Paradise Lost* when he described the figure of Sin, a woman seated at the gates of Hell; she is very nice from the waist upward but 'foul' below. 'And in her womb are kennelled the Hounds of Hell, the fruit of her being raped by her own offspring, Death'— a thought to put even the hardest-boiled gallant off his stroke. In *Samson Agonistes*, Delilah served as a good excuse for Milton to close in on the villain of Creation:

> ... into the snare I fell
> Of fair fallacious looks, venereal trains,
> Softened with pleasure and voluptuous life;
> At length to lay my head and hallowed pledge
> Of all my strength into the lascivious lap
> Of a deceitful concubine ...

Sadly for all concerned, Milton married, had three daughters, and took in also a sister-in-law and his mother-in-law. And, just as Delilah was a Philistine, so Milton's wife came from the enemy camp: she was a Cavalier. The amorous Cavalier showed a different attitude—cynical, clever, irreverent:

> Then thus think I
> Love is the fart
> Of every heart:
> It pains a man when 'tis kept close,
> And others doth offend when 'tis let loose.

Sir John Suckling, 'Love's Offence'

Love was also the world of Restoration comedy, of patches and the pox, of fine manners and much flourishing of lace handkerchiefs, of well bred indecency —'A Barbary shape, and a jut with her bum would stir an anchorite,' says Valentine appreciatively in Congreve's *Love for Love* (1695). In the eighteenth century love was a world of aristocratic adultery: Lady Oxford's progeny were known as 'the Harleian Miscellany'.

And English love had its nobler side, in the passionate friendships that were able to develop, in the unashamed complaisance of Lord Hamilton towards the adultery between his friend, Lord Nelson, and his wife, Emma; and, as a late flowering of this spirit, in the intense love between Harold Nicolson and Vita Sackville-West, despite the fact that both of them had homosexual relationships with others.

The higher-minded Victorians had a much more difficult time of it. On top of puritanical queasiness they were burdened with ideals of chivalry and womanly purity. In *Idylls of the King* Tennyson's King Arthur made his knights swear

*82*

To lead sweet lives in purest chastity,
To love one maiden only, cleave to her
And worship her by years of noble deeds,
Until they won her; for indeed I knew
Of no more subtle master under heaven
Than is the maiden passion for a maid,
Not only to keep down the base in man,
But teach high thought, and amiable words
And courtliness, and the desire of fame,
And love of truth, and all that makes a man.

Whereas a medieval *preux chevalier* could keep his hand in by ravishing the odd wench from below the salt and still claim to be *sans peur et sans reproche*, this agreeable moral arrangement was not available to the English gentleman. Moreover, since a young man would avoid self-pollution because it led inevitably to disfiguring diseases and early death (much as today he would shun smoking and cholesterol), the more reflective Englishman might have problems when it came to grappling with corporeal reality. Charles Kingsley and his wife spent the first month of their honeymoon in prayer and study before taking the plunge. John Ruskin took one look at his naked wife on his wedding night and refused to take it. He explained that he did not want to tire her, so that she would be fit for their Alpine walks together. He continued to spare her the exhaustion of marital relations for the rest of their married life, until she divorced him for failing in his conjugal duties.

A much more romantic story is that of the painter and poet, Dante Gabriel Rossetti, who married the 'Beatrice' of his paintings, Elizabeth Siddal, after a long engagement. Only two years later, in 1862, she was dead of an overdose of laudanum, and in his grief he placed a notebook full of poems he had written for her beside her face in the coffin. Seven years later, he had the coffin in Highgate cemetery disinterred and recovered the book, which was published to great acclaim.

In the nineteenth and twentieth centuries, love was also a world of discreetly managed affairs conducted over weekend country parties. Discreet on the whole, at least. Lord Palmerston, known as 'Lord Cupid', who belonged to the Tally Ho! and the swish-of-the-riding-crop school of seduction, was never forgiven by Queen Victoria for attempting to apply his technique one night on a guest at Windsor Castle.

By and large, the Englishman is no more a connoisseur of the erotic than he is of anything else. He has certainly nothing to match the depravity of the French, except of course for a particular interest in flogging. Demanded the gentleman of his mistress in Thomas Shadwell's *The Virtuoso* (1676): 'Where are the instruments of pleasure? . . . I was so used to it at Westminster School I could never leave it off since . . . Do not spare thy pains. I love castigation mightily.'

Another Westminster man was John Cleland, the author of *Fanny Hill, or the Memoirs of a Woman of Pleasure* (1748–9), probably the most widely read work of top-quality pornography in English. When Cleland followed this success with *Memoirs of a Coxcomb* (1751), the Privy Council offered him a pension of £100 if he would only stop producing any more villainous literature.

In the eighteenth century, the demi-monde was highly visible. What Casanova called 'English overcoats' were freely available, and members of the 'Cyprian' community advertised in such publications as *Harris' List of Covent Garden Ladies, or Man of Pleasure's Kalendar.* There were flagellants' clubs, of course, and what were called 'molly houses', described by a visitor in 1718: 'The men calling one another "my dear", and hugging, kissing and tickling each other, as if they were a mixture of wanton males and females, some telling others they ought to be whipped for not coming to school more frequently.'

Homosexuals had a more difficult time in the late nineteenth century, though they could no longer be hanged. Even Oscar Wilde's friend, the poet Ernest Dowson, wanted to wean the celebrated sodomite onto a 'more wholesome taste'. When the two of them were in Dieppe after Wilde's release from prison, Dowson packed him off to a brothel, cheered on, according to Yeats, by an enthusiastic crowd. Wilde was not converted. 'It was like cold mutton,' he muttered as he emerged. 'But tell it in England,' he let the crowd hear him say, 'for it will entirely restore my character.'

# PUBLIC LIFE

Where the amorous Englishman cannot afford to be caught with his trousers down is in the realm of public life. It is here that the censorious injunction, 'No sex please, we're British', applies most forcibly. As Macaulay so rightly said, 'We know of no spectacle so ridiculous as the British public in one of its periodical fits of morality' ('On Moore's Life of Byron', 1830). It is all a question of how one carries it off.

Charles II and his brother James were as promiscuous a pair of rogues as ever ruled the country, but Charles at least handled his affairs with a light French touch. Of James, Charles remarked shrewdly, 'He will lose his kingdom by his bigotry, and his soul for a lot of trollops.' Where this left Charles's own soul it is hard to guess, unless it be that James seemed such a *sad* profligate—'Dismal Jimmy,' as Nell Gwyn called him. Also, James liked ugly women—or, should we say, unusual-looking women—and Charles suggested that his brother was given his mistresses by his priests, as a penance.

The representatives of the House of Hanover started off by being quietly uxorious. George I arrived in England with two German mistresses, one very fat even by the standards of the day, when everyone who could afford it was at least portly, and the other thin and ugly. Both were well into middle age. 'Two considerable specimens of the King's bad taste and strong stomach,' commented Lord Chesterfield, but it is more probable that they were specimens of the Hanoverians' strong suit: loyalty. Nevertheless, this definite predilection for the matronly led to Napoleon's remark, '*Il parait que vous aimez less vieilles femmes en Angleterre.*'

George II was devoted to his wife. When she was dying, she told him he must marry again. 'Never,' he sobbed. 'I shall have mistresses.' George III confined his attentions, with painful self-restraint, entirely to his homely Queen. We must hope that he had his reward in heaven, for he had none from his sons.

The Prince of Wales, later George IV, fell in love with expensive regularity. At last, having amassed debts of over half a million pounds, he submitted in 1795 to an arranged marriage with Princess Caroline of Brunswick. He had not been warned that she was fat and vulgar and had a powerful body odour. The Earl of Malmesbury introduced them before the wedding:

> She very properly, in consequence of my saying to her it was the right way of proceeding, attempted to kneel to him. He raised her (gracefully enough) and embraced her, said barely one word, turned round, and retired to a distant part of the apartment and calling me to him, said: 'Harris, I am not well; pray get me a glass of brandy.'

The Prince had to drink himself into a stupor in order to steel himself for his nuptial duties, and was found the following morning on the floor with his head in the grate. The couple separated after two weeks, and in 1814 she went abroad, where she proceeded to misbehave on a fairly spectacular scale.

In 1820, the now George IV had her tried for adultery to prevent her joining him for the coronation. She had not improved with age, but there was such wild popular support for her that divorce proceedings had to be dropped. The Duke of Wellington, surrounded by men with pick-axes demanding an oath of loyalty from him to his Queen neatly outflanked them: 'Well, gentlemen, since you will have it so—God save the Queen!—and may all your wives be like her.'

It is said that, when Napoleon finally passed away on St Helena, George IV's groom made a bit of a meal of the news. 'Sir,' he said, 'your greatest enemy is dead.'

'Is she, by God!' roared the king joyfully.

We have to go back to Charles II to find a roué of Edward VII's stature. (It is notable that both of them would perhaps have regarded France as their true spiritual home.) While Prince of Wales, Edward, like others before him, helped to bring his father's grey hairs in sorrow to the grave by embarking at the earliest opportunity on a career of idleness and fornication. When at length he acceded to the throne, *The Times* commented drily that he must often have prayed 'lead us not into temptation' with a feeling akin to hopelessness.

Perhaps the most touching and typically English manifestation of the chivalric spirit, at its most self-effacing and seedy, is the traditional trip to Brighton with a tart and a couple of private detectives to take notes, so that the wife can sue for divorce and appear to be the injured party. When in 1936 it became clear that King Edward VIII wanted to marry Mrs Simpson, sure enough, Mr Ernest Simpson was discovered in a hotel, sharing a bed with a certain 'Buttercup' Kennedy. He remarked, 'My only regret is that I have but one wife to lay down for my King.'

And this is perhaps the essentially English lover, for whom love is neither 'a durable fire, in the mind ever burning' (Raleigh) nor 'a squirt of slippery delight', but does perhaps offer an opportunity for behaving decently and graciously. He would also perhaps agree with W. H. Auden: 'Among those whom I like or admire, I can find no common denominator, but among those whom I love, I can: all of them make me laugh.' Yes, passion and laughter may make excellent bed-fellows, but unfortunately Tennyson's dismal prediction rings horribly true:

> He shall hold thee, when passion shall have spent its novel force,
> A little closer than his dog, a little dearer than his horse.

## THE ROMANTIC ENGLISHMAN

Romance can flower, however, even in the sturdiest English breast. In a letter to George Lewes, Anthony Trollope wrote with a touching and tipsy happiness of his own marriage:

> There is a sweet young blushing joy about the first acknowledged reciprocal love, which is like the bouquet of the first glass of wine from the bottle—it goes when it has been tasted. But for all that, who will confuse the momentary aroma with the lasting joys of the still-flowing bowl? May the bowl still flow for both of us, and leave no touch of headache . . .

There is, of course, many a rewarding relationship that must be accompanied by an occasional monumental hangover. Looking at the *ménage à trois* between Lord and Lady Hamilton and Admiral Nelson it is difficult to credit the harmony of their life together, but it seems that the earthy passion of Emma and Nelson was matched only by the unalloyed affection for them both of old Lord Hamilton. They maintained a bizarre fiction of a 'pure and platonic' relationship even when Emma produced a sudden crop of children—and after it had become clear that, if Nelson and Emma were capable of a pure and refined love, it was not a quality in them that leaped to the attention. Indeed, even in a loud, colourful and unbridled age, Nelson and Lady Hamilton were a social embarrassment. And yet his last thoughts as he died were noble ones, as befitted the national hero, and she was among those thoughts.

An earlier pair of particularly English star-crossed lovers was Dorothy Osborne and William (later Sir William) Temple, who met and fell in love on the Isle of Wight in 1648. Fate decreed that his father should be a Royalist while hers sat in the Puritan Long Parliament. Despite the attentions, over a period of six years, of an extensive series of admirers, many encouraged by her father, she remained obdurately faithful, writing charming letters to him as he travelled abroad. Then, just when the two lovers were about to marry, William's fidelity was tried. Dorothy fell ill with the smallpox, and although she survived, her beauty was gone. He passed the test with flying colours and they married.

A dreadful tale is told by Mark Girouard in *The Return to Camelot*:

> In 1859 Edward Heneage Dering, a rich young officer in the Coldstream Guards, fell in love with Rebecca Dulcibella Orpen. He went to her aunt and guardian Lady Chatterton, the widow of an Irish baronet, to ask permission to pay his addresses to her ward. Lady Chatterton misunderstood him (whether deliberately or not remains unestablished), took the proposal as addressed to herself, and accepted it. Heneage Dering was far too chivalrous a gentleman to cause her the pain and embarrassment of disillusioning her. He married her, even though she was old enough to be his mother.

It was only 26 years later that Heneage and Rebecca Orpen were free to marry as originally planned. The most fearful aspect of this affair is actually the sheer unlikelihood, given the scrupulous impulse that produced it, of its ever coming to light in the normal course of things. How many other English gentlemen have been so slow in getting to the point, or so delicate and roundabout in tackling the sticky subject, that they have been taken up on an offer of marriage they never meant to make?

In *Right Ho, Jeeves* (1934) Bertie Wooster shows how it is done. He is attempting to press Gussie Fink-Nottle's suit for him with the soupy Madeline Basset. After some preliminary persiflage, Wooster begins to work round to Fink-Nottle's aching heart:

> . . . it may interest you to know that there is an aching heart in Brinkley Court.'
> . . . She unshipped a sigh that sounded like the wind going out of a rubber duck.
> 'Ah, yes. Life is very sad, isn't it?'
> 'It is for some people. This aching heart, for instance.'
> 'Those wistful eyes of hers! Drenched irises. And they used to dance like elves of delight. And all through a foolish misunderstanding about a shark. What a tragedy misunderstandings are. That pretty romance broken and over just because Mr Glossop would insist that it was a flatfish.'

Portrait of Lady Emma Hamilton by George Romney, 1785. Impossibly vulgar, irresistibly sexy,
Lady Hamilton had the face of a mischievous angel and a breast fit for English heroes
to lay their laurelled heads upon. Fifteen years after this portrait was painted,
a Swedish diplomat remarked that she was the fattest woman he had ever
laid eyes on, though increasing size had no diminishing effect on Nelson's ardour.

I saw that she had got the wires crossed.

'I'm not talking about Angela.'

'But her heart is aching.'

'I know it's aching. But so is somebody else's.'

She looked at me, perplexed.

'Somebody else's? Mr Glossop's, you mean?'

'No, I don't.'

'Mrs Travers's?'

The exquisite code of politeness of the Woosters prevented me clipping her one on the ear-hole, but I would have given a shilling to be able to do it. There seemed to me something deliberately fatheaded in the way she persisted in missing the gist.

'No, not Aunt Dahlia's, either.'

'I'm sure she is dreadfully upset.'

'Quite. But this heart I'm talking about isn't aching because of Tuppy's row with Angela. It's aching for a different reason altogether. I mean to say— dash it, you know why hearts ache!'

She seemed to shimmy a bit. Her voice, when she spoke, was whispery:

'You mean—for love?'

'Absolutely. Right on the bull's-eye. For love.'

'Oh, Mr Wooster!'

'I take it you believe in love at first sight?'

'I do, indeed.'

'Well, that's what happened to this aching heart. It fell in love at first sight, and ever since it's been eating itself out, as I believe the expression is.'

There was a silence. She had turned away and was watching a duck out on the lake. It was tucking into weeds, a thing I've never been able to understand anyone wanting to do. Though I suppose, if you face it squarely, they're no worse than spinach. She stood drinking it in for a bit, and then it suddenly stood on its head and disappeared, and this seemed to break the spell.

'Oh, Mr Wooster!' she said again, and from the tone of her voice, I could see that I had got her going.

'For you, I mean to say,' I proceeded, starting to put in the fancy touches. I dare say you have noticed on these occasions that the difficulty is to plant the main idea, to get the general outline of the thing well fixed. The rest is mere detail work. I don't say I became glib at this juncture, but I certainly became a dashed sight glibber than I had been.

'It's having the dickens of a time. Can't eat, can't sleep—all for love of you. And what makes it all so particularly rotten is that it—this aching heart—can't bring itself up to the scratch and tell you the position of affairs, because your profile has gone and given it cold feet. Just as it is about to speak it catches sight of you sideways, and words fail it. Silly, of course, but there it is.'

I heard her give a gulp, and I saw that her eyes had become moistish. Drenched irises, if you care to put it that way.

'Lend you a handkerchief?'

'No, thank you. I'm quite all right.'

It was more than I could say for myself. My efforts had left me weak. I don't know if you suffer in the same way, but with me the act of talking anything in the nature of real mashed potatoes always induces a sort of prickly sensation and a hideous feeling of shame, together with a marked starting of the pores.

I remembered at my Aunt Agatha's place in Hertfordshire once being put on the spot and forced to enact the role of King Edward III saying good-bye to that girl of his, Fair Rosamund, at some sort of pageant in aid of the Distressed Daughters of the Clergy. It involved some rather warmish medieval dialogue, I recall, racy of the days when they called a spade a spade, and by the time the whistle blew, I'll bet no Daughter of the Clergy was half as distressed as I was. Not a dry stitch.

My reaction now was very similar. It was a highly liquid Bertram who, hearing his *vis-à-vis* give a couple of hiccups and start to speak, bent an attentive ear.

'Please don't say any more, Mr Wooster.'

Well, I wasn't going to, of course.

'I understand.'

I was glad to hear this.

'Yes, I understand. I won't be so silly as to pretend not to know what you mean. I suspected this at Cannes, when you used to stand and stare at me without speaking a word, but with whole volumes in your eyes.'

If Angela's shark had bitten me in the leg, I couldn't have leaped more convulsively. So tensely had I been concentrating on Gussie's interests that it hadn't so much as crossed my mind that another and unfortunate construction could be placed on those words of mine. The persp., already bedewing my brow, became a regular Niagara.

My whole fate hung upon a woman's word. I mean to say, I couldn't back out. If a girl thinks a man is proposing to her and on that understanding books him up, he can't explain to her that she has got hold of entirely the wrong end of the stick and that he hadn't the smallest intention of suggesting anything of the kind. He must simply let it ride. And the thought of being engaged to a girl who talked openly about fairies being born because stars blew their noses, or whatever it was, frankly appalled me.

Note that Bertie Wooster, usually so reliable when it comes to Bible knowledge, has got his kings of England muddled up. 'Fair Rosamond' was the mistress of Henry II, in much more rude and brutal times than those of Edward III. Henry's son John, for example, himself a busy rapist, had his queen's lover and two go-betweens killed and hung their bodies over her bed.

Edward III, by contrast, was keen to see some more manners and courtesy about him. To this end, in 1344 he held a tournament on St George's Day and, when the Countess of Salisbury's garter slipped off during the dancing, he picked it up. Glaring at his smirking courtiers, he put it on his own leg, announcing, *'Honi soit qui mal y pense'*—thus founding the Order of the Knights of the Garter. This, at least is the official version. Whatever the truth of the matter, it is quite natural that Edward should have become associated with any medieval romantic chivalry going.

# DIRTY OLD ENGLISHMEN

From the fourteenth century to the twentieth. John Betjeman, asked at the end of his life if he regretted anything, said, 'Not enough sex.' Certainly yearning, nostalgia and innocent longing play a large part in his appeal to the great English middle-brow. This feeling is present even in the stories of his days at Oxford. He apparently used to beg Gaitskell, 'Hugh, may I stroke your bottom?' To which the reply would be, as if indulging a child: 'Oh, I suppose so, if you *must*.' His dirty old man is an innocent mixture of enthusiasm and anguish:

> The sort of girl I like to see
> Smiles down from her great height at me.
> She stands in strong, athletic pose
> And wrinkles her *retroussé* nose.
> Is it distate that makes her frown,
> So furious and freckled, down
> On an unhealthy worm like me?
> Or am I what she likes to see?
> I do not know, though much I care.
> ειθε γενοιμην ... would I were
> (Forgive me, shade of Rupert Brooke)
> An object fit to claim her look.
> Oh! would I were her racket press'd
> With hard excitement to her breast
> And swished into the sunlit air
> Arm-high above her tousled hair,
> And banged against the bounding ball
> 'Oh! Plung!' my tauten'd strings would call,
> 'Oh! Plung! my darling, break my strings
> For you I will do brilliant things.'
> ·And when the match is over, I
> Would flop beside you, hear you sigh;
> And then, with what supreme caress,
> You'ld tuck me up into my press.
> Fair tigress of the tennis courts,
> So short in sleeve and strong in shorts,
> Little, alas, to you I mean,
> For I am bald and old and green.

John Betjeman, 'The Olympic Girl'

Chaucer, too, knew what could be reasonably expected of love—and what could not. His dirty old man, January, has married young May, and after the wedding night wakes up thinking that he's love's young dream:

> And upright in his bed then sitteth he,
> And after that he sang ful loude and clere,
> And kiste his wyf, and made wantoun chere,

> He was al coltish, ful of ragerye,
> And ful of jargon as a flekked pye.
> The slakke skin about his nekke shaketh,
> Whyl that he sang, so chaunteth he and craketh.
> But god wot what that May thoughte in her herte,
> When she him saw up sittinge in his sherte,
> In his night-cappe and with his nekke lene;
> She preyseth not his pleying worth a bene.

'The Merchant's Tale'

It is curious that Samuel Pepys, the architect of the British navy, should have come to be best known for his diary. The fascination of this document comes about because of his honesty with himself, his detailing of all his petty deceptions and his human weaknesses and vanities—all those things most people do not even want to know about themselves, let alone write down. On Sunday, 18 August 1667, Pepys recorded:

> I walked toward Whitehall; but being weary, turned into St Dunstan's church, where I hear an able sermon of the minister of the place. And stood by a pretty, modest maid, whom I did labour to take by the hand and body; but she would not, but got further and further from me, and at last I could perceive her to take pins out of her pocket to prick me if I should touch her again; which seeing, I did forbear, and was glad I did espy her design. And then I fell to gaze upon another pretty maid in a pew close to me, and she on me; and I did go about to take her by the hand, which she suffered a little and then withdrew. So the sermon ended and the church broke up, and my amours ended also.

In January 1668 Pepys visited Martin, his bookseller in the Strand, and 'saw the French book which I did think to have had for my wife to translate, called *L'escholle des filles*, but when I came to look in it, it is the most bawdy, lewd book that ever I saw . . .' Overcoming his moral outrage, he bought the book three weeks later ('in plain binding') and took it home for a one-man debauch. Sunday, 9 February 1668:

> Up, and at my chamber all the morning and the office, doing business and also reading a little of *L'escolle des filles*, which is a mighty lewd book, but yet not amiss for a sober man to read over to inform himself of the villainy of the world.

Pepys usually signalled that he was up to some indecency by writing in a sort of souped-up franglais: Sunday, 6 August 1665:

> Dressed and had my head combed by my little girle [the maid], to whom I confess que je sum demasiado kind, nuper ponendo saepe mes mains in su

> dos choses de son breast. Mais il faut que je leave it, lest it bring me to alguno major inconvenience.

He used his position shamelessly to further his amorous intentions: 7 August 1663:

> I stayed walking up and down, discoursing with the officers of the Yard of several things; and so walked back again, and on my way young Bagwell and his wife waylayd me to desire my favour about getting him a better ship; which I shall pretend to be willing to do for them, but my mind is to know his wife a little better.

Not only Mrs Bagwell but also Mrs Daniel, Mrs Martin and Mrs Burrows were all too willing to compromise their virtue to help their husbands get on. It seems miraculous that such a decent, warm and kindly gentleman, as in so many respects Pepys was, should have, for one thing, allowed himself such villainy and, for another, should have left such a full record of it for posterity. But then Pepys was obviously highly susceptible. Seeing the petticoats of the luscious Lady Castlemaine, one of Charles II's mistresses, hanging out to dry, he noted, 'It did me good to look on them.'

On only one occasion was he discovered by his wife in any manner of flagrante delicto. This was with their maid, Deb Willet. Sunday, 25 October 1668:

> At night W. Batelier comes and sups with us; and after supper, to have my head combed by Deb, which occasioned me the greatest sorrow to me that ever I knew in this world; for my wife, coming up suddenly, did find me imbracing the girl con my hand sub su coats; and endeed, I was with my main in her cunny.

A long and terrible rumpus arose from this indiscretion (though Pepys made the interesting note that he had slept with his wife 'as a husband more times since this falling-out than in I believe 12 months before—and with more pleasure to her than I think in all the time of our marriage before'). Always Pepys profoundly regrets, not what he does, but the fact that he has been found out. What is horribly human about him is that he never learns. He remains a lovable hypocrite, and a pillar of respectable society.

## FIRST THINGS FIRST

In the seventeenth century Richard Lovelace put his amorous nature firmly in its place:

> Tell me not (Sweet) I am unkinde,
>   That from the Nunnerie

Of thy chaste breast, and quiet minde,
  To Warre and Armes I flie.

True; a new Mistresse now I chase,
  The first Foe in the Field;
And with a stronger Faith imbrace
  A Sword, a Horse, a Shield.

Yet this Inconstancy is such,
  As you too shall adore;
I could not love thee (Deare) so much,
  Lov'd I not Honour more.

'On Going to the Warres'

'Hark Backward!', which ran over several weeks in J. B. Morton's 'Beachcomber' column in the *Daily Express*, is an abbreviated romance recounting the rivalry for the hand of Petunia Pewce between Nigel Barriscale, a cricket and rugby Blue with a 'fourth' in archaeology, and Captain 'Nark' Fiendish:

### CHAPTER VII

### *On the Rink*

Little gasps of admiration went up from the crowds gathered at the Nie-derschwein rink-side as Captain 'Nark' Fiendish skimmed like a swallow across the smooth surface, cutting figures as he went. He wrote the figure *396* backwards, crossed it out, wrote it again—and all with the skill of a master. But his performance was intended only for the eyes of Petunia, who watched from the outskirts of the crowd. Nor could she restrain her admiration for this daring skater, who did what he would with the ice.

It was now evident that 'Nark' had harboured his strength for a supreme effort. Like a bolt from the blue he shot across the ice, zig-zagging and whirling round like a top, and only when he had arrived at the far corner and disappeared among the groups of spectators did anyone realise what he had done. There, in the centre of the rink, cut by the skate of a master, were the words:

*I love you, Petunia*

Hardly had the crowd recovered from its surprise when a huge figure emerged from a group and took the rink. It was Nigel! What would he do? Petunia clasped and unclasped her hands, and stood first on one leg, then on another. Nigel, supremely unconscious of the sensation he was producing, leapt into the middle of the rink and began to go round like a top. All watched breathlessly. After three minutes he shot away again, leaving a tangled mass of scrawls on the ice.

'What has he done?' queried several voices.

An Oxford don supplied the answer.

'He has written, "Play Up, You Fellows," in ancient Aramaic,' he said.

Not for nothing had Nigel studied archæology.

Later that night Petunia said to Nigel, 'Did you mean what you wrote on the ice?'

'Oh, I say, yes,' replied Nigel, filling his pipe.

The sheer sportsmanship of the man! Petunia knelt mentally at his feet.

# CONSOLATIONS

The amorous Englishman has largely to make do with what he can get. In Leigh Hunt's case this was evidently not a lot. But when he received an unexpected tribute from Thomas Carlyle's wife, he expressed a consoling joy:

> Jenny kissed me when we met,
>     Jumping from the chair she sat in
> Time, you thief, who love to get
>     Sweets into your list, put that in:
> Say I'm weary, say I'm sad,
>     Say that health and wealth have missed me,
> Say I'm growing old, but add,
>     Jenny kissed me.

'Rondeau'

A similar note was struck by Adrian Mitchell in 'Celia, Celia':

> When I am sad and weary,
> When I think all hope has gone,
> When I walk along High Holborn
> I think of you with nothing on.

Sir Frank Swettenham, portrait by John Singer Sargent. Swettenham
was the very model of the Imperial pro-consul. As British Resident-
General in Malaya till he retired in 1901, he built the first railway,
completely reformed the administration, and introduced 'habits of
orderliness and punctuality' in the natives.

# CHAPTER SIX

———— • ————

# THE IMPERIAL ENGLISHMAN

The very word 'Empire' has a ringing glory to it that drowns out the obstinate fact about Empire—the fact which made the idea, until it became too thrilling to be resisted, a terribly un-English notion, associated with the grandiose schemes of tyrants who took themselves much too seriously. Inescapably, Empire is an imposition by one people over another; gratifying at a vulgar, superficial level, but a troubling conceit for a nation with an instinct for liberty.

Edmund Burke viewed 'the establishment of the English colonies on principles of liberty, as that which is to render the kingdom venerable to future ages'. He is not far wrong. Liberty, for whom, though? For Americans, Canadians, Australians and New Zealanders, perhaps. But there were others, whose culture the English swept aside as so much childish nonsense, and, *in loco parentis* as it were, had to educate to value freedom, justice and respect for the individual. Not all Englishmen recognized that this programme begged a few questions. Many were rather pleased with the idea of the Empire as an educational establishment; a realization of Milton's plea in *The Doctrine and Discipline of Divorce* (1643): 'Let not England forget her precedence of teaching nations how to live.' Many also found a stern, chivalric purpose in Palmerston's lofty claim: 'The real policy of England . . . is to be the champion of justice and right.'

Unfortunately, all this noble-browed, white-man's-burden, 'I assure you this is going to hurt me more than it's going to hurt you' sort of gammon won't quite do. The English are dull and decent, confined in a damp, secure little island, and they are only too susceptible to the barbarism, the gaudy pomp, the adventure-book of Empire. This is playtime, and eventually they will be called in to have their tea. Meanwhile, they can act their roles for all they are worth, particularly the rip-roaring, fancy-dress ones, like 'El Laurens', the Bedouin; or the Afghan tribesman, suspiciously pink-faced and blue-eyed beneath his puggaree, playing 'The Great Game' against the Russians; or the Viceroy himself, assuming despotic ceremonials for his five-year term, before returning to the comfort of his London club.

John Bright reduced the Empire to 'a vast system of outdoor relief for the upper classes'. Maud Cecil, daughter of Lord Salisbury, demurred: 'Of course the best class of English don't come out to the colonies, and those that do are apt to be bounders' (a bounder being, according to Lord Curzon, 'one who succeeds in life by leaps and bounds'). Hilaire Belloc was, typically, to the point:

> We had intended you to be
> The Next Prime Minister but three:
> The stocks were sold; the Press was squared;
> The Middle Class was quite prepared.
> But as it is! . . . My language fails!
> Go out and govern New South Wales!

'Matilda', from Cautionary Tales, 1907

The Empire was like an adventure playground for the middle classes—not to mention an approved school for 'black sheep' and a dumping-ground for hopeless cases. You might be a bigamist or a bankrupt; you might have been caught cheating at cards, or been turned down by a woman. Either way, you could disappear with your gun into the heart of Africa or self-consciously go to seed in some remote trading station.

On the other hand, you might be an enterprising engineer; you might have a religious mission; you might like the idea of kicking people around (no problem). You might want to play at being a knight in shining armour (Lawrence of Arabia carried a copy of Malory with him in the desert); or at being an aristocrat ('If you aren't firm with your bearer, he will insist on dressing and undressing you like a tailor's dummy'); or even at being royalty (back in England, on the train, a child puzzles, 'Mummy, why hasn't the guard come along and asked your permission to start the train?').

## IF I RULED THE WORLD

While one was unlikely to achieve the official status of royalty—as did Sir James Brooke (1803–1868), First White Rajah of Sarawak, late of the East India Company Army—merely as 'British Resident' one had a splendid opportunity of playing 'If I ruled the world'. Or, as Gonzalo ruminates in *The Tempest*:

> Had I plantation of this isle, my lord . . .
> And were the King on't, what would I do? . . .
> I would with such perfection govern, sir,
> T'excel the Golden Age.

As British Resident on Cephalonia, and in effect a military dictator, Sir Charles

Napier had, like so many Englishmen, a touching confidence in his own incorruptibility:

> My kingdom is sixty thousand people and martial law exists. This is a fearful power in the hands of one man; but feeling no inclination to be unjust or cruel (except over their horrible trick of maiming animals out of spite for their owner) it does not annoy me. I even like it.

Charles Metcalfe, as Resident—or King, as he was usually styled—at Delhi between 1811 and 1819, ended capital punishment, sent pickpockets to a special camp to learn a trade, and collected up swords and spears, literally to turn them into ploughshares. In this last procedure he was clearly guided by *Isaiah* 11, *iv*, which might have served also as the inspiration of the more megalomaniac English imperialists:

> And he shall judge between the nations, and shall reprove many peoples: and they shall beat their swords into plowshares, . . . nation shall not lift up sword against nation, neither shall they learn war any more.

Isaiah's wonder-worker was of course God, but the imperial Englishman would hardly be abashed by the implication that he was attempting something which the Good Lord Himself was reserving for the Latter Days. Humorists evidently considered it appropriate to interpret the acronyms for the decorations that all good colonials aspired after—CMG, KCMG and GCMG—as, respectively, 'Call Me God', 'Kindly Call Me God' and 'God Calls Me God'.

No respecter of pretensions to divine status, the College of Heralds once declared smugly: 'The Aga Khan is held by his followers to be a direct descendant of God. English Dukes take precedence.' However, one of the secret pleasures of the imperial Englishman was the occasional deification of, if not himself personally, then perhaps someone who had fagged for him at school —or, at the very least, his homely little head of state, the 'Great White Queen'.

One local deity was the Collector of Jessure between 1781 and 1789, Tilman Henckel, who was worshipped in the form of a graven image after his death. The most celebrated was John Nicholson, who so confused the Punjabis by his occasional Christian mercy, interspersed with the sort of capricious brutality which was what they understood as good government, that he was declared to be an incarnation of Brahma. (In England too he was idolized. Mortally wounded at the Kashmir Gate, Delhi, in 1857, he was enshrined in the canon of English commanders who have died in their hour of victory.) A more piercing image, though, is that of the remote Indian hill tribe which sacrificed a goat to a great and beneficent god they called 'The Judicial Committee of the Privy Council', before which, as the final arbiter of justice for the myriad legal systems of the Empire, an appeal was being made over forestry rights. An

Englishman could not help experiencing, unworthy though it might be to do so, a slight Olympian glow as he contemplated the spell-binding sorcery of the English through the amazed eyes of 'ignorant savages'.

This sorcery, however, depended on an imperial role which had to be underplayed if it were to achieve its full dramatic effect. It represented a quality of patience and endurance, of bone-headed sticking at it, which underpinned the whole enterprise and was awesome by anyone's standards.

In *Farewell the Trumpets* (1978) Jan Morris records a brief exchange during a local armistice in South Africa, in 1900:

> . . . while the dead and wounded were being recovered from the battlefield, a Boer soldier engaged a British officer in conversation. 'We've all been having a rough time,' he remarked. 'Yes, I suppose so,' replied the other, 'but for us of course it's nothing. This is what we're paid for. This is the life we always lead—you understand?'
>
> 'Great God,' simply said the Boer.

## JOHN COMPANY

Also during this early period, in 1607 the first envoy of the new East India Company was approaching the court of the great Moghul. This was the plausible William Hawkins, who, despite having been robbed of his presents for the Moghul and having had his letter of introduction translated into Persian for him by, of all people, a Portuguese Jesuit, managed to settle down very easily, and roistered happily with Jehangir for several years. His successor, Sir Thomas Roe, was a representative of the other line of English imperialist. He wrote home: 'This is the dullest basest place that ever I saw and maketh me weary of speaking of it.'

'John Company' chose its servants well. A man who was bored at the court of the Moghul Emperor might be hard to satisfy as a tourist but, as a diplomat, he was not going to be easily overawed—despite the embarassing paltriness of the gifts with which he had been equipped. Roe must have wished that he, too, could have claimed that they had been stolen rather than having to present them to a man who clearly had everything, most of which he wore on his person:

> His sash was wreathed about with a chain of great pearl, rubies, and diamonds drilled. About his neck he carried a chain of most excellent pearl, three double (so great I never saw); at his elbows, armlets set with diamonds . . . his gloves, which were English, stuck under his girdle.

Gifts like this pair of gloves, always very acceptable in England—to sweeten a

---

*Right:* Englishman shooting a tiger. Kalighat School. To the Indians, the employees of the East India Company were just another set of masters (if curiously dressed—the artist has had trouble with the top hat).

rich aunt or even a domesticated monarch—were not received by Jehangir with the pleasure he reserved for more sparkling or imaginative presents.

The English soon learnt that the Moghuls' interest in 'presents' was very serious; indeed, under Aurangzebe, it was complacently insatiable. So, withdrawing the velvet hand of diplomacy, they revealed, if not the iron fist (which they could not afford), at least a naval operator of the old school—untutored, determined and audacious. In 1687 a hopelessly outnumbered Job Charnock defeated the Moghuls by bluff: when reinforcements arrived in the shape of a solitary ship, his men beat drums, blew trumpets and roared so loudly that the enemy was persuaded to offer a truce.

Afterwards, Charnock founded Calcutta, and, according to Captain Alexander Hamilton in *A New Account of the East Indies* (1710), 'reigned more absolutely than a Rajah, only he wanted much of their humanity'. He liked to dine to the cries of natives being whipped in the next room.

In the middle of the eighteenth century came Robert Clive. He was shaped in the same mould: a ruthless, greedy, brilliant opportunist. Rising from suicidal obscurity and morbid homesickness for Shropshire, he attained opulence, a title and finally a successful suicide. While Canada was being won, largely by sea, he and Eyre Coote nudged the French off the subcontinent at Plassey and Wandewash.

'John Company' was composed of merchant adventurers. The ideal they fought for was a fat percentage. Left alone with the decaying corpse of the Moghul Empire, they held their noses and helped themselves. So long as astronomical 'presents' kept coming their way, they avoided the trouble and expense of cleaning up the administration. The whiff of corruption carried as far as England, where the nabobs' parvenu vulgarity soon had the Establishment sharpening its hatchets. In 1788, Warren Hastings was impeached for gross misgovernment and corruption; in fact, in 1795 he was shown to be innocent, but during the course of his seven-year trial the Establishment had accidentally landed itself with extremely high imperial ideals.

These ideals sat a little unsteadily on what had always been meant as a money-making concern, but with their flair for hypocrisy the English nevertheless maintained them. They could afford to be sublimely impartial in administrating their trading outposts since technologically they were so far in advance of other nations. They gave all traders a fair and sporting chance, because they knew that at the end of the day the English traders would come out on top. They played by the rules, but those were European rules, and sometimes had to be enforced: the Chinese required military persuasion before the English were allowed to sell them opium.

The English want to be virtuous as much as they want to be rich; not a bad thing really, except that it meant trade had to be spiritualized. Richard Cobden likened the effect of commerce on the 'moral world' to 'the principle of gravitation in the universe—drawing men together, thrusting aside the antagonism of race and creed and language, and uniting us in the bonds of eternal peace'. Sir John Bowring, from 1849 the British consul in Hong Kong, was even more emphatic: 'Jesus Christ is Free Trade, and Free Trade is Jesus Christ.'

# PATERNALISM

If the English could afford to be suspicious of the profit motive, their administrators were plainly directed by a benevolent and chivalrous altruism, even in 1770. As Harry Verelst wrote in that year:

> Amongst the chief effects which are hoped for . . . are to convince the Ryot (the peasant) that you will stand between him and the hand of oppression; that you will be his refuge and the redresser of his wrongs . . . and finally to teach him a veneration and affection for the humane maxims of our government.

Thomas Pattle, Collector of Lashkarpur, responded to the spirit of these instructions by developing a seigneurial affection for his ryots. In 1774 he noted that '[for] my ryots I shall always feel a degree of partiality, and I trust that there is no impropriety in the avowal'. Indeed not. The Empire was run on the cheap. From the first envoys, with their wretched gifts, to the civil servants of Empire starved of the means to get anything done, a lot of reliance had to be placed on the enterprise and enthusiasm with which the man on the spot motivated local resources. Two centuries later, the Governor of Hong Kong, John Pope-Hennessy, had little respect for the Colonial Office and even less for the interests of the great English business 'taipans', but to the poor Chinese he was 'Number One Good Friend'. And Hubert Berkeley ruled Upper Perak in Malaya from 1891 to 1927 with the warm and proprietorial commitment of an old English country squire—fathering a lot of half-caste children and foiling all attempts at official interference. Visitors might find their way obstructed by fallen trees blocking the road, but assuming they reached him they would on occasion find themselves received by the great man in his lavatory (built for two), seated beneath a large photograph of the formidable Resident-General of the Malay States, Sir Frank Swettenham, placed there by Berkeley to help his bowel movements.

For a country that prides herself on her sense of justice and her parliamentary democracy, England has produced her fair share of brisk despots, of whom Sir Charles Napier was among the most cavalier. In Scinde, which he annexed in 1842, he showed scant respect for the venerable tradition of 'Suttee': 'My nation also has a custom. When men burn women alive, we hang them.' And he was shamelessly frank about the double standards under which he operated: 'We break treaties, but that is not a reason for letting others do the same.'

There might be a lot of head-wagging and tut-tutting in Whitehall over their unbiddable envoys and administrators, but the people at home also understood that their power in the world depended on the confidence of the man on the spot that, whatever he did, he would be backed up. And so he would be, unless he committed a moral blunder that was visible for all the world to see or, as in the case of the Jameson Raid, the high-handed mavericks fell flat on their faces.

Warren Hastings had sufficient respect for the Hindus and their culture as to be uneasy about the prospect of English dominion of all India—'an event which I may not mention without adding that it is what I never wish to see'. There was a tone of unpretentious, humane quietism at this time, later to be rather drowned out by the sturdy Victorian cries of 'philanthropy and five per cent'. Compare the protest of Thomas Munro (1761–1837)—'neither the face of the country, its property, nor its society, are things that can be suddenly improved by any contrivance of ours, though they may be greatly injured by what we mean for their good'—with Winston Churchill's waistcoat-stretching rhetoric in *The River War* (1899):

> What enterprise that an enlightened community may attempt, is more noble and more profitable than the reclamation from barbarism of fertile regions and large populations? To give peace to warring tribes, to administer justice where all was violence, to strike the chains from the slave, to draw the richness from the soil, to plant the earliest seeds of commerce and learning . . . ? The act is virtuous, the exercise invigorating and the result often extremely profitable.

Churchill has the honesty then to bring our attention to the sinister figures lurking in the shadows of this vision: '. . . the greedy trader, the inopportune missionary, the ambitious soldier and the lying speculator . . .'

# IMPERIAL RULE

Fortunately, the old aristocratic policy—'Do nothing, have nothing done, and let nobody do anything'—remained as the essential ballast of Empire. It did, though, lose the struggle waged for the collective soul of the imperial Englishman between Gladstone and Disraeli.

It seems unlikely that such a sedate, simple, sincere person as Queen Victoria—'an immovable sideboard in the huge saloon of state', as Lytton Strachey called her in *Eminent Victorians* (1918)—could have been so seduced by the glitter, facility and vanity of Disraeli's political persona that she should have allowed herself to be crowned Empress of India. But those were intoxicating times. By 1897, even the Americans, according to the *New York Times*, wanted to be 'a part, and a great part, of the Greater Britain which seems so plainly destined to dominate this planet'.

Gladstone, by contrast, was a more aware and responsible imperialist, anxious to develop the native people to a position from which they could govern themselves and thereafter, wherever possible, to leave them alone. However, he lashed his moral integrity to the issue of Irish Home Rule, and went down when the issue foundered on the ever-present political hazard of sexual scandal. (As a result the English maintained their astonishing record in Ireland, summed up by Sydney Smith: 'The moment the name of Ireland is mentioned, the English seem to bid adieu to common feeling, common prudence, and common sense, and to act with the barbarity of tyrants, and the fatuity of infants.')

However, Gladstone's austere banner was taken up on the other side of the House by Lord Salisbury, for whom ruling the country was a duty rather than a destiny, and for whom British policy was 'to drift lazily downstream, occasionally putting out a boathook to avoid a collision'. This aristocratic prime minister worked in harness with a flashy, rather Disraeli-like upstart of a colonial secretary Joseph Chamberlain, who announced in 1896: 'I don't know which of our enemies we ought to defy, but let us defy someone.'

Accumulated in 'a fit of absence of mind', the Empire had no overall plan. It was literally eccentric. There were dozens of different governments and all sorts of different forms of law. Nigeria was governed by a commercial company, the African Gold Coast by a despotism of English officials, and Malta and Gibraltar by military governors. Ascension Island became HMS *Ascension Island*, under the command of a ship's captain. Egypt came to be ruled by the British Consul-General, who 'advised' the Egyptian government; in Sarawak there reigned an hereditary English Rajah; while Tristan da Cunha was basically in the hands of the Society for the Propagation of the Gospel. Some places were simply rented. Victoria was Empress only in India: she ruled the rest of her 'Empire' as Queen.

It was a virtuoso performance. With vast responsibilities and little more than an appearance of military power, the English, as we have seen, governed largely through the individual, very often on his own for long periods in some bleak outpost. He was left to get on with it in his own style, to bend and even break the rules when necessary, and to act without orders; he fulfilled the functions of policeman, judge, vet, public health inspector, civil engineer, agricultural adviser, philosopher and friend, while at the same time being ready to deal with anything else that might come up, like shooting a man-eating tiger.

There were two faces of the Englishman in this situation. On the one hand, there was ample room for an odd-ball to really spread himself. On the other, the imperial Englishman carefully developed and preserved a quasi-religious ethos based on his nationality and class. This was easily recognized and even crudely imitated, but in difficult situations it impressed others with its aura of unflappable confidence. It had its mysterious rituals and its powerful disciplines: always dressing for dinner, passing the port (and only to the left), never showing emotion (particularly fear or excitement), arranging games of cricket at every

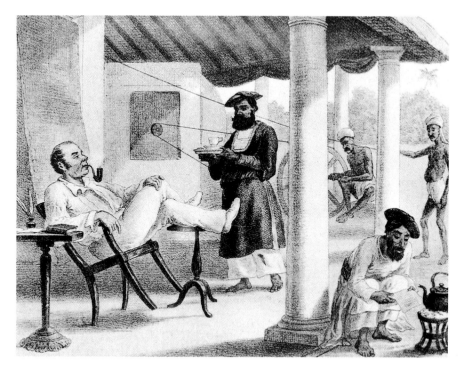

*The Colonel* (from *British Social Life in India*, 1938). At ease with his
pipe, the Colonel can be confident that his chota peg will be prepared
just as he likes it by his quick-witted, docile and utterly loyal Indian
servant. Independence came ten years later.

opportunity with the zeal of a priest performing a rite that is compellingly
necessary to himself but baffling to others—in fact, observing all the bred-in-the-
bone ceremonies, especially when they were quite clearly more trouble than
they were worth.

Together these qualities and practices served to maintain what the Indians
called the 'iqbal' of the English, or what in chivalric terms would have been
called their 'virtue'; it was their moral strength, and it gave them, against all the
odds, power over hundreds of millions of people. Even the secret Indian society
of ritual murderers, the Thugs, had to submit to this more powerful spiritual
force: 'Before the sound of your drums, sorcerers, witches and demons take
flight. How can Thuggee stand?', as one captured Thug admitted to the self-
appointed hunter of the Thugs, Captain William Sleeman—whose power actually
existed only in his rectitude, his sense of mission, and his painstaking
investigations.

# EGYPT: PEN-PUSHERS AND HEROES

The real strength of the Empire lay not so much in its heroes and fanatics as in the pen-pushers and regular officers who accommodated them. In Cairo, in World War I, was General Edmund Allenby, known as the 'Bull' and regular army through and through. One can imagine him looking across his desk at the mannered deviant in his precious Bedouin robes as he heard him out. 'At the end he put up his chin, and said quite directly, "Well, I will do for you what I can," and that ended it.' (T. E. Lawrence, the mannered deviant in question, was an imperial type that cropped up from time to time. 'Hodson's Horse', the legendary Punjabi irregular cavalry, had been raised back in the 1850s by a similarly bookish fellow with a taste for native costume: William Hodson, son of an archdeacon of Lichfield.)

Between 1883 and 1907 Lord Cromer reigned in Cairo. As British Consul he had no official power, but nevertheless he ruled as absolutely as anyone anywhere in the Empire. He was the still, efficient point around which the weird and unstable Egyptian world revolved, and from which the even weirder and more unstable English generals went steaming down the Nile in various heroic attitudes.

First, General Gordon, ('half-cracked', Cromer called him) set off on his own to do something about the Sudan. He ended up holding together the Egyptian garrison at Khartoum against the Sudanese, to no apparent purpose except perhaps to show how an Englishman—albeit as unhinged a case of muscular Christianity as ever licked a Chinese army into shape—could impose his will on the least promising material. 'A more contemptible soldier than the Egyptian never existed,' he noted in his journal, even as he confided in a merchant of the city, with a boyish pleasure in assuming the Arab machismo:

> When God was portioning out fear to all the people in the world, at last it came to my turn, and there was no fear left to give me; go tell all the people in Khartoum that Gordon fears nothing, for God has created him without fear.

General Sir Garnet Wolseley, another Christian soldier, was despatched to rescue his old friend Gordon. He approached the job with his customary minute planning and the boot-thwacking positiveness that he brought to all his tidy little campaigns. (One of these, against the Ashanti, was reported by the *United Services Gazette* to have resulted in 'the capture of an umbrella'.) It was Wolseley who turned the old conception of duty as the genial disregard of personal danger into a neat maxim for military advancement: 'The first business of any ambitious young officer is to try and get himself killed . . .'

Wolseley, however, was too late to save Gordon from his martyrdom, and a third English general turned up in 1897 to avenge England's imperial saint.

Kitchener sent his troops in chanting 'Remember Gordon!', killed about 10,000 'fuzzy-wuzzies' at Omdurman, and held a memorial service at Khartoum, the high point of which was the massed rendering of Gordon's favourite hymn, 'Abide with Me'.

Unperturbed by these grand imperial gestures, Cromer carried on the task of bringing some kind of order and prosperity to Egypt. In the end he was only brought down by an odd-ball coming from the other direction.

Wilfred Scawen Blunt was a poet who adopted both a Bedouin lifestyle and Arab nationalist politics. He was enjoyed by Cromer as an amusing pet nuisance until, in 1901, Blunt's servants were arrested for assaulting some English officers who had chased a fox into his garden. In 1906 Blunt got his revenge when he used his pen to raise a storm over four Egyptian villagers hanged for attacking English officers (one of whom died) who had been out shooting and had bagged some of the villagers' tame pigeons.

# IMPERIAL RECREATIONS

Poets and thoughtful characters like Wilfred Blunt were rather on their own. The Empire was never a forcing house for the arts. Anything that smacked of reflection was inimical to imperial rule and the maintenance of order—although allowances were made for viceroys, who were expected to charm the native princes with their liberal views, and put them at their ease with perhaps a hint of oriental decadence.

In his *British Social Life in India* (1937) Dennis Kincaid told of a distinguished member of the Indian Civil Service who, lecturing in Oxford during the 1920s, 'was asked how a young man with liberal sympathies would fare in India. "Well," said the distinguished official with a confiding smile, "I don't mind admitting I was a bit of a liberal myself, but once out there you soon forget all about that sort of thing. Too many other interests. Big-game shooting, for instance."'

If the imperial Englishman had not got his values in order at the start, he would soon be put straight. Philip Mason recalled his first morning at Saharanpur:

> I met my Collector for the first time at breakfast. He came in from his morning ride and said, 'Hello Mason, I've got a pony for you that you can buy immediately after breakfast if you like . . . Work? . . . no, you don't need to do any work your first year. Here's a book about polo, you can read that and I'll examine you on it this evening.'

As for pig-sticking, the reader is referred to Baden-Powell's book on the subject—*Pigsticking; or Hoghunting: A Complete Account for Sportsmen; and Others; illustrated by the author* (1889)—in which it is commended as a 'manly tip-top sport'. But of even greater importance than pig-sticking—and many army officers seriously could not imagine such a thing—were team games. These formed one of the chief instruments of British imperialism, by use of which it attempted to introduce pluck, backbone and decency into the natives, and without which they would never be able to govern themselves. The introduction of cricket to Tonga, for example, had a dramatically beneficial effect: it seems that petty pilfering virtually ceased. Unfortunately, so did work on the plantations. The King of Tonga was driven to forbid his subjects to play more than once a week.

When Warren Hastings laid down the principle for the East India Company—'It is on the virtue, not the ability of their servants that the Company must rely'—he did not foresee what abysses of ignorance would be countenanced for the sake of the simpler virtues inculcated through sport; nor that, when looking for recruits, the Colonial Office would be more interested in a man's batting averages than in his examination results. The qualities sought in a young applicant may be inferred from this passage from a sermon preached in the chapel of Stowe House, Broadstairs, on 5 July 1914:

> For here now 'we see through a glass darkly', so darkly that try as we will, we cannot see the score; so darkly that we can hardly see to play the game; but not so darkly that we are going to appeal against the light—nor so darkly that we cannot be sportsmen and glory in the difficulties we have to overcome. Who wants an easy victory? Who wants a life of full-pitches to leg? Do you think the Great Scorer is going to give you four runs every time for those? I believe with all my heart and soul that in this splendidly difficult Game of Life it is just the cheap and easy triumph which will be written in water on the score-sheet. And the way we played for our side, in the bad light, on the difficult pitch: the way we backed up and ran the other man's runs; . . . surely, surely it is these things above all that will count, when the innings is over, in the Pavilion of Heaven.
>
> Reported in S. Chichester (ed.), *E. W. Hornung and his Young Guard, 1914*, 1936

If sport was akin to a spiritual discipline, one may well shudder to think what these men did for recreation. 'We were capable of being pretty frivolous,' admitted Baden-Powell in his *Indian Memories* (1915). In a jape called 'The Fire Alarm' the unfortunate fellow to be ragged—'either he is dirty and needs washing, or he has got some characteristic that needs toning down'—would be thrown out of the window to be caught by some other fellows waiting underneath. Occasionally—very amusing this—he would be thrown out of the wrong window. Another well known game involved piling the furniture in the middle of the room with the writing-desk in front; each member of the mess (for this is the army) had then to clap his hands three times, shout 'I am a bounding brother of the Bosphorus!', turn head-over-heels on the writing-desk, and more or less hurt himself in the shambles beyond. 'Visiting generals would be shot off the ends of mess tables wrapped in blankets and if, in full flight you could not succeed in striking a match it was a misfire and you were shot again' (Charles Allén, *Plain Tales from the Raj*, 1975).

The Indian Civil Service should have been a more contemplative or at least a more rational body of men. In 1862, in a letter to his fiancée, William Hunter, one of the new breed of 'competition wallahs', observed the discomfiture of the old type in the examination hall:

> After eyeing their papers with a blank, dreary gaze, they slowly take out a cigar case, examine its contents, smell its Russian delicacy, extract a cigar, put on their hats and march out. 'Cabby, drive to Morley's.' And this is repeated twice daily; meanwhile they eat like prize fighters to support the waste of body and of the mind.

However, Hunter found that the rational faculties so rigorously tried in England seemed hardly to survive the journey to Calcutta:

> . . . after a tiffin, consisting of soup, two or three kinds of meat with an immense heap of curry, no end of fruit, with beer and sherry ad lib, they went to the cricket ground and played for three hours in the burning sun. Dinner lasted from 7.30 till nearly midnight–ice pudding with champagne. Then, till 2 am they played a wild game of loo.

## SPIRITUAL DUTY

In general the early imperialists, as opposed to the colonists of North America, were the servants of mammon. If they had ideals, they were limited, humanist ideals. Warren Hastings saw his duty as 'to protect the Hindus from wrong and to leave their religious creed to the Being who has so long endured it, and who will in his own time reform it'. Christian missionaries were actively discouraged. In 1801 the English in Calcutta celebrated the Peace of Amiens by making a procession to the shrine of the goddess Kali, where they made a thanksgiving offering.

The Evangelical movement changed all this and brought a fresh vigour to imperial service. It also brought about the Great Mutiny.

The natural arrogance of the English imperialist has been universally remarked, and by the English themselves even encouraged, as in the unblushing precept of Cecil Rhodes: 'Always remember that you are an Englishman, and consequently have worn first prize in the lottery of life.' In William Wilberforce, speaking to Parliament in 1813, this conceit is rather touching in its optimism:

> Let us endeavour to strike our roots into the soil by the gradual introduction and establishment of our own principles and opinions; of our laws, institu-

tions, and manners; above all, as the source of every other improvement, of our religion, and consequently of our morals . . . Are we so little aware of the vast superiority even of European laws and institutions, and far more of British institutions, over those of Asia . . . and can we doubt that it would be bound even by the ties of gratitude to those who have been the honoured instruments of communicating them?

The English now had moral and spiritual carte blanche to interfere with foreign cultures and be utterly confident that they were 'doing good'−ever an important consideration. Even Wilberforce might have blenched, though, at Cecil Rhodes' arrogation of total superiority to the English: 'We happen to be the best people in the world, with the highest ideals of decency and justice, and liberty and peace, and the more of the world we inhabit, the better it is for humanity.' And when in 1897 G. W. Stevens of the *Daily Mail*, noting the 'ugliness' and 'stupidity' of some Indian seamen, concluded that 'it is because there are people like this in the world that there is an Imperial Britain. This sort of creature has to be ruled, so we rule him, for his good and our own' the humanitarian veneer was thin indeed.

In 1857 many sepoys, already made jittery by an evangelical gleam appearing here and there in the eyes of even some of their own officers, were unable to take a little slip-up like their cartridges being greased with animal fat as anything less than a deliberate attempt to undermine their religious code. The result−the Indian Mutiny−was fought with all the nauseating ferocity and zeal that have always characterized religious wars. Afterwards, Queen Victoria herself (Lord Lytton thought she was 'really a better Englishman than any of her subjects') added a clause to the proclamation that passed the rule of India from the East India Company to the Crown: 'Firmly relying ourselves on the truth of Christianity, and acknowledging with gratitude the solace of religion, we disclaim alike the right and the desire to impose our convictions upon any of our subjects.'

Serious Christians there were who saw the Great Mutiny in quite the opposite terms. Sir Herbert Edwardes was one. He was convinced that the uprising was a punishment inflicted by Providence on the East India Company for its refusal to have anything to do with spreading the gospel−a view he repeated so insistently that Lord Canning was moved to say of him that he was exactly the man that the prophet Mohammed would have been if the prophet had been born at Clapham instead of Mecca.

## THE IMPERIAL LOVE LIFE

The Englishman's realization that he possessed the sole means of salvation for the poor benighted heathen did not make for social ease between the two cultures. Another social link was broken when the British resolved to go forth and sin no more.

Traders and freebooters of Empire certainly accepted that one of the perks of working outside the bounds of Christendom was the possibility of exploring a world of uncomplicated and imaginative sexual experience beyond the Victorian polarities of matrimonial felicity and the services of degraded prostitutes. In his *History of Jamaica* (1774) Edward Long wrote of the sexual skills of Jamaican women: 'Many are the men, of every rank, quality, and degree, who would much rather riot in these goatish embraces, than share the pure and lawful bliss derived from matrimonial, mutual love.' In India, 'sleeping dictionaries' were taken as a matter of course, even several. However, moral and spiritual confusion arose out of too close an intimacy with unregenerate natives: Job Charnock rescued a Rajput princess from her husband's pyre, where, aged just 15, she was about to commit suttee, and married her. After she died, he made the vaguely Hindu gesture of sacrificing a fowl in her mausoleum every year on the anniversary of her death.

In an undated letter to Lady Salisbury, Lord Lytton (son of the novelist) wrote:

> The moral prejudice and middle class propriety of the later Indian administrators have practically put an end to the illicit connection between the British officials and native women which was formally universal, and have thus destroyed one of the few, and at the same time one of the strongest channels of social intercourse, and sympathy, left open to a conquering race.

Regular cargoes of nice English girls were now being shipped out to spike colonial frailties of the flesh by offering the enticement of decent wedlock. Decent, perhaps, but dull – at least for the Viceroy, Lytton, who wrote in 1876 that

> Our own social surroundings here are so grievously good. Members of Council and heads of departments hold prayer meetings at each others' houses thrice a week, and spend the rest of their time in writing spiteful minutes against each other.

Many of the expatriates now married – if at all – late in life. Kitchener and Rhodes would accept around them only unmarried men. One feels there is something lacking in these men, who felt it necessary to put duty before pleasure for years on end because a wife would get in the way, a mistress was a sin, self-abuse rotted the spine and turned you blind, and homosexuality was an unspeakable vice. Their energy, their self-denial and their intense friendships were all admirable, but England's men abroad were also very often unhappy, if not a little mad.

There is a touching innocence about their affection for boys. Sir James Brooke took a fond interest in adolescent midshipmen; General Gordon spent several years looking after urchins in London, and hoped to retire to teach the Christian faith to poor Syrian boys; Baden-Powell founded the Scout Association in 1908, appointing his lifelong friend, Malcolm 'The Boy' McClaren as chief administrator. Henry Stanley was another of those who, essentially a noncomba-tant in the sexual field, turned his affection towards young boys, one of whom he even wanted to accompany him on his expedition to find Livingstone in 1869. And Kitchener called his young officers 'my happy family of boys' and had bronze sculptures of boys in his garden.

'Not since the heroic days of Greece, has the world had such a sweet, just, boyish master,' wrote the American George Santayana (*Soliloquies in England*, 1922) of the rule of the English imperialist: 'It will be a black day for the human race when scientific blackguards, conspirators, and fanatics manage to supplant him.' The trouble was that these eternal schoolboys very often had the responsi-bility of providing for the needs of men who did not share their sense of restraint. As the English sense of morality came to a climax towards the end of the century, official military brothels were virtuously closed down. Even so, in 1897 over 50 per cent of those in the army in India received treatment for VD—and this despite a pitiless prescription of football to sweat the sex out of the men.

Thereafter, if we are to believe Somerset Maugham's tales of lust in the rubber plantations of Malaya and the legends of aristocratic high jinks in Kenya's Happy Valley, at least parts of the Empire started going down hill. The 'boyish masters' disappeared in the mud of Flanders. A tight-lipped George V put his finger on the cause of this moral decay: he had heard that men who should have known better had taken to dining in pyjamas.

# THE IMPERIAL BEASTLINESS

In Australia, the Aborigines were treated like vermin: they were hunted for sport if there was a shortage of other game—and sometimes even if there was not. Yet to John Stuart Mill British rule was 'not only the purest in intention, but one of the most beneficent in act ever known among mankind'.

The British Government was always concerned to foster this idea. Hence its concern over the fate of the Tasmanians, a separate race from the Australian Aborigines, at the hands of British settlers: 'The adoption of any line of conduct having for its avowed or for its secret object the extinction of the native race could not but leave an indelible stain on the character of the British government.' Nevertheless, it remained realistic about the aborigines' chances: '. . . it is not unreasonable to apprehend that the whole race of these people may at no distant period become extinct'. It was not unreasonable at all, for they were entrusted to the protection of a Wesleyan called George Augustus Robinson, who—in order to save them from the hunters—went one worse by rounding them up, stranding them on a little island, and instructing them in Christian faith and morals. By 1850 all but a handful were dead, and these survivors were obviously too traumatized to take in any more of Christ's message. The last of the pure-blooded Tasmanians died in 1876.

It is instructive to pass from Robinson to another 'protector of aborigines', Governor Eyre. Eyre was genuinely considerate and humane towards the Australian Aborigines. However, being transferred to the West Indies, he put down a bloody little insurrection in Jamaica with such appalling brutality that he was relieved of his post. Marx wrote to Engels: 'The Jamaican incident is characteristic of the beastliness of the "true Englishman".' The Indian Mutiny was likewise defeated by the sheer ferocity of the English response. When, in 1919, General Reginald Dyer ordered troops to open fire on an unarmed crowd in the Jalienwallah Bagh at Amritsar, killing 375 people, he was applying the same principle. For it *was* a principle: the 'Punjab principle', or 'a shot in time saves nine', or 'severity always, justice when possible', or 'butcher and bolt' or, in Charles Napier's schoolmasterly interprretation, 'a good thrashing first, and great kindness afterwards'. Dyer intended 'to create a sufficient moral effect from a military point of view throughout the Punjab'. Lord Elgin's decision to destroy the Summer Palace in Peking was made in the same calculating spirit: a sort of cultural corporal punishment. The strategically unnecessary fire-bombing of Dresden in 1945, destroying Germany's most beautiful city, was presumably meant to serve a similar function.

> However good they may be, they must, as a people, be ruled with a hand of iron in a velvet glove; and if they writhe under it, and do not understand the force of it, it is no use to add more padding—you must take off the glove for a moment and show them the hand. They will then understand and obey.
>
> Lord Baden-Powell, *The Downfall of Prempeh*, 1896

This sort of attitude was the despair of the old school. Queen Victoria, who waged a lifelong struggle against the racial and religious fatuities expressed and committed by her more bigoted subjects, castigated 'the snobbish and vulgar, overbearing and offensive behaviour of our Civil and Political Agents'.

Even before the nineteenth century mated Christianity with imperialism there had been an awareness of the equivocacy of the moral position; but the earlier imperialist was more concerned with being self-perceivedly humane than with moral absolutes. In the entry in his diary for 7 October 1842, Charles Napier wrote, of the Amirs of Scinde: 'They are tyrants, and so are we, but the poor will have fairer play under our sceptre than under theirs . . . We have no right to seize Scinde, yet we will do so, and a very advantageous, useful, humane piece of rascality it will be.'

The more serious imperialists who followed Napier felt so uncomfortable in their role as rascals that a curious dislocation started to take place. In *Pax Britannica* (1968) Jan Morris recalled boarding the Cairo train at Port Said

> with an English colonel of particular gentleness of manner and sweetness of disposition. As we walked along the corridor to find a seat we found our way

blocked by an Egyptian, offering refreshments to people inside a compartment. Without a pause, apparently without a second thought, the colonel kicked him, quite hard and effectively, out of our way.

Queen Victoria, viceroys, the British Government and the more enlightened of the public at home in Britain did not have to believe in the racial superiority of the white man. (As early as 1828, black and white in South Africa were declared equal before the law 'in the most full and ample manner', according to Jan Morris.) At the sharp end of Empire it was a different matter. The less sophisticated Englishman reckoned that he had a larger brain than the natives and consequently a thinner skull, and so he would never be seen outside without his protective pith helmet. Others, though, were aware that the whole thing was a bluff. They carried on showing the flag, looking imperturbable and resolute, and continued to assume an impenetrable persona of unbending conformity in the most outlandish circumstances, in the knowledge that their power was, in Nehru's phrase, 'a psychological triumph', and that they would one day have to abjure their 'rough magic'. India was conquered not by the English but by the sepoys. And Sir Arthur Grimble wrote from the Gilbert Islands that 'We did not stop to think then how much more the maintenance of the Pax Britannica owed to their [the islanders'] marvellous patience and courtesy with us than to the inherent virtue of ourselves or our system' (*A Pattern of Islands*, 1952).

When their bluff was finally called, the English generally submitted with good grace. E. M. Forster wrote in *Two Cheers for Democracy* (1951) of his friend Syed Ross Masood:

> There is a story that he was once involved in a 'railway carriage' incident. He was stretched full-length in an empty compartment when a British officer bounced in and said 'Come on! get out of this.' Masood looked up quietly and said, 'D'you want your head knocked off?', whereupon the officer exclaimed, 'I say, I'm awfully sorry, I didn't know you were that sort of person,' and they became excellent friends.

# MATTERS OF HONOUR

Warren Hastings observed with concern that 'There is a fierceness in the European manners, especially among the lower sort, which is incompatible with the gentle temper of the Bengalee'. One may admire the bulldog charm of one of Sir Thomas Roe's early servants at the Moghul court, who stretched his master's powers of diplomacy when, as the emperor's brother went by with his retinue, greeted him drunkenly: 'How now, thou heathen dog?' But one can only draw a veil over the myriad discourtesies inflicted by the English when *they* were top dog. Sometimes they got their come-uppance. An incident in the Taiping Rebellion was reported in *The Times* in 1860:

Some Sikhs and a private of the Buffs (the East Kent Regiment) having remained behind with the grog-carts, fell into the hands of the Chinese. On the next morning they were brought before the authorities and commanded to perform the 'kotow'. The Sikhs obeyed; but Moyse, the English soldier, declaring that he would not prostrate himself before any Chinaman alive, was immediately knocked on the head, and his body thrown on a dunghill.

Sir Francis Doyle was swift to riposte with a poem celebrating the honour of the plain Englishman, 'The Private of the Buffs':

> *Last night,* among his fellow roughs
>     He jested, quaffed, and swore;
> A drunken private of the Buffs,
>     Who never looked before.
> *Today,* beneath the foeman's frown,
>     He stands in Elgin's place,
> Ambassador from Britain's crown,
>     And type of all her race.
>
> Poor, reckless, rude, low-born, untaught,
>     Bewildered, and alone,
> A heart, with English instinct fraught,
>     He yet can call his own.
> Ay, tear his body limb from limb,
>     Bring cord, or axe, or flame,
> He only knows, that not through *him*
>     Shall England come to shame.
>
> For Kentish hop-fields round him seem'd,
>     Like dreams, to come and go;
> Bright leagues of cherry-blossom gleam'd,
>     One sheet of living snow;
> The smoke, above his father's door,
>     In gray soft eddyings hung;
> Must he then watch it rise no more,
>     Doom'd by himself, so young!
>
> Yes, honour calls! with strength like steel
>     He puts the vision by.
> Let dusky Indians whine and kneel,
>     An English lad must die.
> And thus, with eyes that would not shrink,
>     With knee to man unbent,
> Unfaltering on its dreadful brink,
>     To his red grave he went.
>
> Vain, mightiest fleets of iron framed;
>     Vain, those all-shattering guns;

Unless proud England keep, untamed,
  The strong heart of her sons.
So let his name through Europe ring—
  A man of mean estate,
Who died, as firm as Sparta's king,
  Because his soul was great.

# THE CLASSICAL HERITAGE

The natural snobbery of the English middle classes was gratified beyond its wildest dreams by the necessity of having to accommodate themselves to the fastidious anxiety about caste and precedence traditional to Hindu society. However, above this struggle for position, there was a more classical ideal, which Philip Mason uncovered in the ethos of the 'heaven-born', the Indian Civil Service: 'Plato had entrusted his Republic to a class of guardians specially trained and chosen. They were to be persuaded that the god who created them had mixed gold in their composition to distinguish them from the common people . . .' The English guardians were rather similarly

> a corps of men specially selected, brought up in a rigour of bodily hardship to which no other modern people have subjected their ruling class, trained by cold baths, cricket, and the history of Greece and Rome, a separate race from those they ruled, aloof, superior to bribery, discouraged from marriage until they were middle-aged, and then subjected to long separations . . .
>
> Plato taught that the guardians of the state should not know their parents; the English did not go as far as that, but when they were eight years old the children from whom rulers were to be chosen were taken away from home for three-quarters of every year, taught not to mention their mothers or their own Christian names, brought up in the traditions of the Sparta which Plato had admired. And the children grew up to be true guardians; no other people in history can equal their record of disinterested guardianship.

Philip Mason, The Men Who Ruled India, 1963

The British public considered Palmerston extreme and high-handed when in 1850 he sent a fleet into the harbour at Piraeus to confiscate Greek shipping, in retaliation for the ill-treatment by the Greeks of a Portuguese Jew named Don Pacifico, who happened to have been born in Gibraltar. The public changed their tune when Palmerston explained the Classical precedent for his action. He concluded his speech with a celebrated peroration:

> As the Roman, in days of old, held himself free from indignity, when he could say '*Civis Romanus sum*', so also a British subject, in whatever land he may be, shall feel confident that the watchful eye and the strong arm of England will protect him against injustice and wrong.

Even Indians responded to this idea. Nirad Chaudhuri dedicated his *Diary of an Unknown Indian* (1987)

> To the memory of the British Empire in India, which conferred subjecthood on us but witheld citizenship, to which yet every one of us threw out the challenge *Civis Britannicus sum*, because all that was good and living within us was made, shaped, and quickened by the same British rule.

However, Baden-Powell bucked the Classical trend by founding the Scout Movement specifically in order to avoid the decadence of the Romans, who became, as he warned his young scouts, 'wishy-washy slackers without any go or patriotism about them'.

# THE INIMITABLE IMPERIALIST

Victor Jaquemont, a French traveller of the early nineteenth century, wrote of the arrogance of the English being so transcendent that it appeared unassuming:

> The English, who inspire so much respect in the natives of India by their power, strength, wealth and morality (always true to their word, upright and just, ninety-nine times out of a hundred), who . . . receive from them so many Asiatically servile demonstrations of respect and submission . . . are the only European people that do not take a pleasure in these marks of respect. They esteem themselves too highly, they despise the coloured races too much, to be flattered by their homage.
>
> *Letters from India, 1829–32*

In *The Seven Pillars of Wisdom* (1935), T. E. Lawrence discerned a similar sense which the English have of being in a category of their own, inimitable:

> The Englishmen in the Middle East divided into two classes. Class one, subtle and insinuating, caught the characteristics of the people about him, their speech, their conventions of thought, almost their manner. He directed men secretly, guiding them as he would. In such frictionless habit of influence his own nature lay hid, unnoticed.
>
> Class two, the John Bull of the books, became the more rampantly English the longer he was away from England. He invented an Old Country for himself, a home of all remembered virtues, so splendid in the distance that, on return, he often found reality a sad falling off and withdrew his muddle-headed self into fractious advocacy of the good old times. Abroad, through his armoured certainty, he was a rounded sample of our traits. He showed the complete Englishman. There was friction in his track, and his direction

was less smooth than that of the intellectual type: yet his stout example cut a wider swathe.

Both sorts took the same direction in example, one vociferously, the other by implication. Each assumed the Englishman a chosen being, inimitable, and the copying him blasphemous or impertinent. In this conceit they urged on people the next best thing. God had not given it them to be English; a duty remained to be good of their type. Consequently we admired native custom; studied the language; wrote books about its architecture, folklore, and dying industries. Then one day, we woke up to find this chthonic spirit turned political, and shook our heads with sorrow over its ungrateful nationalism‑ —truly the fine flower of our innocent efforts.

The French, though they started with a similar doctrine of the French‑ man as the perfection of mankind (dogma amongst them, not secret instinct), went on, contrarily, to encourage their subjects to imitate them; since, even if they could never attain the true level, yet their virtue would be greater as they approached it. We looked upon imitation as a parody; they as a compliment.

The Englishman is, of course, used to putting up with the vagaries of the weather, whether it be in his own country or far from home. In 'Mad Dogs and Englishmen' Noel Coward took this one stage further:

> In tropical climes there are certain times of day,
> When all the citizens retire
> To tear their clothes off and perspire.
> It's one of those rules that the greatest fools obey,
> Because the sun is much too sultry
> And one must avoid its ultry-violet ray . . .
> The natives grieve when the white men leave their huts,
> Because they're obviously definitely nuts!

> Mad dogs and Englishmen
> Go out in the midday sun.
> The Japanese don't care to,
> The Chinese wouldn't dare to,
> Hindoos and Argentines sleep firmly from twelve to one,
> But Englishmen detest a
> Siesta.
> In the Philippines there are lovely screens
> To protect you from the glare.
> In the Malay States there are hats like plates
> Which the Britishers won't wear.
> At twelve noon
> The natives swoon
> And no further work is done,
> But mad dogs and Englishmen
> Go out in the midday sun.

In *The Man of Destiny* (1898), George Bernard Shaw took a hard look at the Englishman's moral pretensions as an imperialist:

> When he wants a thing, he never tells himself that he wants it. He waits patiently until there comes into his mind, no one knows how, a burning conviction that it is his moral and religious duty to conquer those who have got the thing he wants. Then he becomes irresistible. . . . He is never at a loss for an effective moral attitude. As the great champion of freedom and national independence, he conquers and annexes half the world and calls it colonization. When he wants a new market for his adulterated Manchester goods, he sends a missionary to teach the natives the Gospel of Peace. The natives kill the missionary: he flies to arms in defence of Christianity; fights for it; conquers for it; and takes the market as a reward from heaven.

The ideal colony for the English, strangely enough, proved to be the United States; ultimate independence remained their very unimperial ideal. For a short while the Empire had seemed to some people quite solid and real; subject to decay and ultimate ending, like all empires, but a substantial entity nevertheless. It was never meant to be. The English did not put down roots. Finally they went home to die, with a few curios, a hunting trophy, an assegai or a taste for curries . . . and a working knowledge of some obscure dialect from the other side of the world. They must have wondered what it was all for.

Yet the radical anti-imperialist Wilfred Blunt had *some* idea. Even he could not resist 'the sentiment of Empire', admitted by no less unlikely a person than Gladstone to be 'innate in every Briton'. Blunt expressed it in the sestet of his sonnet 'Gibraltar':

> Ay, this is the famed rock, which Hercules
> And Goth and Moor bequeathed us. At this door
> England stands sentry. God! to hear the shrill
> Sweet treble of her fifes upon the breeze,
> And at the summons of the rock gun's roar
> To see her red coats marching from the hill!

# BIGOTS AND BULLIES

In *Burmese Days* (1934) George Orwell showed the rough edges and frayed ends of the small-time English imperialist at the end of his tether:

> 'How much ice have we got left?'
>      ' 'Bout twenty pounds, master. Will only last today, I think. I find it very difficult to keep ice cool now.'
>      'Don't talk like that, damn you—"I find it very difficult!" Have you swallowed a dictionary? "Please master, can't keeping ice cool"—that's how you

ought to talk. We shall have to sack this fellow if he gets to talk English too well. I can't stick servants who talk English . . .'

'Oh, hell! I'd snivel psalms to oblige the padre, but I can't stand the way these damned native Christians come shoving into our church . . . What bloody fools we were ever to let those missionaries loose in this country! Teaching bazaar sweepers they're as good as we are. "Please, sir, me Christian same like master." Damned cheek.'

'I remember when we paid our butler only twelve rupees a month, and really that man loved us like a dog.'

'In my young days, when one's butler was disrespectful, one sent him along to the jail with a chit saying "Please give the bearer fifteen lashes".'

'Our burra sahib at Mandalay always said . . . that in the end we shall simply *leave* India. Young men will not come out here any longer to work all their lives for insults and ingratitude. We shall just *go*.'

'We could put things right in a month if we chose. It only takes a pennyworth of pluck. Look at Amritsar. Look how they caved in after that. Dyer knew the stuff to give them. Poor old Dyer! That was a dirty job . . .'

# RELICS OF EMPIRE

Geoffrey Moorhouse, travelling to the North-West frontier in the early 1980s, visited the officers' mess of the Chitral Scouts and found relics of the imperial Englishman still lovingly preserved in modern Pakistan:

On one wall was a boyish pictorial map of the district, drawn by some artistic British officer whose winters clearly pivoted on the Chitral Ski Club. The words were formed by human figures bent into alphabetical shapes, and similar whimsy marked various features of the terrain. 'Crappo's Slalom' was depicted by a line of flags down a mountain. The 'Nursery Slopes' had a Nanny pushing a pram uphill. The young men who officered the frontiers of Empire had left behind them a still powerful whiff of schoolboy humour . . .
    'And look at this. Tell me if you have seen anything quite like it before?' Major Quamber was pointing to the billiards table. The timber edges, the pockets and the green baize on top were conventional enough, supplied by a firm in Bombay. The rest of the table had been made of cement.
    'You see, it was impossible to transport a proper billiards table across Lowari in those days. So they made one themselves out of that.'
    He was speaking like an archaeologist, turning over some specimens with considered care . . .

Cavalry Charge, Omdurman. The last British cavalry charge took place,
fortunately perhaps, against the Sudanese, who were without the
means to do much damage. As so often, the effect of the exercise on
the final outcome was virtually nil, but the young Winston Churchill,
present on this occasion, enjoyed himself hugely.

Moorhouse also visited the Khyber Pass:

> Of all places where fighting had occurred, this probably was the corridor
> which had seen most blood spilt. That, perhaps, was why just beyond it there
> appeared the strange collection of regimental badges decorating the rock
> faces beside the road . . . In one clump, the Dorset Regiment, the Royal
> Sussex Regiment, the Essex Regiment, the South Wales Borderers, the
> Cheshire Regiment and the Gordon Highlanders stood together.
>
> They stirred me more than they should have done . . . The soldiers who
> fought in those regiments may have been engaged in an essentially immoral
> enterprise, yet they were strangely respected . . . and the respect seemed not
> to have dissolved, though a full generation had passed since last they were
> here. The latest coat of paint on the badges couldn't have been more than
> twelve months old.

# AN IMPERIAL PRAYER

If you ask the imperial Englishman what he believes in, he will more than likely refer to Rudyard Kipling's 'If':

If you can keep your head when all about you
    Are losing theirs and blaming it on you,
If you can trust yourself when all men doubt you,
    But make allowance for their doubting too;
If you can wait and not be tired by waiting,
    Or being lied about, don't deal in lies,
Or being hated, don't give way to hating,
    And yet don't look too good, nor talk too wise:

If you can dream—and not make dreams your master;
    If you can think—and not make thoughts your aim;
If you can meet with Triumph and Disaster
    And treat those two imposters just the same;
If you can bear to hear the truth you've spoken
    Twisted by knaves to make a trap for fools,
Or watch the things you gave your life to, broken,
    And stoop and build 'em up with worn-out tools:

If you can make one heap of all your winnings
    And risk it on one turn of pitch-and-toss,
And lose, and start again at your beginnings
    And never breathe a word about your loss;
If you can force your heart and nerve and sinew
    To serve your turn long after they are gone,
And so hold on when there is nothing in you
    Except the Will which says to them: 'Hold on!'

If you can talk with crowds and keep your virtue,
    Or walk with Kings—nor lose the common touch,
If neither foes nor loving friends can hurt you,
    If all men count with you, but none too much;
If you can fill the unforgiving minute
    With sixty seconds' worth of distance run,
Yours is the Earth and everything that's in it,
    And—which is more—you'll be a Man, my son!

*The Sleeping Congregation*: print by William Hogarth, 1728. The vicar
is preaching on the text, 'Come unto me all ye that are heavy laden,
and I shall give you rest'. A sermon within a sermon. It's hard to tell
whether Hogarth is lashing contemporary standards of worship, or
simply casting a Donald McGill-like eye over everyday behaviour.

# CHAPTER SEVEN

# THE ENGLISHMAN
# AT PRAYER

An Englishman may or may not be aware of his mortality—and, if he is, on the whole he would rather not talk about it. As for morality, Lord Melbourne spoke for many when, after listening to an Evangelical preaching on the consequences of sin, he blustered, 'No one has more respect for the Christian religion than I have, but really, when it comes to intruding it into private life . . .' When asked as to his religion, Benjamin Disraeli proclaimed it to be 'that of all reasonable men'. The fact that he was on his death-bed had clearly not affected his dandyish alertness to the requirements of Englishness.

An Englishman may very well not be able to say exactly what the 39 Articles are, let alone subscribe to them. If he attends Church at all, it may possibly be from a sense of duty, rather in the spirit of the Army Regulations: 'Every soldier, when not prevented by military duty, is to attend the worship of Almighty God according to the forms prescribed by his own religion.'

But, whatever the Englishman's faith—or lack of it—the Church is there in physical form in every town and village, built by his uncouth ancestors in the belief that the Christian religion kept sparks of conscience alive in an otherwise barbarous world, or at least terrified oppressors with the horrors of Hell; that it was the source of civilization, the rule of law, education, technology, the arts . . . There may be no rare Roman bricks in the fabric of the local church, no rough Saxon stones, no squat Norman arches or Gothic tracery; no crusader lying awkwardly cross-legged within, no brass carving or bas-relief of a Jacobean divine, no prolix stone inscriptions to Georgian squires or busy Victorians, quietly confident of the life to come, no ancient yew-trees among tilting headstones. The local church or chapel may be inscribed 1882, optimistically forestalling the antiquarian guesswork of future ages, and commemorate little more than the vanity of civilization in long lines of local names and 'the old lie'—'*Dulce et decorum est pro patria mori*'. Yet even so, the Church in England remains the linchpin of English culture, if only because one has merely to open the Authorized Version or the Book of Common Prayer to be connected with the rootstock of the national life—what George Borrow termed 'England's sublime liturgy':

> . . . defend us, thy humble servants, in all assaults of our enemies, that we, surely trusting in thy defence, may not fear the power of any adversaries . . .

## THE ENGLISH CHURCH MILITANT

Inevitably, the popular English spiritual ideal is a heroic one. To the Anglo-Saxons, Christ's humility was a laughable model. He had to be presented instead as a young warrior, covered in blood and glory. Even then, of all the pagan tribes, the Anglo-Saxons were the most fractious. In the early seventh century King Sigbert of East Anglia was killed by his vassals for being 'too ready to forgive his enemies'.

However, with a little chivalric adjustment, initiated in the ninth century by Alfred the Great, who mystified the Danes with his magnanimity, the English taste for battle was accommodated to the New Testament. Typifying the Englishman's peace of mind when called upon to stand up and fight is Sir Jacob Astley's manly last-minute prayer to a kindly and indulgent god before the battle of Edgehill (1642): 'O Lord, thou knowest how busy I must be this day. If I forget thee, do not forget me . . . March on, boys!' At the battle of Chilianwala (1849), the British cavalry, bungled into shameful retreat by a superannuated officer, were halted only by the chaplain, who pointed out that 'the Almighty God would never will it that a Christian army should be cut up by a pagan host'.

Later in the nineteenth century, William Booth struck gold when he managed to weld the kindness and the militarism of the English into one bizarre unit—the Salvation Army. His mission-halls became 'barracks', while prayer was euphemized into 'knee-drill' and death into 'promotion to glory'. Uniforms and brass bands, the motto 'Blood and Fire', and the *War Cry*—such puerile Sunday-school stratagems provided an unlikely front for a series of worldwide initiatives in social relief: food distribution, night shelters, legal aid, the first labour exchange, a missing-persons bureau, and schemes to help discharged prisoners in Australia, alcoholics in New York, prostitutes in Tokyo and earthquake victims in San Francisco. But then an Englishman is often at his most serious when he is at his most absurd.

## A BROAD CHURCH

In *Areopagitica* Milton wrote: 'I cannot praise a fugitive and cloistered virtue, unexercized and unbreathed, that never sallies out and sees her adversary, but slinks out of the race . . .' This is the English spiritual vision—practical, open to criticism, trusting to experience and common sense, and scorning what Coleridge called 'vain philosophy's aye babbling spring'.

Dr Johnson is naturally magisterial on the subject:

> Human experience, which is constantly contradicting theory, is the great test of truth. A system, built on the discoveries of a great many minds, is always of more strength than that which is produced by the mere workings of any one mind, without the aid of prior investigators.

The English greet religious disorder with as little relish as they greet disorder at a bus-stop. As John Selden put it in his *Table Talk* (1689), 'men say they are of the same religion for quietness' sake'. Spiritual values are best served not by insisting upon one's own idea of the truth, should one be so presumptuous as to have one, but by not causing any trouble:

> That private reason 'tis more just to curb,
> Than by disputes the public peace disturb.

> Dryden, 'Religio Laici'

If Dryden's attitude is that of a spiritual police constable, Thomas Hobbes, in *Leviathan* (1651), is more like a regimental sergeant-major in his prescription for a Church: 'A company of men professing Christian religion, united in the person of one sovereign, at whose command they ought to assemble, and without whose authority they ought not to assemble.' (Charles II remarked happily that young clergymen were set to worry over Hobbes as dogs were exercised by being encouraged to bait a bear.)

What is significant is not that this idea should be entertained, but that most Englishmen have little difficulty in adjusting their beliefs, when necessary, to conform with the interests of the state—although they might not express themselves as insensitively as Lord Thurlow (1731–1806) did on being approached, as Lord Chancellor, by a deputation of Non-conformists:

> I'm against you damme! I am for the established Church by God! Not that I have any greater regard for the established Church than for any other Church, except because it is established. If you can get your damned religion established, I'll be for that too.

Typically, English Christians have rarely lost sleep over their official adherence to the uncompromisingly Calvinist 39 Articles. The important thing, as Hobbes pointed out, is not to think too hard about them: 'It is with the mysteries of our religion as with wholesome pills for the sick; which swallowed whole, have the virtue to cure; but chewed up, are for the most part cast up again without effect.' Even Percy Bysshe Shelley, an outspoken atheist, was in 1815 attracted to the idea of taking orders, on account purely of the social functions a parson may fulfil ' . . . in his teaching as a scholar and a moralist; in his example as a gentleman and a man of regular life; in the consolation of his personal intercourse and of his charity among the poor . . . And am I to deprive myself of the advantages of this admirable institution because there are certain technicalities . . .' (quoted by Thomas Love Peacock).

Alas, the Church of England, even at its broadest, boggles at atheism. However, when they were given the opportunity of sewing up a religion of their own, the English settled for a capacious, hold-all establishment, with room for as many differing mentalities as possible. Cleverly, they contrived a reformation of their faith which was fuelled by forceful Puritan personalities, but firmly directed by rather conservative civil servants disguised as prelates.

One of the most robust in the former category was Dr Rowland Taylor, rector of Hadleigh in Suffolk and blessed with the build and the belligerence of a commando. When it came to his 'degradation' before going to the stake in February 1555, he intimidated Bishop Bonner into forgoing the customary ritual of striking him on the breast with his crozier: 'My lord,' warned Bonner's chaplain, nervously regarding the massive Puritan presence before them, 'strike him not, for he will sure strike again.' Taylor backed up this intuition: 'Yea, by St Peter will I. The cause is Christ's and I were no good Christian, if I would not fight in my Master's quarrel.'

Less pugnacious but no less staunch and buoyant were the immortal words of Latimer to his fellow-martyr: 'Be of good comfort, Master Ridley, and play the man. We shall this day light such a candle by God's grace in England as I trust shall never be put out.'

Thomas Cranmer, the architect of the Church of England and the author of its liturgy, was not quite the stuff these martyrs were made of. He was a diplomat, after all. He made seven grovelling recantations in the hope of dodging the stake. At the last, though, when he learned that his efforts had been in vain, he retracted them all and made a brave show of holding steadily in the fire his right hand, which had been guilty of signing them.

# PURITANS AND PAPISTS

Cranmer was an exception. The English, if they have to burn anyone at all, prefer to burn men of principle. As Sydney Smith remarked in a letter to Lady Mary Bennet, describing a prison visit in 1821 with the Quaker, Elizabeth Fry, 'She is very unpopular with the clergy. Examples of living active virtue disturb our repose, and give birth to distressing comparisons: we long to burn her alive.' This suspicion of unnatural virtue is expressed for all Englishmen by Sir Toby Belch: 'Dost thou think because thou art virtuous, there shall be no more cakes and ale?' Moreover, there is something about a Puritan that makes an Englishman like Sir Toby's companion in *Twelfth Night*, Sir Andrew Aguecheek, want to 'beat him like a dog'.

> **SIR TOBY**: What, for being a Puritan? Thy exquisite reason, dear knight?
> **SIR ANDREW**: I have no exquisite reason for't, but I have reason good enough.

Nearly ten years after the Restoration, the Puritans were still being ridiculed, even at Lambeth Palace. There, on 14 May 1669, Pepys was privileged to witness a private performance:

> Most of the company gone, and I going, I heard by a gentleman of a sermon that was to be there; and so I staid to hear it, thinking it serious, till by and by the gentleman told me it was a mockery by one Cornet Bolton, a very gentleman-like man, that behind a chair did pray and preach like a Presbyter Scot that ever I heard in my life, with all the possible imitation in grimaces and voice. And his text about the hanging up their harps upon the willows; and a serious good sermon too, exclaiming against Bishops . . . till it made us all burst . . .

And by now Papists were if anything worse. The word itself started off by being almost a synonym for 'agents of a foreign power', eventually declining until it became a general term of abuse and Catholicism a common bugbear. The attitude was later typified by Uncle Matthew in Nancy Mitford's *The Pursuit of Love* (1945), as, upset by the tragic denouement of *Romeo and Juliet*, he surveyed the Roman Catholic content of Shakespeare's play:

> 'All the fault of that damned padre', he kept saying on the way home, still wiping his eyes. 'That fella what's 'is name, Romeo, might have known a blasted papist would mess up the whole thing. Silly old fool of a nurse too, I bet she was an RC, dismal old bitch.'

A whiff of treason still clung to the 'old religion' in the late 1820s, when Lord Wellington, the Prime Minister, 'called out' Lord Winchilsea for accusing him of popery during the debates on Catholic Emancipation, which Wellington staunchly supported. While they waited at Battersea Park for Winchilsea's party to arrive (very late, having thought the venue was to be Putney Heath), Wellington instructed his anxious second, Viscount Hardinge, who had lost an arm at Waterloo: 'Now then Hardinge, look sharp and step out the ground. Damn it! Don't stick him up so near the ditch. If I hit him he will tumble in.' (Much of the Duke's success as a commander had been a result of his sharp eye for the lie of the land.) When it came to it, however, Wellington fired wide. Winchilsea then fired into the air and apologized. The affair was widely deplored, and it is doubtful whether Wellington was really serious about it.

Fighting a duel, however feebly, seems an odd way to stand up for one's religious principles; but not if one sees one's religion as a sort of dignified old lady, whose honour must be defended and to whom all respect must be accorded. Dr Johnson summed it up when he spoke approvingly of Dr John Campbell: 'I am afraid he has not been in the inside of a church for many years; but he never passes a church without pulling off his hat; this shows that he has good principles.'

## GOD IS ALIVE AND WELL AND LIVING IN ENGLAND

If the Church of England was something of a muddle from the beginning, that was because God wanted it that way. Archbishop Parker did not think it unreasonable, 'where God is so much English as he is', to demand allegiance to the new Anglican faith. And Milton, in *Areopagitica*, was equally aware of the special relationship the English enjoyed with their Creator, even under the more coherent direction of 'devout and holy men':

> God is decreeing to begin some new and great period in his Church, even to the reforming of Reformation itself; what does he then but reveal himself to his servants, and as his manner is, first to his Englishmen?

Perhaps it is only natural that some felt able to drop God altogether, and find themselves still moved by a patriotism that took on the aspect of divinity. One such was the apparently cynical Marquess of Halifax (1633–1695), known as the 'Trimmer', on account of his ability to trim the boat, and his principles, in his service to the state. In *The Character of a Trimmer* (1699) he wrote of himself:

> Our Trimmer is far from Idolatry in other things, in one thing only he cometh near it, his Country is in some degree his Idol; he doth not worship the Sun, because 'tis not peculiar to us, it rambles about the World, and is less kind to us than others; but for the Earth of England, tho perhaps inferior to that of many places abroad, to him there is Divinity in it, and he would rather dye, than see a spire of English grass trampled down by a Foreign Trespasser . . .

There have been those who have refused to submit their principles to this deity, and regrettably have had to be sacrificed to it: As the 'Trimmer' remarked, 'there is in many, and particularly in Englishmen, a mistaken pleasure in resisting the dictates of rigorous authority, a stomach that riseth against a hard imposition.'

## REBELS

Medieval English kings did not mind owing theoretical allegiance to Rome. In 1157 Henry II, ably supported by his chancellor, Thomas Becket, was in dispute with Bishop Hilary of Chichester. When the bishop denied the royal right to depose abbots, Henry roared, 'Depose, No; shove out, Yes!' This was the way to settle nice questions of ecclesiastical jurisdiction, and Henry presumed that Becket was taking notes. He had little idea that the Thomas with whom he played chess and rode out hawking would drop this diplomatic approach to religion and develop cocky ideas of becoming a saint.

If one is to believe the testimony of his secretary, William Fitzstephen, Becket was so far from being troubled by urgent spiritual promptings that on at least one occasion saintliness had to be, as it were, thrust upon him. Riding through the streets of London on a wintry day, the king and the chancellor encountered a beggar, and Becket agreed with Henry's suggestion that it would be great charity to give him a thick warm coat. But Henry went on, 'You indeed shall have the grace of this great charity.' It took a tussle before the king could relieve Becket of his cloak and pass it to the bemused beggar, who wandered off, resplendent in scarlet and ermine and giving thanks to God. One imagines Becket knew how to laugh this off while inwardly seething at his loss of dignity.

Suddenly finding himself Archbishop of Canterbury, however, Becket fulfilled the requirements of this position with the same dedication that he had brought to his duties as chancellor, and with greater success—his weaknesses, of obduracy and theatricality, leading him inexorably to a martyr's crown. In 1163, when he insisted on carrying his own episcopal cross to his last meeting with the king before fleeing into exile, one of his clerks appealed to Gilbert Foliot, Bishop of London, to relieve Becket of this unnecessary stageprop. 'My dear man,' Foliot replied, 'he has always been a silly ass, and always will be.'

The second version of this very English tragedy took place nearly 400 years later. Thomas More was another unlikely English saint; uxorious, pragmatic, ironic and agreeable, he was a model of the essentially balanced virtues of the Englishman. Robert Whittington's contemporary eulogy is justly celebrated: 'More is a man of angel's wit and singular learning. I know not his fellow. For where is the man of that gentleness, lowliness and affability? And as time requireth, a man of marvellous mirth and pastimes and sometime of a sad gravity. A man for all seasons.'

This tragedy also had its idyll before the storm, with Henry VIII holding his chancellor in the warmest of regards. It was observed once that the king 'walked in Sir Thomas More's garden by the space of an hour and held his arm about Sir Thomas More's neck'. More had no illusions though: 'If my head could win his majesty a castle in France—it should not fail to go.' Even as he dealt with heretics, which as chancellor it was his business to do, More had a fellow-feeling with them that was unusual in that age of self-righteousness:

> I pray God that some of us, high as we seem to sit upon the mountains treading heretics under our feet like ants, live not to see the day that we would

gladly be at league and composition with those whom you call heretics to let them have their churches quietly to themselves so that they would be content to let us have ours quietly to ourselves.

And, while his crisis drew from him a more forthright declaration of liberty of conscience – 'I leave every man in his conscience and methinketh that in good faith so were it good conscience every man should leave me to mine' – England's power in future ages to stand up for liberty and to be a home for refugees from tyranny required not only the repudiation of papal jurisdiction but also the heads of those who were too stubborn in their old loyalties.

One of the Catholic martyrs under Elizabeth I was Robert Colton, a boy from Wisbech. Showing a maturity beyond his years, he made this point: 'I hear say that England hath been a Catholic Christian country a thousand years afore this queen's reign and her father's. If that were the old highway to heaven, then why should I forsake it?'

The English are not generally given to witch-hunts and torture, and during the persecution of the Catholics they needed to be assured by the 1st Lord Cecil that the warders 'whose office it is to handle the rack' were 'specially charged to use it in as charitable a manner as such a thing might be'. And, if this vision of kindly torturers seems like typical English hypocrisy, it is worth recording the reply of Bishop Bonner, the notorious persecutor of Protestants under Bloody Mary, to someone who taxed him with allowing an old man to be whipped: 'If thou hadst been in his case, thou wouldst have thought it a good commutation of penance to have thy bum beaten to save thy body from burning.'

However, it is apparent that English Roman Catholics were not in the least interested in fulfilling the Pope's command that Elizabeth I be deposed. Most were of the mettle of Sir Thomas Tresham, who begged in 1588, when nearly 70, to be allowed to fight for queen and country against his co-religionists.

As the ideal of religious toleration was essentially impracticable at this time in England, it was exported to the New World. But even the Puritan emigrants of the 1620s still identified with the Church of England. In his *A True Relation of the Last Voyage to New England*, published in the 1630s, Francis Higginson declared, 'We will not say . . . "Farewell Babylon!" "Farewell Rome!" but we will say, "Farewell, dear England!" . . . We do not go to New England as Separatists from the Church of England . . .'

And those Puritans who remained, in due course to overthrow and execute their monarch, performed this sacrifice with the greatest reluctance. For most of the Civil War, the Parliamentarians were conservative, even Royalist. At late as 1647, less than two years before having him beheaded, Cromwell called Charles I 'the uprightest and most conscientious man of his three kingdoms'.

Things changed after James II's futile attempt to reimpose Catholicism. For example, it was said of George Frederick Handel that he often spoke of it as one of the great good fortunes of his life that he lived in a country where men suffered no 'molestation or inconvenience' on account of their own religious principles. Voltaire shared this view:

> England is the land of sects. An Englishman, like a free man, goes to heaven by the way which pleases him . . . If there was only one religion in England its despotism would be a matter for fear; if two, they would cut each other's throats; but there are thirty, and they live in peace, and are happy.
>
> *Letters on the English*

This despite the subversive, democratic notions of Non-conformists.

Methodism was a clean, belt-tightening new broom of a religion for the spiritual heirs of John Ball, Wycliffe and Bunyan. The Wesley brothers brought a stern, improving aspect to popular religion. On his mother's death, John Wesley was refreshingly unsentimental: 'I am absolutely sure God does not condemn me for any want of duty towards her, except only that I have not reproved her so plainly and fully as I should have done.' His brother Charles, a tireless hymnographer, was equally unshaken by the Great Leveller:

> Ah, lovely appearance of death!
> What sight upon earth is so fair?
> Not all the gay pageants that breathe
> Can with a dead body compare.
>
> 'On the Sight of a Corpse'

With the occasional bathos went spiritual vigour—and political vigour, too, leading eventually to the trades union movement. John Wesley appealed to the pride and independence of the working man. 'Do not affect the gentleman. You have no more to do with this character than that of a dancing master.' And the feeling was mutual: a curate in Charlotte Brontë's novel *Shirley* (1849) announces that 'the circumstance of finding himself invited to tea with a Dissenter would unhinge him for a week'.

The established Church soon found itself infected with the new zeal. Lord Melbourne was afraid to go to church 'for fear of hearing something very extraordinary'. And the same energy that exposed and insisted on the reform of scandalous social conditions at home also imposed Sunday observance and the missionary position on South-Sea Islanders.

## SELF-INFLICTED WOUNDS

The characteristic attitude of the Englishman at his devotions—benign, optimistic, equable, with a preference for dull social virtues over spiritual fervour—was prefigured in the form of the fifth-century British heresiarch, Pelagius, whom

Bertrand Russell found 'a cultivated and agreeable ecclesiastic', and who spoke from the twilight of the Roman age, after the sack of the capital, with an urbane reasonableness on the sticky subject of free will and original sin: 'He [God] has not willed to command anything impossible, for he is righteous; and he will not condemn a man for what he could not help, for he is holy.'

Hair-shirts and scourges were standard equipment for those who took their devotions seriously in the Middle Ages, and the monks who found the body of Thomas Becket outstretched on the floor of Canterbury Cathedral were thrilled to discover that he wore a hair-shirt and drawers, crawling with vermin, and sewn tightly round the body and thighs; the opening was at the back, so that he could have his daily scouring. They surmised that being murdered must have been something of a relief for their archbishop. Canonization would be a mere formality.

However, the stock-in-trade of a martyr never caught on as a general thing with the English. If they disciplined themselves, it would be in private; and disciplining others was simply the pleasant or unpleasant duty of a school-master. Even at the time of the Black Death, when the rest of Europe was gripped by a craze for mass public flagellation, England remained unaffected. A delega-tion of flagellants from the Low Countries performed their bloody devotions in front of St Paul's to what must have been bemused indifference. Their spectators certainly did not rush to try it themselves.

Gladstone was one of the few Englishmen known to have taken a scourge to himself without the object of pleasure. To the eighteenth-century 'Hell-Fire' (Sir Francis) Dashwood – notorious as a satanist but who also collaborated with Benjamin Franklin on a simplified Book of Common Prayer (still in use in America as *Franklin's Prayer Book*), and thus had a broad knowledge of religious affairs – it was a decidedly suspect practice. In his posthumously published *Memoirs of the Reign of King George III* (1845), Horace Walpole described a visit to the Sistine Chapel.

> On Good Friday, each person who enters the Sistine Chapel takes a small scourge from an attendant at the door. The chapel is dimly lighted, only three candles, which are extinguished by the priest, one by one. At the putting out of the first, the penitents take off one part of their dress. At the next, still more, and in the dark which follows the extinguishing of the third candle, 'lay on' their own shoulders with groans and lamentations. Sir Francis Dashwood, thinking this mere stage effect, entered with the others dressed in a large watchman's coat, demurely took his scourge from the priest and advanced to the end of the chapel, where in the darkness ensuing he drew from beneath his coat an English horse whip and flogged right and left quite down the chapel – the congregation exclaiming, 'Il Diavolo! Il Diavolo!' – thinking the Evil One was upon them with a vengeance. The consequence might have been serious had Dashwood not immediately fled the Papal dominions.

# THE ANGLICAN VISION

The English developed a sensible and sanguine theology. 'Ethics are defined to be the art of living well and happily,' wrote Henry More after the Restoration. Brushing off the Dark Night of the Soul, they looked on the bright side. 'It is a happy world after all,' wrote William Paley at the end of the eighteenth century: 'If we look to what the waters produce, shoals of the fry of fish . . . These are so happy that they do not know what to do with themselves.' Paley, one of the most influential Establishment theologians of the nineteenth century, had a short way with the clerical ideals of poverty and humility: 'Rich and splendid situations in the Church have been justly regarded as prizes held out to invite persons of good hopes and ingenuous attainments to enter into its service.' However, this bland and eminently acceptable spiritual fare was accompanied by the sort of unguarded and barbed remarks one might expect from a native of Giggleswick. He once likened the property system to a flock of pigeons all collecting grain to feed one superior pigeon. George III refused to consider him for a bishopric: 'What? Pigeon Paley? Not orthodox, not orthodox.'

The primary enthusiasm of an eighteenth-century man of God was not

*The Resurrection, Cookham* by Stanley Spencer, who singlemindedly represented Biblical events, including the end of all things, as taking place in a small dormitory town on the Thames. The English tend to shy away from the idea of eternal damnation, and the unregenerates of Cookham appear to have a very mild fate in store for them, as befits a suburban Last Judgement.

always a professional one. For Gilbert White the study of natural history was consistent with his cloth, but Laurence Sterne could hardly have claimed the same consistency for his risqué novels. Dr Johnson had a friend, the Reverend John Taylor (at whose table the Doctor nearly died of over-eating), whose 'talk was all of bullocks'. And Sydney Smith felt that many of his brothers in Christ had attained an expertise in horsemanship unbecoming to their cloth: 'I see so little of any clever men here that I have nobody to recommend. But if you have any young horses to break I can find many clergymen who will do it for you' (Letter to Henry Brougham, 1826).

Sustaining the dignity of a powerful ecclesiastical hierarchy while refusing to vex themselves with celibacy, Anglican divines lacked the glamour of seminary-trained priests or hell-fire preachers. Indeed, there was something irresistibly droll about Anglican parsons and prelates, thrust into the world with little more than a classical education. Jane Austen, in a letter, remarked: 'How can a bishop marry? How can he flirt? The most he can say is "I will see you in the vestry after service."' Sydney Smith suggested that there were in fact three sexes, 'men, women, and parsons'. They retained a consciousness, however, that they were in possession of the only really sound and respectable faith for an Englishman. For Fielding's Parson Thwackum in *Tom Jones* (1749) the Church of England had got it just right: 'When I mention Religion, I mean the Christian Religion; and not only the Christian Religion, but the Protestant Religion; and not only the Protestant Religion, but the Church of England.'

While Gerard Manley Hopkins, the Catholic priest, was composing his superb record of spiritual despair, the 'terrible sonnets', the blither serenity of the Anglican vision was captured in *Pippa Passes* (1841) by Robert Browning:

The Year's at the Spring,
And day's at the morn;
Morning's at seven;
The hill-side's dew-pearled;
The lark's on the wing;
The snail's on the thorn:
God's in his heaven—
All's right with the world!

In AD 627, King Edwin's High Priest was prepared to give Christianity a trial. According to Bede's *History of the English Church and People* (731), Chapter 13, the priest Coifi presented a good case to Edwin:

' . . . for I verily declare to you, that the religion which we have hitherto professed has, as far as I can learn, no virtue in it. For none of your people has applied himself more diligently to the worship of our gods than I; and yet there are many who receive greater favours from you, and are more preferred than I, and are more prosperous in all their undertakings. Now if the gods were good for any thing, they would rather forward me, who have been more careful to serve them. It remains, therefore, that if upon examination you find those new doctrines, which are now preached to us, better and more efficacious, we immediately receive them without any delay,'

Another of the king's chief men, approving of his words and exhortations, presently added: 'The present life of man, O king, seems to me, in comparison of that time which is unknown to us, like to the swift flight of a sparrow through the room wherein you sit at supper in winter, with your commanders and ministers, and a good fire in the midst, whilst the storms of rain and snow prevail abroad; the sparrow, I say, flying in at one door, and immediately out at another, whilst he is within, is safe from the wintry storm; but after a short space of fair weather, he immediately vanishes out of your sight, into the dark winter from which he had emerged. So this life of man appears for a short space, but of what went before, or what is to follow, we are utterly ignorant. If, therefore, this new doctrine contains something more certain, it seems justly to deserve to be followed.' The other elders and king's councillors, by Divine inspiration, spoke to the same effect.

But pagans becoming Christians is a reversible process. A lot of sturdy obstreperous paganism lurked beneath the popular heresies, such as the medieval Lollardry. Much later, W. E. Henley's enormously popular poem, 'Invictus', found the English going back to the cold stormy night of pagan ignorance with stoic acceptance:

> Out of the night that covers me,
> Black as the pit from pole to pole,
> I thank whatever gods may be
> For my unconquerable soul.
>
> In the fell clutch of circumstance
> I have not winced nor cried aloud.
> Under the bludgeonings of chance
> My head is bloody, but unbowed.
>
> Beyond this place of wrath and tears
> Looms but the horror of the shade,
> And yet the menace of the years
> Finds, and shall find, me unafraid.
>
> It matters not how strait the gate,
> How charged with punishments the scroll,
> I am the master of my fate:
> I am the captain of my soul.

Religious trends come and go, but in practice the English tend to follow the dictum of 'Trimmer' Halifax: 'Men must be saved in this world by their lack of faith.' This was well understood by the Vicar of Bray in the anonymous song:

> In good King Charles's golden days,
>     When loyalty no harm meant,
> A zealous High-Churchman I was,
>     And so I got preferment:
> To teach my flock I never missed—
>     Kings are by God appointed,
> And damned are those who do resist
>     Or touch the Lord's annointed.
>         And this is law, I will maintain,
>             Until my dying day. Sir,
>         That whatsoever king shall reign,
>             I'll be the Vicar of Bray, Sir.
>
>
> When royal James obtained the crown,
>     And Popery came in fashion,
> The penal laws I hooted down,
>     And read the declaration:
> The Church of Rome I found would fit
>     Full well my constitution,
> And had become a Jesuit—
>     But for the Revolution.
>         And this is law, etc.
>
>
> When William was our king declared
>     To ease the nation's grievance,
> With this new wind about I steered,
>     And swore to him allegiance.
> Old principles I did revoke,
>     Set conscience at a distance:
> Passive obedience was a joke,
>     A jest was non-resistance.
>         And this is law, etc.
>
>
> When gracious Anne became our queen,
>     The Church of England's glory,
> Another face of things was seen—
>     And I became a Tory:
> Occasional Conformists base,
>     I scorned their moderation,
> And thought the church in danger was
>     By such prevarication.
>         And this is law, etc.

When George in pudding-time came o'er,
　　And moderate men look big. Sir,
I turned a cat-in-pan once more—
　　And so became a Whig, Sir:
And thus preferment I procured
　　From our new faith's defender,
And almost every day abjured
　　The Pope and the Pretender.
　　　　And this is law, etc.

The illustrious house of Hanover,
　　And the Protestant succession.
To these I do allegiance swear—
　　While they can keep possession:
For in my faith and loyalty
　　I never more will falter,
And George my lawful King shall be—
　　Until the times do alter.
　　　　And this is law, etc.

# *LAITY*

In *Brief Lives* John Aubrey recorded a gross example of religious opportunism of the kind to which the laity had to resort in order to survive. At the dissolution of the monasteries, Wilton Abbey went to the Earl of Pembroke:

> In Queen Mary's time, upon the return of the Catholic religion, the nuns came again to Wilton Abbey, and this William Earl of Pembroke came to the gate (which looks towards the court by the street, but is now walled up) with his cap in hand and fell upon his knee to the lady abbess and the nuns, crying 'I have sinned.' Upon Queen Mary's death the earl came to Wilton (like a tiger) and turned them out, crying 'Out, you whores, to work, to work, you whores, go spin.'

The unpretentious vigour of spiritual life at this time is exemplified in another of Aubrey's *Brief Lives*. Aubrey's abbreviated prose particularly suits the informal character of Bishop Richard Corbet:

> One time, as he was Confirming, the country-people pressing in to see the Ceremonie, sayd he, 'Beare off there, or I'le confirm yee with my Staffe.' Another time, being to lay his hand on the head of a man very bald, he turns to his chaplaine, Lushington, and sayd, 'Some Dust Lushington' (to keepe his hand from slipping). There was a man with a great venerable Beard: sayd the Bishop, 'You, behind the Beard.'
> 　His Chaplain, Dr Lushington, was a very learned and ingeniose man, and

they loved one another. The Bishop sometimes would take the key of the wine-cellar, and he and his Chaplaine would goe and lock themselves in and be merry. Then first he layes downe his Episcopall hat–'There lyes the Doctor.' Then he puts off his gowne–'There lyes the Bishop.' Then 'twas 'Here's to thee, Corbet,' and 'Here's to thee, Lushington.'

He married Alice Hutton, whom 'twas sayd he bigott. She was a very beautiful woman, and so was her mother . . .

The last words he sayd were, 'Good night, Lushington.'

The English do not like to leave ecclesiastical matters to clerics. Henry II told the monks of Winchester, when a new bishop was required, 'I order you to hold a free election, but forbid you to elect anyone but Richard my clerk.' In the nineteenth century Ralph Waldo Emerson noted that

> The Bishop is elected by the Dean and Prebends of the cathedral. The Queen sends these gentlemen a 'congé d'élire', or leave to elect; but also sends them the name of the person whom they are to elect. They go into the cathedral, chant and pray, and beseech the Holy Ghost to assist them in their choice; and, after these invocations, invariably find that the dictates of the Holy Ghost agree with the recommendations of the Queen.
>
> *English Traits*, 1865

The laity maintained its grip at the local level, too, as the eighteenth-century poet William Cowper observed in one of his letters:

> . . . the Squire . . . like the King, may be styled Head of the Church in his own parish . . . and I know one parish where the preacher has always the complaisance to conclude his discourse, however abruptly, the minute that the Squire gives the signal, by rising up after his nap . . .

Joseph Addison, a journalist with the *Spectator* in the early years of the eighteenth century, celebrates a country Sunday under the watchful eye of 'Sir Roger de Coverley':

> As Sir Roger is Landlord to the whole congregation, he keeps them in very good order, and will suffer no body to sleep in it besides himself: for if by chance he has been surprised into a short nap at sermon, upon recovering out of it he stands up and looks about him, and if he sees any body else nodding, either wakes them himself, or sends his servants to them. Several other of the old knight's particularities break out upon these occasions: sometimes he will be lengthening out a verse in the singing-psalms, half a minute after the rest of the congregation have done with it; sometimes, when he is pleased with the matter of his devotion, he pronounces *Amen* three or four times to the same prayer; and sometimes stands up when every body else is upon their knees, to count the congregation, or see if any of his tenants are missing.

It is hardly surprising that Non-conformist chapels became so popular with the independent-minded working classes.

Dr Johnson—melancholic, and terrified at the prospect of Hell-fire—was nevertheless unimpressed by excessive mourning: 'We must either outlive our friends or our friends outlive us; and I see no man that would hesitate about the choice.' He was scathing about any idealization of poverty: 'Sir, all the arguments which are brought to represent poverty as no great evil, show it to be evidently a great evil. You never find people labouring to convince you that you may live very happily upon a plentiful fortune.' And, according to Mrs Thrale's *Anecdotes* (1786), his charity was as unconditional as he might have wished his God's to be:

> He loved the poor as I never yet saw any one else do, with an earnest desire to make them happy. What signifies, says someone, giving halfpence to common beggars? They only lay it out in gin or tobacco. 'And why (says Johnson) should they be denied such sweeteners of their existence? it is surely very savage to refuse them every possible avenue to pleasure, reckoned too coarse for our own acceptance. Life is a pill which none of us can bear to swallow without gilding; yet for the poor we delight in stripping it still barer, and are not ashamed to show even visible displeasure, if ever the bitter taste is taken from their mouths.' In consequence of these principles he nursed whole nests of people in his house, where the lame, the blind, the sick, and the sorrowful found a sure retreat from all the evils whence his little income could secure them.

Despite doubts raised by Darwinism or anything else, the English continued—as they still do—to convert primitive tribal societies, just as they themselves were once converted by early missionaries from Rome. They also gradually discovered the more elegant religions of the East, largely impervious to facile evangelism. The 'Sea of Faith' began its 'melancholy, long, withdrawing roar', as Matthew Arnold put it in 'Dover Beach', and it left behind the flotsam and jetsam of 1000 years of spiritual direction and ecclesiastical mummery, of holiness and humbug, of kindness and cant.

Churches and chapels still stand, convenient and solid, looking as if they would like to help, but arousing impure thoughts in property developers. Christmas remains, still suspiciously 'merry' for a wholly Christian festival. Church fêtes are still held for the organ fund. There is still a glass of sherry for the vicar after matins. Bishops still take their place in the House of Lords.

The English took from the Christian faith what they needed, a religious and moral justification for their resistance to bigotry, hysteria and too many celibate clerics.

Portrait of John Keats by Joseph Severn. The painter Severn sat with
his friend Keats throughout the poet's last illness at Rome. He it was
who received Keats' famous injunction that his gravestone be
inscribed 'Here lies one whose name was writ in water'.

# CHAPTER EIGHT

# THE CREATIVE ENGLISHMAN

The poet's eye, in a fine frenzy rolling,
Doth glance from heaven to earth, from earth to heaven . . .

*A Midsummer Night's Dream*

This sort of unstable character is not one that is looked upon with approval in England. He may be admired once dead, or as long as he confines his artistic behaviour to places like Italy, where they understand and even appreciate that kind of thing. But the highly strung and ethically adventurous spirit does not contribute to the ordered society that has developed as an English ideal.

Lord Macaulay went further in an essay in the *Edinburgh Review*: 'Perhaps no person can be a poet, or even enjoy poetry, without a certain unsoundness of mind.' The Victorian age favoured really sound men of letters like Anthony Trollope, who would knock out a few thousand words before breakfast, leaving the rest of the day free for sensible pursuits like fox-hunting. It is a curious paradox, however, that the political liberty and freedom of speech, and the general confidence that these allow to the creative Englishman to be as wayward and unsound as he likes, depend upon what Walter Bagehot identified in 1852 as 'the essential mental quality for a free people', which is 'much stupidity': 'What we opprobriously call stupidity, though not an enlivening quality in common society, is Nature's favourite resource for preserving steadiness of conduct and consistency of opinion.' From this paradox arises the Janus-face of the essential Englishman: on the one hand the bowler-hatted, brolly-flourishing conformist, with his MCC tie and his neatly folded copy of *The Times*; and on the other the equally English eccentric or man of artistic temperament, thriving atop the unwaveringly solid base of English 'stupidity'. Thus the creative Englishman is rarely hindered. Queen Elizabeth I employed William Byrd, a Roman Catholic, to compose Church of England music for the Chapel Royal—a quite remarkable instance of Elizabethan blurred vision when it came to religion. And some of the credit for *Paradise Lost* should really go to Charles II, who allowed England's greatest Republican propagandist to go free and get on with his work.

# PROPHETS IN THEIR OWN COUNTRY

The other side of the coin is that neither is the English artist necessarily likely to be appreciated by the stolid defenders of his liberty. The fount and guardian of this splendid stodginess is the House of Hanover. 'Was there ever—' cried George III, as recorded by Fanny Burney, 'Was there ever such stuff as the great part of Shakespeare? Only one must not say so! But what think you—What?—Is there not sad stuff? What?—What?'

The greatest work of sustained historical narrative in the English language was received with no more comprehension. The Duke of Gloucester, George III's brother, on being presented with the second volume of *The Decline and Fall of the Roman Empire*, gazed at the heavy quarto blankly: 'Another damned, thick, square book! Always scribble, scribble, scribble! Eh! Mr Gibbon?'

This spirit seems to have been passed down through the generations quite undiluted. The late Duke of Gloucester, seeing Tosca (sung by the legendary Maria Callas) plunge to her death, looked up happily: 'Well, if she's really dead, we can all go home.'

Charming as this unapologetic philistinism might be, it seeps down through society till one is left with an aristocracy of blockheads, or 'upper-class twits'. 'I am always glad when one of these fellows dies,' said the otherwise very astute and able Lord Melbourne on the death of the poet George Crabbe in 1832, 'for then I know I have the whole of him on my shelf.' It has even been said of Elgar that he might have been a great composer if he had not been such a perfect gentleman.

The conductor Sir Thomas Beecham used cunningly to give the impression of being at times a philistine and a bigot, a policy that could be calculated to endear him to the British public; 'I am not the greatest conductor in this country. On the other hand I'm better than any damned foreigner,' he once remarked. On one occasion, at Covent Garden, he asked Douglas Steele to turn the pages for him while he went through *Gotterdämmerung*: 'When I missed a turn,' Steele later recounted, 'he cursed not me but the *Ring*. "Damn awful thing, what? Barbarian lot of Nazi thugs, aren't they?"'

Despite Beecham's oft-expressed distaste—'Isn't Wagner an old bore?' he sighed resignedly during a rehearsal with two eminent German vocalists—he was much in demand as an interpreter of Wagner. On one occasion though, the critic Neville Cardus complained that he had ruined a performance of *Siegfried* by galloping through the last act. Beecham expostulated:

> You critics are very inhumane. My orchestra had been in the pit on a hot summer night since 5.30. At the beginning of the last act I took note of the time—after 10 o'clock. And the pubs about to close at 11! My orchestra had not had a drink for hours. And many of the dear people in my audience had to get back home to Woking and Pinner. So I said to my orchestra 'Whoops!'

It seems, though, that a fast tempo could be motivated as much by malice as by kindness. Conducting for the Diaghilev ballet, he pulled the orchestra to a halt after a furious account of the *Polovtsian Dances* and beamed at the leader: 'We made the buggers hop, what?'

Beecham's aristocratic hauteur is quite acceptable. What is not is the languid, orchidaceous cosmopolite with his foreign aesthetic ideas, as characterized in Gilbert and Sullivan's *Patience* (1881):

> A most intense young man,
> A soulful-eyed young man,
> An ultra-poetical, super-aesthetical,
> Out-of-the-way young man!
>
> A Japanese young man,
> A blue-and-white young man,
> Francesca da Rimini, mimini-pimini,
> *Je-ne-sais-quoi* young man!
>
> A pallid and thin young man,
> A haggard and lank young man,
> A greenery-yallery, Grosvenor Gallery,
> Foot-in-the-grave young man!

Typically, the English public was able to signal its disapproval of effeminate decadents through the courts. Oscar Wilde was packed off to Reading Gaol for sodomy, while Whistler made the mistake of suing John Ruskin for the latter's celebrated criticism, in 1877, of one of Whistler's atmospheric paintings: 'I have seen and heard, much of Cockney impudence before now; but never expected to hear a coxcomb ask two hundred guineas for flinging a pot of paint in the public's face.' Justice required that judgement be for the plaintiff, but Whistler was awarded damages of a farthing.

Patronage did not come easily to many creative Englishmen. One of the main reasons was that the upper-class young gentlemen received their aesthetic education on the Continent. It seemed to be self-evident that, if one had ventured abroad to study the fine arts and gone to the trouble of learning off all the sonorous foreign names and shipping the canvases home, then surely, in the interests of *bon ton*, one should not bother too much with the home-grown talent.

William Hogarth *Self Portrait with Pug*. Hogarth's inspiration was
Shakespeare, Swift and Milton. But as for his dog Trump – pugnacity?
. . . doggedness? . . . fidelity to truth? Hogarth also deliberately made
this small dog's face an echo of his own blunt features, as if to say,
'Nothing fancy or foreign about me! But look how I paint!'

In a letter to the *St James's Evening Post* of 7 June 1737, William Hogarth, who despised what he termed 'foreign rubbish', bitterly sketched an enthusiastically camp art-dealer, up to the eternal tricks of his ancient trade:

> If a man, naturally a judge of painting . . . should cast his eye on one of their sham virtuoso-pieces, he would be very apt to say: 'Mr Bubbleman, that grand Venus (as you are pleased to call it) has not beauty enough for the character of an English cook-maid.' Upon which the quack answers, with a confident air, 'O Lord, sir, I find that you are no connoisseur—that picture, I assure you, is in Alesso Baldovinetto's second and best manner, boldly painted, and truly sublime; the contour gracious; the air of the head in the high Greek taste; and a most divine idea it is.' Then spitting on an obscure place, and rubbing it with a dirty handkerchief, takes a skip to the other end of the room and screams out in raptures, 'There is an amazing touch! A man should have this picture a twelve-month in his collection before he can discover half its beauties . . .'

Sir Joshua Reynolds attempted to be cosmopolitan, with his Royal Academy and his lofty Classical ideals, but in practice he ran off mainly quiet, atmospheric portraits like any other English painter of the time, even if he tarted them up with the odd Classical touch. Almost as soon as it was formed, the Royal Academy lost control: grand gestures and fancy dress are simply not part of the creative Englishman's language. And they were certainly not part of Hogarth's. Belligerently a man of the people, self-trained and independent, Hogarth saw himself as a man first and an artist a long way behind. Like Dickens, he liked to tell a story with a powerful moral content. Through making engravings of his works he ensured that his message would reach as many people as possible, and this freed him from the constrictions of patronage.

Aristocratic patronage was irretrievably discredited when Lord Chesterfield wrote a couple of magazine articles in recommendation of Dr Johnson's *Dictionary*. His Lordship's testimonials received the well aimed Johnsonian boot:

> My Lord, . . . When, upon some slight encouragement, I first visited your lordship, I was overpowered, like the rest of mankind, by the enchantment of your address, and could not forbear to wish that I might boast myself *le vainqueur du vainqueur de la terre*—that I might obtain that regard for which I saw the world contending; but I found my attendance so little encouraged, that neither pride nor modesty would suffer me to continue it. When I had once addressed your lordship in public, I had exhausted all the art of pleasing which a retired and uncourtly scholar can possess. I had done all that I could; and no man is well pleased to have his all neglected, be it ever so little.
>
> Seven years, my lord, have now passed since I waited in your outward rooms, or was repulsed from your door; during which time I have been

pushing on my work through difficulties, of which it is useless to complain, and have brought it at last to the verge of publication, without one act of assistance, one word of encouragement, or one smile of favour. Such treatment I did not expect, for I never had a patron before.

The shepherd in Virgil grew at last acquainted with Love, and found him a native of the rocks.

Is not a patron, my lord, one who looks with unconcern on a man struggling for life in the water, and when he has reached ground encumbers him with help? The notice which you have been pleased to take of my labours, had it been early, had been kind; but it has been delayed till I am indifferent, and cannot enjoy it; till I am solitary, and cannot impart it; till I am known, and do not want it. I hope it is no very cynical asperity not to confess obligations where no benefit has been received, or to be unwilling that the public should consider me as owing that to a patron which Providence has enabled me to do for myself.

Having carried on my work thus far with so little obligation to any favourer of learning, I shall not be disappointed though I should conclude it, if less be possible, with less: for I have been long wakened from that dream of hope, in which I once boasted myself with so much exultation, my Lord—Your lordship's most humble, most obedient servant,

Sam Johnson

Lord Chesterfield, to his credit, recognized this letter to be a masterpiece of its kind and showed it to all his friends.

# THE MUSICAL ENGLISHMAN

Elgar's A-flat Symphony was described by Beecham—probably not unfairly—as the musical equivalent of St Pancras Station. But Elgar had also a 'Malvern Hills' side, as he said himself: 'English music should have about it something broad, noble, chivalrous, healthy, and above all an out-of-doors spirit.' Through this Boy Scout language one glimpses another essential strain in the creative Englishman—a lyrical, pastoral quality. We find it, too, in the anonymous medieval round

> Sumer is icumen in,
> Lhude sing cucu . . .

The great Elizabethan composers—Tallis, Byrd, Orlando Gibbons, Morley, Bull, Tye, Dowland, Weelkes and Tomkins—all contributed to make England the most musical country in Europe. With a 'Fa la la' and a 'hey nonny no', the Italian forms of madrigal and canzonet were vigorously anglicized. And the lute songs, from 'Greensleeves' (perhaps by Henry VIII) onwards, and particularly those of Dowland, achieved a perfection of plangent melancholy, spilling over into the bittersweet boy-girl comedies of Shakespeare.

Dowland's mastery, and Purcell's after him, was in his extreme sensitivity to the words he set. Naturally, this sophisticated lyrical instinct was offended by Italian opera – 'An exotic and irrational entertainment' as Dr Johnson sweepingly dismissed it. Sir Thomas Beecham recognized the difficulty of presenting opera to the English: 'One of the drawbacks of opera in English, where everything that is sung or said can be instantly understood, is that our public, which has a lively sense of humour, never misses an opportunity for a laugh.'

The trouble is that the quality and complexity of the English theatre, which learned both to dazzle the court gallants and to distract the sweaty groundlings in the absence of royal or aristocratic patronage, made Italian opera seem very unsatisfactory. Swift complained of 'that unnatural taste for Italian music among us which is wholly unsuitable to our northern climate and the genius of the people, whereby we are over-run with Italian effeminacy and Italian nonsense'. And what could be more un-British than the nasty Romish tradition of castrati?

> But never shall a truly British age
> Bear a vile race of eunuchs on the stage . . .
>
> Charles Churchill, *The Rosciad*, 1761

Opera was as ridiculous in Italian as in translation: 'There is no question but our grand-children will be very curious to know the reason why their forefathers used to sit together like an audience of foreigners in their own country, and to hear whole plays acted before them in a tongue which they did not understand.' When Addison wrote this in 1707 he was admittedly particularly bitter on account of the recent humiliating failure of his own attempt at an opera libretto, *Rosamond*.

And Sydney Smith slid elegantly out of an engagement to go to the opera with Lady Holland in November 1842:

> My Dear Lady Holland,
>     I have not the heart, when an amiable lady says, 'Come to *Semiramis* in my box', to decline; but I get bolder at a distance. *Semiramis* would be to me pure misery. I love music very little – I hate acting: I have the worst opinion of Semiramis herself, and the whole thing (I cannot help it) seems so childish and foolish that I cannot abide it. Moreover it would be rather out of etiquette for a Canon of St. Paul's to go to an opera, and where etiquette prevents me from doing things disagreeable to myself, I am a perfect martinet. All these things considered, I am sure you will not be a Semiramis to me, but let me off.

Handel understood his adopted audience. 'You have taken too much trouble over your opera,' he told Gluck, who asked him what he thought of *La Caduta de' Giganti*: 'Here in England, that is mere waste of time. What the English like is something they can beat time to, something that hits them straight on the drum of the ear.'

It is said that the tradition of standing for the 'Hallelujah Chorus' was initiated by George II who, not having followed the English libretto of *The Messiah* very well up to this point, assumed that the words 'And he shall reign for ever and ever' were meant for him. But Handel certainly stretched himself trying to get to the great English eardrum. The 'Hallelujah Chorus' may well have been carefully calculated to echo Thomas Arne's big hit of 1740, 'Rule Britannia!', from the grossly patriotic opera *Alfred*, itself a nugget from the same seam as Purcell's *King Arthur* (1691). Certainly there is an uncanny resemblance between the two anthems, both of which bring the British public to their feet. Wagner was a little unfair, however, when he claimed that 'the first eight notes of "Rule Britannia" express the whole character of the British people'.

Oratorio has remained extraordinarily popular in England, as a morally unimpeachable way of enjoying something that can so easily get out of control. Jeremy Collier, in *A Short View of the Immorality and Profaneness of the English Stage* (1697), expostulated about how a susceptible gentleman might be corrupted by less respectable kinds of music: 'This Sort of Musick warms the Passions, and unlocks the Fancy, and makes it open to Pleasure like a Flower in the Sun . . .' And he concluded, all too reasonably: ''Tis possible a publick Regulation might not be amiss.'

In the nineteenth century serious composers virtually locked themselves away in the Victorian Gothic cathedrals and churches to compose grand puddingy works for the organ and for vast amateur choirs. Here was music that was uplifting, irreproachable in a morally nervous age, Gladstonian and middle-class, the whole edifice supported on a series of massive musical pillars, dear to the heart of every 'serious' musical Englishman: *The Messiah*, Mendelssohn's *Elijah*, Elgar's *The Dream of Gerontius*, Walton's *Belshazzar's Feast* . . . Only Arthur Sullivan slipped out guiltily to knock out potboilers in conjunction with his librettist, William Gilbert. Surprisingly, their collaborations provided the most vigorous music of the age.

The ultimate synthesis of the religious and the patriotic was achieved with the hymn 'I Vow to Thee My Country', in the setting from Holst's *Planets* suite. It was a superbly sustained melody of the purest and darkest treacle. In the Victorian drawing-room, aspidistra on the piano, the treacle was spread with an even less sparing hand, as in the setting of the 'Indian Love Song', Laurence Hope's 'Pale Hands I Loved':

> Pale hands I loved
> Beside the Shalimar,
> Where are you now?
> Who lies beneath your spell?

Meanwhile, the saucy, jaunty, strutting music-hall songs were reaching their vacantly uproarious apogee:

> My Old Man said follow the van,
> And don't dilly dally on the way . . .

During the two world wars the 'home front;' was sustained by songs like 'Keep the Home Fires Burning', 'The White Cliffs of Dover', and

> There'll always be an England,
> While there's a country lane,
> Wherever there's a cottage small
> Beside a field of grain.

English troops themselves, though, would never march to such stuff. Instead they sang 'I Want to Go Home' or songs about what a bastard the sergeant-major was. During the Christmas truce of 1914 the troops responded to the lachrymose German renderings of '*Stille Nacht, Heilige Nacht*' with a hymn to words of their own:

> We are Fred Karno's Army,
> The ragtime infantry,
> We cannot fight, we cannot shoot,
> What bleedin' use are we?
> And when we get to Berlin
> The Kaiser he will say
> '*Hock! Hock! Mein Gott!*
> What a bloody rotten lot
> Are the ragtime infantry!'

In *The Victorian Age in Literature* (1913) G. K. Chesterton pointed out, correctly enough, that

> The Germans, like the Welsh, can sing perfectly serious songs perfectly seriously in chorus; can with clear eyes and clear voices join together in words of innocent and beautiful personal passion for a false maiden or a dead child. The nearest one can get to defining the poetic temper of Englishmen is to say that they couldn't do this even for beer. They can sing in chorus, and louder than other Christians; but they must have in their songs something, I know not what, that is at once shamefaced and rowdy. If the matter be emotional, it must somehow be also broad, common, and comic, as 'Wapping Old Stairs' and 'Sally in Our Alley'. If it be patriotic, it must somehow be openly bombastic and, as it were, indefensible, like 'Rule, Britannia!' . . . But our greatest bards and sages have often shown a tendency to rant it and roar it like true British sailors; to employ an extravagance that is half conscious and therefore half humorous. Compare, for example, the rants of Shakespeare with the rants of Victor Hugo. A piece of Hugo's

eloquence is either a serious triumph or a serious collapse: one feels the poet is offended at a smile. But Shakespeare seems rather proud of talking nonsense.

The pawky humorous lyric—brought to a dizzying perfection in the offerings of the D'Oyly Carte Company, a sort of English equivalent of Bayreuth—was perhaps first seen on the English stage in John Gay's *The Beggar's Opera* (1728)—unheroic, cocky and satirical—which burst into the world of Handelian opera and oratorio like a bucket of cold water. Even Handel had to admit that he was put off his stride: 'Ballad opera pelted Italian opera off the stage with "Lumps of Pudding" [one of the hits from the show].' The notorious weakness of English aristocrats for chorus girls, responsible for a clutch of extremely unsuitable Victorian and Edwardian duchesses, began when the leading lady in *The Beggar's Opera* married a duke.

Looking even further back, we can find the dim and curious origins of the music hall in the diaspora of church organs during the Commonwealth: an awful lot of them seemed to find their way into taverns.

The high-brow end of the market had similarly insalubrious beginnings. Most English music had been amateur. An experience which Pepys recorded (1 May 1663) encapsulated this: 'I took leave and went to hear Mrs Turner's daughter (at whose house Sir J. Mennes lies) play on the Harpsicon; but Lord, it was enough to make any man sick to hear her; yet I was forced to commend her highly.'

Royal patronage had always been frankly skimpy, and standards slipped badly during the Interregnum. Pepys, attending the Chapel Royal shortly after the accession of Charles II, noted that 'one Dr Crofts made an indifferent sermon, and after it, an anthem, ill sung, which made the king laugh'. The choirmaster was a certain Captain Cooke, whose main qualification for his post seemed to be that he'd had a good war. But his choirboys on that inauspicious occasion include John Blow, Humfrey, and the father of the sublime Henry Purcell—who would later produce the only really first-rate English opera to appear before the twentieth century, *Dido and Aeneas* (1689).

However, the English led the way where public concerts were concerned, even if the way led to what Roger North called 'a nasty hole in Whitefriars', the scene of John Bannister's becoming the world's first musical impresario, in 1670. And the every-man-for-himself English musical scene did throw up a sort of patron saint of amateur music enthusiasts, Thomas Britton, 'the Small-coal man'. A hawker of coal from a sack on his back, he converted the hay-loft above his coal storage in Clerkenwell into a concert hall; this operated from 1678 until 1714. Access was by crawling up an outside stairway, but this did not deter even the nobility. On his first trip to England, Handel was one Britton's visitors and probably performed himself, no doubt reflecting how different this was from the home life of a continental musician serving in the great courts of Europe.

It was not until comparatively recently that English concert halls began to lose their unsavoury notoriety among musicians. The great pianist Artur Schnabel used to give lectures about his experiences of English provincial concert tours; apparently the main hazard was icy draughts. English audiences would wrap up well, confident that they would enjoy plenty of fresh air with their music, as if briskly distrustful of its sensual snares and determined to remain alert to its languorous blandishments.

Nevertheless, twentieth-century English music—when at its most English—ranks with the best in the world. Referring back to the great Elizabethans, the modern renaissance of English music involves songwriting as well as lush pastoral idylls such as Delius' 'In a Summer Garden'. Vaughan Williams, Gurney, Warlock, Butterworth, Tippett—all drew inspiration from Cecil Sharp's rediscovery of English folk-song. And, when that stream began to run dry, along came Lennon and McCartney, who combined an easy lyrical gift with a crafty northern urban wit to produce what Shostakovich, among others, suggested were the best songs to have been written since Schubert's *lieder*.

However, the most distinguished post-war English composer has certainly been Benjamin Britten. Despite his originality, Britten remained vigorously conservative, setting his face against the electronic age, and composing above all—in his operas, his choral works, and his songs—for the human voice. In a 1965 speech he said:

> I want my music to be of use to people, to please them . . . I do not write for posterity—in any case, the outlook for that is somewhat uncertain. I write music, now in Aldeburgh, for people living there, and further afield, indeed for anyone who cares to play it or listen to it.

## AN INHABITED LANDSCAPE

England is still a country of enthusiastic amateurs. The only full copy of Michelangelo's masterpiece on the ceiling of the Sistine Chapel in Rome is on the ceiling of a post-war pre-fab building, the English Martyrs Catholic Church at Goring-by-Sea. It is the work of Gary Bevans. In an interview which appeared in *The Independent* on 16 January 1989, Mr Bevans revealed some of the secrets of his art:

> I sign-write on a lot of big lorries so I've a good eye for size. I've done all the articulated vehicles for Luckings Theatrical Removals based up the road. I also do long shop fronts, like Richmond Cycles of Worthing, so I'm not frightened of tackling something large.

This might appear to dish Sir Nikolaus Pevsner's contention that English amateurism manifests itself only in minor achievements, like miniatures and water-colours. But not if one puts Gary Bevans among the builders of religious monuments.

England has produced one style of architecture which outdoes all others in sheer panache, and that is fifteenth-century perpendicular. The walls reach across to form the roof as if at the last moment. Flying buttresses are delicate and fantastic. The fan-vaulting is sheer bravura. Windows everywhere, according to Pevsner, 'make churches of that age veritable glasshouses, clear, light, vast, and not in the least mysterious'; Osbert Lancaster described them as 'ecclesiastical conservatories'.

English parish churches from that period are very often square-topped — another peculiarly English characteristic — so that they give the impression of being grounded, earthbound, attached to the landscape: 'matter-of-fact' in their 'absence of demonstrated aspiration', as Pevsner described it. Pevsner directs our attention also to the roofs:

> Hearts of oak are not only the ships, but also the mighty and ingenious roofs of the churches of England . . . A timber vault, in imitation of stone, such as exists at York Minster in the transept and in the chancel at St Albans, seems ignominious to a Frenchman. But then he has nothing like the double hammerbeam roofs of East Anglia.

The English are generally unaware that they have much architecture to brag about. Actually they have, among others, Inigo Jones, who imported Classical ideas to England (rather late in the day, but all the better for it) and Sir Christopher Wren, who was perhaps ultimately responsible for every nice street in the country not to mention the marvels of inventiveness and elegance that can still remind one of civilization even in the City of London, with their ingenious, almost ludicrous, 'Classical' spires poking up between the great blank-faced monuments to Mammon.

However, despite, or perhaps partly because of, the nation's extensive industrialization, the English artistic achievement is essentially romantic and rural — or, at least, sporting and agricultural. In this latter context we have the great English tradition of painting breath-taking prodigies of animal husbandry, vast barrels of pork perched on the merest suggestion of trotters, and majestic bovine monsters helpless before the inexorable march of agricultural progress. This is where the specialist knowledge acquired by the House of Hanover came into its own: Queen Victoria and Prince Albert, viewing Thomas Sidney Cooper's *Victoria Jersey Cow*, were able, while complimenting the likeness, to point out that the dock leaves in the painting were evidence of poor farming practice and that the puddle of water in which the beast stood suggested bad drainage.

The central place of the horse in English life is evidenced by the fact that the nation's best horse painter is also one of its very greatest artists. George Stubbs' human figures, too, ruddy with porter and stuffed with the roast beef of old England so ably advertised by lesser animal painters, are caught in an attitude of mystical stillness.

The portrait in a landscape, and the human, inhabited landscape, the speciality of Stubbs and Gainsborough, are thoroughly English. As with the English landscaped garden created by Lancelot Brown (called 'Capability' because, when looking over an estate, he would invariable announce sagely, 'there are great capabilities here'), the effect is one of human liberty. The '*jardin anglais*' is irregular and informal, with serpentine lakes, winding, lyrical walkways, and trees. Brown planted hundreds of thousands of trees. More than 100 years later, the French historian H. Taine, visiting a country estate, was astounded by the trees he saw. In his *Notes on England* (1872) he commented:

> They have been cared for like children of rich parents; they have always had full liberty to grow, all their needs catered for, nothing has ever checked their growth or hindered their luxuriance; they breathe the air and consume the soil like rich noblemen to whom that air and soil belong by right.

The master of English portrait painters, Thomas Gainsborough, certainly felt constrained by city life. He wrote in a famous letter:

> I am sick of Portraits and wish very much to take my viol-da-gamba and walk off to some sweet village where I can paint landskips and enjoy the fag-end of life in quietness and ease. But these fine ladies and their tea-drinkings, dancings, husband huntings etc etc etc will fob me out of the last ten years.

But then Thomas Gainsborough—like Cotman, Crome and Constable—came from East Anglia, where vast moving skies offer endless drama.

Constable, too, could write lyrically of his art, as when in a letter to Archdeacon Fisher he expressed a keenness to see foreign parts. However, he went on: 'But I was born to paint a happier land, my own dear old England; and when I cease to love her, may I, as Wordsworth says, "never more hear her green leaves rustle, and her torrents roar".'

Like Wordsworth, Constable was engaged on a ruthless programme of ridding his artistic medium of useless conventions. As Delacroix put it, 'the Englishmen seem to be pursuing Nature, while we are merely occupied in imitating pictures'. The effect was shockingly vivid, and to some eyes in poor taste. The whole point of a painting was that it should have that overall well varnished, old-violin look.

Predominant in the work of Constable is a minute and direct observation of atmosphere and of weather—and, being English weather, it has to be caught on the move. Fuseli said of Constable's work, 'He makes me call for my greatcoat and umbrella.'

This rendering of atmosphere was taken to its extreme in the paintings of J. M. W. Turner. Turner may have been a revolutionary, but he was not a boorish one. On one occasion two typically muted, well bred portraits by Sir Thomas Lawrence were suddenly made to look dowdy when one of Turner's stunning bursts of colour was hung between them at an exhibition. Turner kindly adumbrated the brilliance of his golden sky with a thin covering of lamp-black (which he was able to wash off afterwards). And the close depiction of weather remained a permanent feature of English art into the twentieth century, giving rise to another example of the House of Hanover school of aesthetics. George VI, at an exhibition of paintings by John Piper, examined with the artist a picture of Windsor Castle and commiserated, 'Pity you had such bloody awful weather.'

Truth to nature was taken to bizarre lengths in some of the works of the Pre-Raphaelite Brotherhood, a Victorian sort of *Boy's Own Paper* secret society, devoted to making the world a better place. Holman Hunt, for example, travelled all the way to the Holy Land to paint an unattractive biblical goat by the shores of the Dead Sea. He called it *The Scapegoat*, and it was considered at the time to be, if only by a short head, the most baffling and ghastly painting produced by the movement.

Blake represented a quite different English essay in the arts from that of the Pre-Raphaelites: 'Shall Painting be confined to the sordid drudgery of facsimile representations of merely mortal and perishing substances . . . ?' he asked. To a visionary like himself, the answer was obviously not. Like Shelley, his feet left the ground; inhabiting a higher realm of being, as he certainly did, he was often clumsy as a painter and a poet. Samuel Palmer, who followed him with his glowing, mysteriously fecund, orange twilights, communicated more simply, being untrammelled by anything like Blake's apparatus of ideas.

Holman Hunt's *The Scapegoat*, however, exemplified a very important strand in the creative Englishman—his dottiness, somehow going a bit further than mere eccentricity. One can point to such works as *Tristram Shandy*, the Brighton Pavilion, Blake's portrait of the ghost of a flea, the Tudor poet John Skelton's requiem and lament for a pet bird ('Philip Sparrow'), the nonsense verse of Edward Lear, Lewis Carroll's philosophical puzzles posing as children's literature, some of the more lunatically inspired verses of William Gilbert, and Christopher Smart's hymn to his cat:

> For I will consider my cat Jeoffry,
> For he is the servant of the Living God . . .

Significantly, these peculiar things tend to be hugely popular in England.

# *ENG. LIT.*

The English language, like the people, is a great mongrel breed. The stark and melancholy Anglo-Saxon can be played endlessly against the grand and stylish Latin. The language has no pedigree or purity. It has no official guardian or 'Academy'. It lies open to every passing fancy. It is the ideal medium for the coupling of thought and feeling. It comes alive when the natural instinct of the educated Englishman to reproduce Classical forms is sweetened into song or broken up by a passionate engagement. The English language embodies the variety, the freedom, the miscegenated individuality of the English. Spenser and Milton may sail their stately poetic galleons loaded with the ore of Classicism and biblical themes, but English poetry is essentially lyrical, dramatic, atmospheric and unheroic, with always some irreducible strangeness in the composition.

Geoffrey Chaucer kicked off for England with an unbeatable handling of portraiture—ironic, tender and appreciative, with that close attention to the details of everyday life which can be glimpsed also in the playful marginalia of medieval illustrators and in those church carvings which draw, as by magnetism, the worshipper's straying attention. Blake summed it up: 'As Newton numbered the stars, and as Linnaeus numbered the plants, so Chaucer numbered the classes of men.'

Chaucer's charm and approachability were due in part to his classical restraint and economy. Caxton, in his Proem to *The Canterbury Tales*, wrote, in the sort of mannered verbosity that would gather steam up until the Elizabethan literary explosion: 'He comprehended his matters in short, quick, and high sentences, eschewing prolixity, casting away the chaff of superfluity and showing the picked grain of sentence uttered by crafty and sugared elegance.' Dryden, in his more sensible way, agreed: 'He is a perpetual Fountain of good Sense . . . as he knew what to say, so he knows also when to leave off; a Continence which is practic'd by few writers . . .'

In *The Canterbury Tales* Chaucer depicts himself as a patient, mild character. His rather tiresome effort at a story is brutally interrupted by the Master of Ceremonies, the innkeeper 'Your wretched rhyming isn't worth a turd!' The patience and mildness seem to have been genuine, if we can believe Chaucer's rather average pupils, Hoccleve, and Lydgate, who averred:

> Hym liste not pinche nor gruche at every blot . . .
> Suffering goodly of his gentilnes
> Ful many thing embracid with rudeness.

In short, he did not grumble, but kindly put up with Lydgate's most rubbishy efforts.

'*Albion rose . . .*' by William Blake. A Cromwell without religion, Blake
saw a regenerate and awakened England (Albion) as the Promised
Land. His apocalyptic call to cast off the fetters of government and
Church was set to music and is now one of the most popular of
Anglican hymns.

Both Blake and Milton indulged in an odd sort of transcendental patriotism. Indeed, Blake's concept of 'Albion' is the mystical Englishman's idea of the 'soul' of England.

Blake was sitting in his back-garden once with his wife, both of them stark naked. They were reading passages from *Paradise Lost* when they heard a knock on the door. Visionaries are never thrown by social difficulties. Blake called out, 'Come in. It's only Adam and Eve, you know.' We should not imagine that the Blake's favourite author would have raised his Puritan eyebrows or pursed his Puritan lips at this charming scene.

John Milton is the only English artist to have worked successfully with his head in the clouds—in a baroque firmament. Perhaps this was in part because he went blind in the service of the English Republic. But he was also served by an acutely musical ear. His original idea for a blockbuster, some kind of Arthurian treatment, might have been more immediately popular. As it was, his extraordinary and unique coup, a successful English verse epic—he intended that the world 'should not willingly let [it] die'—was not universally well received. Dr Johnson was thoroughly respectful, but his reservations express the Englishman's impatience with poets who are too obviously attempting an assault on Mount Parnassus: 'None ever wished it longer than it is. Its perusal is a duty rather than a pleasure. We read Milton for instruction, retire harassed and overburdened, and look elsewhere for recreation; we desert our master and seek for companions.' Johnson also noted, in *Lives of the Poets*, that Addison (writing earlier, and still reeling under the blow) was more bitter: 'Our language sunk under him.'

*Paradise Lost* has been balanced by a continuous flow of mock-epics, anti-heroes and satires, from Skelton, Donne, Dryden and Pope to Byron, Browning and T. S. Eliot. The general characteristic of these poets has been a close observation of human and social life, a sense of drama and a dry wit. Their general tone is admiration at their own cleverness. Impenetrability is often a bonus. When the London Poetry Society asked Browning to elucidate a particularly baffling passage in his *Sordello* (published 1840), the poet grappled with it for a few minutes, before admitting himself beaten: 'When I wrote that, God and I knew what it meant, but now God alone knows.'

The English by and large like to be able to follow what is going on. The Swiss painter Fuseli said that there was 'little hope of Poetical painting finding encouragement in England. The people are not prepared for it. Portrait with them is everything. Their taste and feeling all go to realities.' Dr Johnson, as always, was emphatic: 'I had rather see the portrait of a dog I know than all the allegories you can show me.'

Johnson sat at the heart of his age, haunted both by weaknesses of the flesh and by Boswell, and delivering an endless stream of heavily ballasted one-liners from a coffee house somewhere in London. The result is the greatest biography in the language, although this is necessarily at some cost to the reputations of the protagonists, chiefly Boswell's. As Horace Walpole commented in a letter, 'the more one knows of Johnson, the more preposterous assemblage he appears of strong sense, of the lowest bigotry and prejudices, of pride, brutality, fretfulness and vanity—and Boswell is the ape of most of his faults, without a grain of his sense'. Macaulay winced at Boswell's candour: 'Everything the publication of which would have made another man hang himself, was a matter of exaltation to his weak and diseased mind.'

Eighteenth-century novels, like Chaucer's tales, are stuffed with character and incident, as are the eighteenth-century cartoons by artists such as Hogarth, Rowlandson and Gillray. The Victorian age dunked this rich and nourishing fare in moral fervour. Ruskin led his disciples, one of whom was Oscar Wilde, to engage in the honest toil of building a road. William Morris started the Arts and Crafts movement to bring art to the people. *The Awakened Conscience* and Holman Hunt's earnest allegory on the state of the English Church, *The Hireling Shepherd*, were painted.

Alas, the road was not completed. Even in his own lifetime, Morris's work was way beyond the reach of anyone but the rich. And the paintings of the Pre-Raphaelite Brotherhood positively drip with suffocating sensuality. Dickens, by contrast, could propagate an effective moral imperative by sugaring it with stories that could bring the country to a halt.

## *THE BARD*

The English do not like to wipe their feet, take their hats off and sit attentive to their literature. Milton, literature in its Sunday best, gathers dust in its honoured place on the shelf. Shakespeare, who wrote for possibly the most disruptive and distracted of any audience, taught them to expect to be charmed, as did Sir Philip Sidney in *The Defence of Poesie* (1595): 'Now, therein, of all Sciences (I speak still of humane) and according to the humane conceit, is our Poet the Monarch . . . and with a tale forsooth he commeth unto you, with a tale, which holdeth children from play, and olde men from the Chimney corner.'

Of Shakespeare, Ben Jonson—who was rare enough himself—wrote: 'He was not of an age, but for all time.' It might also be said, of course, that Shakespeare is not of a particular nation either, except that he so obviously fulfilled Voltaire's idea of the creative Englishman: 'Their poetical genius resembles a closely grown tree planted by nature, throwing out a thousand branches here and there and growing lustily and without rules. It dies if you try to force its nature and trim it like the gardens of Marly.'

The significant point about English literature is that its highest achievement is in the theatre—and until the reforms of David Garrick in the eighteenth century the theatre was the equivalent of a football league fixture. The Classical proprieties went unregarded. There were often a lot of corpses at the end of an Elizabethan play, but none could be less lamented than the mangled remains of the Classical unities of time, place and action, which the Elizabethan dramatists trampled jubilantly underfoot.

In the Prologue to *Henry V*, Shakespeare confidently invited his audience to use its imagination:

> can this cockpit hold
> The vasty fields of France? or may we cram
> Within this wooden O the very casques
> That did affright the air at Agincourt?

As befits a man of the theatre, the world of shows and shadows, disguises, magic tricks and transformations, cardboard crowns, boy queens, dry ice and tomato sauce, William Shakespeare presented the world as essentially insubstantial, as having no fixed essence of reality. Leaving his work in a muddle of bad quartos and 'foul papers', he retired with the hieratic hero of his last play, *The Tempest*, reminding us that

> The cloud-capp'd towers, the gorgeous palaces,
> The solemn temples, the great globe itself,
> Yea, all which it inherit, shall dissolve,
> And, like this insubstantial pageant faded,
> Leave not a rack behind. We are such stuff
> As dreams are made on; and our little life
> Is rounded with a sleep.

As for Shakespeare's greatest plays, perhaps particularly *King Lear*, the insights into the human condition contained in their dramatic action have the power to move the jaded spiritual sense that leaves the interpreters of religious doctrine stammering foolishly outside the doors to the Englishman's heart.

Portrait of W. G. Grace. If there ever lived a straight, true and pukka Englishman, then surely this is he, the stout patriarch of the game himself. Yet W. G. Grace was the arch 'shamateur' earning more than any professional 'player' of the day. Why did he not turn professional? Because he was a gentleman. It was a question of caste. To this day the game is quietly dominated, from pavilion and committee room, by 'gentlemen'.

# CHAPTER NINE

——— • ———

# THE SPORTING ENGLISHMAN

Sport is common to all men: what the English did was to institutionalize it. Rules were drawn up, often in a pub—the first meetings of the Jockey Club were held in the Star and Garter in Pall Mall, and here, too, the rules of cricket were first drawn up in 1776. Tournaments and championships were organized, and results were recorded. Thus sport developed its own literature and its own history: 1780 became the year Diomed won the Derby, 1882 the year England was first humbled by Australia, 1966 the year England won the World Cup, and so on. Tales of extraordinary feats, mighty contests and large and cavalier characters were preserved to fan the enthusiasm of future generations.

We have to negotiate an ambiguity in the title of this chapter: this is that, as an ideal, the 'Sporting Englishman' may be distinguished from the 'unsporting' one. However, to exclude unsporting Englishman from our brief would probably leave us with a mere handful of reverend gentleman, mostly cricketers, and hardly representative of the passion for idle pursuits that is the essential Englishman's most innocent legacy to the world.

Sadly, the Englishman's sporting instinct is more commonly allied to his vices than to any higher calling. Chaucer's monk,

> Who did not give a hen for the old saw,
> That hunting was against the moral law

was still indulging his moral weakness for savage rural pursuits 600 years later in the familiar figure of the 'hunting parson'. Charles Kingsley, best-selling author and chaplain to Queen Victoria, advocated hunting as particularly beneficial for clergymen. Mind you, this was the age of muscular Christianity: Bishop Tucker of Uganda boasted that at 59 he could still ride six hours in the saddle from one mission station to another and then play three sets of tennis and win them all.

Football came into the world as an excuse for mass hooliganism, it seems. But that desire to make off with an inflated pig's bladder, worthless in itself and vigorously defended by a lot of other people, seems to have been genuine enough to keep it going as a game through the centuries.

When they weren't playing murderous games themselves, the English always enjoyed setting animals to fight each other. In 1809, an MP defended animal-baiting as 'a most necessary foundation of our military spirit'. Just as the English military virtue is pluck rather than dash or initiative, so they loved to test the courage, endurance, and 'bottom' of animals known for those qualities —bears, bulls and badgers.

Horse-racing was for the aristocracy, who also may be said to have matched pugilists against each other as they matched their animals, and with the same heavy wagers. Successful animals and pugilists were cossetted and admired; indeed, John Gully, a very popular champion of England, became an MP.

The nastiest English sports—at least those enjoyed by the lower orders, like bear-baiting and cock-fighting—were banned by 1850. Previous attempts to control English sport had never worked because the restrictions did not apply to 'gentlemen', always a large and loose concept for the English. King Canute felt that only gentlemen should be allowed to possess a greyhound, and passed a law to this effect in 1016. An Act of 1388 prohibited the playing of tennis by servants and labourers on pain of six days' imprisonment. And another Act, finally repealed only in 1845, tried to specify exactly what constituted the kind of 'inferior' people who were not allowed to play bowls (except at Christmas): 'any artificer or craftsman of any handycraft or occupation, husbandman, apprentice, mariner or fisherman, waterman or any serviceman'. But it was really of little use trying to separate the gentlemen from the rest, thanks to the natural self-respect and bumptiousness of the English people from Wat Tyler and John Ball onwards. Ball, probably quoting a verse that had become 'common property', made the point in his revolutionary sermon at Blackheath in 1381:

> When Adam delved and Eve span
> Who was then the gentleman?

Despite the inexorably futile attempts to separate amateurs from professionals, 'gentlemen' from 'players', and the privileged from the patronized, the class-conscious English always relished the relaxation of social distinctions in the heat of sporting rivalry: the king with his courtiers at bowls, a great landowner and a tenant farmer on the hunting field riding hard at the same fence, the local cricket team where a man is valued for his bowling more than for his bank balance. And sport will always bring the cold-blooded, taciturn, essential Englishman to life.

# CRICKET

Cricket is one of those games with little military utility to it. As such, whatever early version of it was being played at the time, along with bowls and other harmless diversions, was roundly condemned by Edward III in his instructions to the Lord Lieutenant of Kent in 1363—Kent being the birthplace of the game, as near as one can tell.

> Whereas the people of our realm, gentle and simple alike, were wont formerly in their games to practise skill in archery and that now the said skill in archery having fallen almost wholly into disrepute, our people give themselves up to the throwing of stones and of wood and of iron and some even to other unseemly sports that be less useful and manly, whereby our realm will soon, as it appeareth, be stripped of archers. We, wishing that a fitting remedy be found in this matter . . . require that every man in the county, sobeit he be able-bodied, shall, upon holidays, make use, in his games, of bows and arrows and learn and practise archery. Moreover, that you prohibit all and sundry in our name from such stone, wood and iron throwing under penalty of imprisonment.

It was found to be a useless prohibition. The king was hardly to know that cricket would be discovered to serve the English need for martial virtues with as much efficacy as practising on the butts. The later Victorians liked to imagine Wellington saying, 'The battle of Waterloo was won on the playing fields of Eton.' he said nothing of the kind, but the idea was a potent one:

> There's a breathless hush in the Close to-night—
>     Ten to make and the match to win—
> A bumping pitch and a blinding light,
>     An hour to play and the last man in.
> And it's not for the sake of a ribboned coat,
>     Or the selfish hope of a season's fame,
> But his Captain's hand on his shoulder smote—
>     'Play up! play up! and play the game!'
>
> The sand of the desert is sodden red—
>     Red with the wreck of a square that broke;
> The Gatling's jammed and the Colonel dead,
>     And the regiment blind with dust and smoke.
> The river of death has brimmed his banks,
>     And England's far, and Honour a name,
> But the voice of a schoolboy rallies the ranks:
>     'Play up! play up! and play the game!'
>
> This is the word that year by year,
>     While in her place the School is set,

> Every one of her sons must hear,
>   And none that hears it dare forget.
> This they all with a joyful mind
>   Bear through life like a torch in flame,
> And falling, fling to the host behind —
>   'Play up! play up! and play the game!'

Newbolt, 'Vitaï Lampada'

With his straight bat and his sense of 'fair play', this noble image of the sporting Englishman still haunts, a little reproachfully, club-houses and pavilions throughout the world. Nor is it an entirely mythical image.

Of Alfred Lyttelton (1857–1913) who played football, cricket (he was considered the best wicket-keeper in England), tennis and golf, it was said that as an MP 'he had an ingrained sense of "the rules of the game" and whatever the provocation, he was no more capable of taking what he thought an unfair advantage of his opponent than of disputing the umpire's decision at Lords'. He died, as he would perhaps have wished, hit in the stomach by a cricket ball.

The unspotted ideal was probably C. T. Studd, who opened the batting for England in his youth and later became a missionary in Africa, where he died. At Ibambi in the Congo, he laid out a grass-roofed church 22 yards long, which proved so popular that neighbouring tribes demanded 'cricket-pitch churches' of their own. He was also gratified to note that those who attended his sermons would come back for a 'second innings'.

What is it about the game that takes it so deep into the English soul? There is surely some inexplicable mystery that allows the two names that come down to us most clearly from the history of the game to be Thomas Lord and W. G. Grace.

First, just as football is the sporting expression of industrial England, the whole ethos of cricket is essentially rural and thus awakens the deeply pastoral and nostalgic element in the English. It seems appropriate that teams are identified by counties rather than by large towns. This practice seems to date from times when great landowners had their own teams. The 3rd Duke of Dorset captained his own side himself, and was commissioned in 1789 by the then Foreign Secretary, the Duke of Leeds, to take a cricket team over to France on a 'goodwill visit'. Unfortunately, the tour had to be cancelled owing to the worsening political situation there. Thus was an early attempt at diplomacy through sport nipped in the bud.

The French never quite appreciated the importance of the game for the national team spirit. Cesar de Saussure observed in 1728, in a letter, 'Everyone plays it, the common people and also men of rank . . . they go into a large open field and knock a ball about with a piece of wood. I will not attempt to describe this game; but it requires agility and skill.'

Even after the French Revolution—of which G. M. Trevelyan wrote, 'If the French noblesse had been capable of playing cricket with their peasants, their châteaux would never have been burnt'—the French had still not quite got the point. When the MCC were in Paris in 1867 a Frenchman remarked to 'Bob' Fitzgerald: 'It is a truly magnificent game, but I cannot understand why you do not engage a servant to field for you instead of having so much running about to do yourself.'

By playing the game, as with sitting in church, all men become, relatively speaking, equal. And so cricket today is still played and studied with an earnest reverence, as if it somehow guaranteed their spiritual salvation or even their political liberty. Neville Cardus, the music critic, was also one of cricket's many philosophers:

> Like the British Constitution, cricket was not made: it has 'grown'. Its rules and its general legal system tell of the English compromise between individual freedom and corporate responsibility; cricket is known as essentially a 'team-game', yet one player may dominate the proceedings for hours, as much the cynosure of all eyes as a prima-donna. On the other hand, the greatest cricketer in the world will sooner or later find himself so anonymously just a part of the whole, the XI, that he is reduced to mute and inglorious inactivity for hours . . .

The game is, of course, immensely complex, and has swallowed up many lifetimes of scholarly research by enthusiasts with a passion for statistics. Vast compendiums of cricketing records go back well over a century. It is also an astoundingly long game. There is a saying, attributed to Lord Mansfield, to the effect that cricket is a game which the English, not being a spiritual people, have invented to give themselves some conception of eternity.

The progress of a match is like the weather, which affects it in such subtle and deep-reaching ways. Nothing much may happen for long periods, and then there will come a sudden upset—or, then again, it might not. Sometimes the interest of a game develops very slowly but surely to a climax of excitement. Often it winds down, after several days' play, to a draw. What is looked for in the game is thus not the result, which may well be indecisive, but the occasional sparkle of athleticism, a stylish flourish, a classically elegant stroke, perhaps a patient display of grit and concentration—an innings being carefully built up—or a heroic and combative stand against long odds, bold tactics or a cautious but cunning strategy. The pressures on a captain over an important five-day match can be considerable. It is little wonder that the most successful English captain of recent years was an academic philosopher who retired from the game to take up psychotherapy.

There is also a certain pressure on the BBC commentary box to hold the attention of listeners to the radio during the inevitable longueurs in a match; if the fast bowlers are on, this can mean between each ball. The commentators do this with a mix of three or four distinct styles, even caricatures, to reflect the depth and complexity of the cricketing experience. There should firstly be a head full of batting averages and bowling figures—Bill Frindall—then a couple of public-school chaps full of boyish enthusiasm, balanced by a bluff Yorkshireman, say Freddie Trueman, and finally there needs to be a prose poet to give the scene a patina of timeless but particular significance—someone like John Arlott.

For John Nyren, in his classic evocation of cricket in the early days, *The Cricketers of my Time* (1833), the richness of the experience necessarily included beer and punch: 'good unsophisticated, John Bull stuff—stark!—that would stand on end—punch that would make a cat speak . . .' Nyren went on to describe the crowd gathered on Broad Ha'penny Down to witness the village of Hambledon play against all England:

> There would this company, consisting most likely of some thousands, remain patiently and anxiously watching every turn of fate in the game, as if the event had been the meeting of two armies to decide their liberty. And whenever a Hambledon man made a good hit, worth four or five runs, you would hear the deep mouths of the whole multitude baying away in pure Hampshire—'Go hard! go hard—*Tich* and turn!—*tich* and turn!' . . . and the smell of that ale comes upon me freshly on the new May flowers.

Nyren's book is a classic because it gets to the heart of the game, which is simply character. He marvels, for example, at one of the immortals of Hambledon, Tom Walker, at his

> hard ungainly scrag-of-mutton frame; wilted, apple-john face . . . his long spider legs, as thick at the ankles as at the hips, and perfectly straight all the way down. Tom was the driest and most rigid-limbed chap I ever knew; his skin was like the rind of an old oak, and as sapless. I have seen his knuckles handsomely knocked about from Harris's bowling; but never saw any blood upon his hands—you might just as well attempt to phlebotomise a mummy.

Though an air of reverence has long pervaded the game, cricket used to be played for high stakes (the straight bat, that ever ready symbol of moral rectitude, did not appear until mid-nineteenth century). Until then winning was very important, decisions were invariably disputed, matches fixed, and the losing side beaten up by their backers. However, if overt gambling was gradually driven out of the hallowed pavilions, there were other ways of adding interest, mainly by a piquant composition of teams. The famous annual match of the 1890s, 'Big Game Hunters versus Worplesden', was probably a tame enough affair. But in 1861 a reporter from *All the Year Round*, a magazine edited by Charles Dickens, saw an announcement in a tobacconist's window near the Elephant and Castle:

*168*

On Saturday,
A Cricket Match will be played at the
Rosemary Branch, Peckham Rye,
Eleven One-armed Men and Eleven One-legged Men.
The Match to begin at Eleven o'Clock a.m.

The year after this match, the England selectors received a letter from a certain Mrs Grace, giving notice of a being who would bestride the narrow world of cricket like a colossus:

> Dear Sir,
>   I am writing to ask you to consider the inclusion of my son, E. M. Grace—a splendid hitter and most excellent catch—in your England XI. I am sure he would play very well and do the team much credit. It may interest you to learn that I have a younger son, now 12 years of age, who will in time be a much better player than his brother because his back stroke is sounder, and he always plays with a straight bat. His name is W. G. Grace.
>
>                                         I am, Sir,
>                               Your obedient servant,
>                                         Martha Grace

Neville Cardus saw W. G. Grace as a kind of fertility god—a pagan embodiment of vernal renewal:

> Morning after morning the summer's sun rose for him, and he went forth and trod fresh grass. Every springtime came and found him ready for cricket; when he was a boy he learned the game in a Gloucestershire orchard white with bloom. He grew in the sunshine and wind and rain; the elements became flesh within him.

What gave Grace his divinity was simply his watchfulness and awareness, seeming preternatural because it could be sustained over hours. Arthur Conan Doyle watched him in his old age, apparently drawing strength and vitality, Antaeus-like, out of the ground as he played:

> It was amazing that a man who was capable of such exertions should carry such weight. As he came towards the wicket, walking heavily with shoulders rounded, his great girth outlined by his coloured sash, one would have imagined that his day was past. 'He may make his twenty or thirty,' one thought, 'and then Nature will dismiss him if the bowler fails.' Never was there a greater fallacy. He seemed slow, stiff and heavy at first. When he had made fifty in his quiet, methodical fashion, he was somewhat younger and fresher. At the end of a century he had not turned a hair, and was watching the ball with as clear an eye as in the first over. Younger batsmen might tire and grow ragged in their strokes, but never the old man. It was his advice to play

Cricket was evidently a consciously created aesthetic experience even in 1820
—the sound of leather on willow echoing across the sunlit sward,
while country life goes on nearby, undisturbed.

every ball as if it were the first—and he lived up to it. There was no feeling for the ball, no half-hits or wild slogs. Everything that he did was firm, definite and well within his strength.

When he was well on towards his sixtieth year I have seen him standing up to Lockwood when man after man was helpless at the other wicket, tapping those terrific expresses away through the slips with the easy sureness with which one would bounce a tennis ball with a racket. Nor was he ever to be frightened by the most dangerous bowler. Poised and firm, he never flinched, but turned the rising ball to leg or patted it to the off. The fastest bowler in England sent one like a cannon-shot through his beard, with only a comic shake of the head and a good-humoured growl in reply.

Even the gods are mortal, though they don't like to admit it. One of the stories in Harry Furniss's book, *A Century of Grace* (1984), tells of a gusty morning when a fast ball eluded W. G.'s bat and snipped a bail, which fell to the ground. 'Windy day today, umpire,' remarked Grace, replacing the bail. 'Make sure it doesn't blow your cap off on the way back to the pavilion,' was the umpire's reply.

Francis Thompson's famous lament, 'At Lords', immortalized the opening batsmen for Lancashire in the 1880s: A. N. Hornby Esq. (a gentleman) and R. G. Barlow (a player). Barlow was the stonewaller of the pair, while Hornby swung the bat.

> It is little I repair to the matches of the Southron folk,
>   Though my own red roses there may blow;

It is little I repair to the matches of the Southron folk,
    Though the red roses crest the caps, I know.
For the field is full of shades as I near the shadowy coast,
And a ghostly batsman plays to the bowling of a ghost,
And I look through my tears on a soundless-clapping host
    As the run-stealers flicker to and fro,
        To and fro:
    O my Hornby and my Barlow long ago!

# FOOTBALL

Football is no longer the combat sport it once was, when hundreds would compete for possession of a wooden ball, boiled in tallow to make it slippery, and calling forth the remark by one observer of a game in Pembrokeshire in 1588, 'If this be but play, I cold wishe the Spaniardes were here to see our plaies in England. Certes they would be oodielyie [utterly] feare of our warre.'

But even then it was being seen in terms of a positive physical culture allied to the Classical ideal of *mens sana in corpore sano* as reinterpreted to accommodate the English need for a good punch-up. The sixteenth-century headmaster of St Paul's School, Richard Mulcaster, wrote of football: 'It strengtheneth and brawneth the whole body, and by provoking superfluities downewards, it dischargeth the head and upper parts. It is good for the bowels, driveth downe the stone and gravel from both the bladder and kidneies.'

This combination of violence and healthful recreation is a difficult one to maintain. Violence on the pitch was eventually given the thumbs down. Nowadays, the realms of healthful recreation and violence are separated by wire fencing—largely the result of the Victorian ideal of the Christian gentleman, which required the game to become a sport played in a spirit of friendly rivalry, with a fixed number on each side to make it 'fair'. This unrealistic ideal gives rise eventually to the sort of supercilious football or rugby martyr remembered by Gerald Davies, in *The Times* of 12 February 1989:

> The embellished tale goes something like this. There was an English lock, a long time ago in the Fifties, who travelled in New Zealand, bowler-hatted and with umbrella rolled. Back home, he was something in the City. His many irreproachable virtues, though esteemed elsewhere, were perhaps not so highly thought of around New Zealand's rugby paddocks and had, in consequence, to be put to the test.
>
> At any rate, at a lineout he had a tasting of a five-knuckle sandwich in the face. The player, undeterred, went on with his own game. No goose ever heard a less-resounding boo.
>
> A Welshman, affronted by the lack of fibre without the necessary right stuff, grilled him afterwards. The gist of which was to ask why he, the offended party, did not give him a good one back. To which the studied reply came from decades of careful breeding: 'I didn't give him one, as you so colourfully

put it, because I wanted the fellow to feel like a cad.'

Such a cool, philosophical response would today be thought of only as coming from a duffer, further reinforcing the idea of the good British loser. The line between fair means and foul is not really so well defined today as it once might have been.

As a staple recreation in the public schools of the nineteenth century, football developed into various forms, and from these descended two of our national games, rugby union and association football. The FA Cup, instituted in 1871, was dominated by teams of Old Boys from the public schools for a decade. In 1882, the Old Etonians met Blackburn Rovers in the Final and won 1–0. The winning goal came early in the match. As this contemporary newspaper report shows, the public school men played a brutal game, leaving their northern working-class opponents to offer a more gentlemanly spirit:

> There was a marked contrast in the style of play of the rival teams and to Blackburn spectators the game revealed features unusual in the north. While the Rovers worked their way towards their opponents' goal by passing, the Etonians did so by rushes, the player securing the ball at the start retaining possession of it until robbed or checked, and his partner bearing him company to render assistance when opposition appeared. The Etonians indulged in none of the dribbling or dodging which forms an interesting and pleasing part of the famous Lancashire team's play, reliance being placed instead on the weight and speed of the forwards. A still greater contrast was afforded in the kicking of the ball when running. While the Rovers sent the leather forward so little raised above the ground as almost to touch it in skimming along, their opponents kicked the ball much higher and springing up at it while dashing along delivered the kick frequently with both feet off the ground. The spring was made whether or not an opponent was close to the ball when it bounded, and the Rovers, unaccustomed to this practice, were badly kicked, particularly towards the finish when the play was mainly in close quarters. To the same fact was probably due the entire absence, or nearly so, of the scrimages almost on the goal-line that are often seen on northern football fields, and while the Rovers used heads, chests, and knees as well as feet in manipulating the ball, the Old Boys relied entirely on kicking . . .
>
> As the time for play gradually shortened, the supporters of the Rovers became less confident, and there were shouts from the grand stand of 'Play up Blackburn', to which admirers of their opponents responded by cries of 'E-e-ton'. But there was ominous silence amongst the Lancashire spectators. For nearly twenty minutes before the close the Etonians were practically penned in their own quarters, and the Rovers were constantly striving to score, but only to be disappointed by seeing the ball go over the line, on the wrong side of the posts or to be stopped by the goalkeeper. All the shots were high, however, and there was no opportunity of judging of Rawlinson's power with his feet. The desperate struggle was continued until the referee's

whistle signalled the expiration of time, and the Etonians were hailed the victors by one goal to none.

But the following year the boot was on the other foot, as it were: Eton, still committed to outmoded bulldozing tactics, succumbed to the more modern football skills of a rival Lancashire side, Blackburn Olympic.

Being pragmatic, the English know how to lose. The way they like to win is expressed in the headline carried by *The Times* in its report of the World Cup final in 1966: 'England surmount final test of morale.' The report described the final stage of the match in the sort of terms that are dearly familiar to the English:

> The climax came in a punishing period of an extra half-hour after the Germans had first led and then saved their necks with an equalizing goal at 2–2 a mere 15 seconds from the end of normal time.
>
> To have the Cup thus apparently dashed from their lips at the very moment of victory was a deep test of England's morale. Psychologically, Germany should have had the edge in that extra time. But Moore and his men rose magnificently to the challenge. Only the two sets of actors down on that

Bobby Charlton (left) and Nobby Stiles, respectively the white knight and 'hard man' of England's 1966 World Cup team. In his time the patrician Charlton, born into a family of Northumberland miners, was the most famous Englishman in the world. The diminutive Stiles, here shown cleaned up and with his teeth in, was a merciless harrier of opposing forwards whatever their reputation.

green stage could have truly felt the bitter disappointment or the elation of that moment.

But as England were yet girding themselves for the extended test, Mr Ramsey, their manager, walked calmly among his men to say: 'All right. You let it slip. Now start again!' They did. They reacted vigorously. How some of them found the resilience and the stamina finally to outstay a German side equally powerful physically, equally determined, equally battle-hardened was beyond praise.

In a book published some 20 years later, *England's Last Glory*, David Miller, Chief Sports Correspondent of *The Times*, remembered the day vividly:

> If the reverse at the 90th minute of the match had been stunning for England, the Germans must now have felt engulfed by the vast wave of opposing emotion. The conventional, restrained English, that strange people across the Channel with their raincoats and their rain, their bowler hats and their orderly queues of two people at a bus stop, their lack of conversation in public or with people they did not know, were revealing their inner self, that cheerful bawdiness which lay so close beneath the surface, that willingness, given the opportunity, to be brash and boastful, which Victorianism had taught them was not the done thing. Out of the shell of moderation, the World Cup hatched an Elizabethan boisterousness of an earlier century: a drinking, uninhibited, almost primitive zest for the moment. Live now, pay later, was the slogan of the time. In the world's most simple and most popular game, the English were winning. And loving it.

# BOXING

The great age of English boxing, of what 'A Yorkshireman' writing to the Editor of *Bell's Life in London* in 1843 called 'a jolly good old-fashioned English mill', began with Jack Broughton's rules of the sport, as laid down in 1743. As a sport, boxing emerged from a cheerful alliance of aristocratic patrons and working-class bruisers like Broughton himself—who started his sporting career by winning the annual race for watermen on the Thames, 'Doggett's Coat and Badge', in 1743.

However, the Huguenot refugee Misson de Valbourg, in his *Memoirs and Observations in England of 1719*, remarked that rules of a sort, and a commitment to fair play, were observed well before they were written down:

> If two little boys quarrel in the street, the passengers stop, make a ring round them in a moment, and set them against one another, that they may come to fisticuffs . . . During the fight the ring of bystanders encourages the comba-tants with great delight of heart, and never parts them while they fight according to the rules. And these bystanders are not only other boys, porters, and rabble, but all sorts of men of fashion, some thrusting by the mob that they may see plainly, others getting upon stalls, and all would hire places, if

scaffolds could be built in a moment. The fathers and mothers of the boys let them fight on as well as the rest, and hearten him that gives the ground, or has the worst. These combats are less frequent among grown men than children, but they are not rare. If a coachman has a dispute about his fare with a gentleman that has hired him, and the gentleman offers to fight him to decide the quarrel, the coachman consents with all his heart. The gentleman pulls off his sword, lays it in some shop with his cane, gloves and cravat, and boxes in the same manner as I have described above. If the coachman gets soundly drubbed, which happens almost always, that goes for payment, but if he is the beater, the beatee must pay the money about which they quarrelled. I once saw the late Duke of Grafton at fisticuffs in the open street, with such a fellow, whom he lambed most horribly. In France we punish such rascals with our cane, and sometimes with the flat of the sword; but in England this is never practised. They use neither sword nor stick against a man that is unarmed, and if an unfortunate stranger (for an Englishman would never take it into his head) should draw his sword upon one that had none, he'd have a hundred people upon him in a moment, that would, perhaps, lay him so flat that he would hardly ever get up again until the Resurrection.

Gentlemen who boxed were not necessarily masters of the art of pugilism (although many of them would don the 'mufflers' at the boxing academies that sprang up). Squire Mytton, the early-nineteenth-century Master of Hounds, used to fight in an uninhibited style that could hardly be graced by the term 'fisticuffs'. But he was seldom bested. His longest fight was 20 rounds with a Welsh miner, which Mytton won after taking a lot of punishment. (He is known also to have fought two dogs 'of exceptional strength and savagery' using his teeth. He won each of these fights by clamping his teeth over the dog's nose.)

Bare-knuckle boxing never became altogether respectable. But the people of England did. Lord John Manners bemoaned this change in his countrymen in 1843, in *A Plea for National Holy Days*: '. . . the English people, who of yore were famous all over Europe for their love of manly sports and their sturdy good humour, have year after year been losing that cheerful character.'

The final pugilistic exhibition of that character came in 1861, when, such was the excitement generated by the bloody and by then illegal bare-knuckle confrontation, that no less august a newspaper than *The Times* published a blow-by-blow account of the fight for the championship of England. Tom Sayers was giving away three stone in weight and 5½ ins in height to the American Challenger Heenan. But, as the Times said: 'Heenan's skin yesterday was, as we have said, fair and white as marble—Sayers' as dark as that of a mulatto; and the "fancy" leant strongly to the opinion that the former was too delicate, and would bruise too much—and this was true . . .'

The report began by sounding a high chivalric note: 'Time was when the championship of England was an office which conferred honour on the highest,

Bareknuckle boxing at the Fives Court in London's Haymarket c. 1820.
The highest in the land took a keen interest in the scrupulously organized,
but wholly illegal, bouts fought here for nearly a century.

when "Marmion, Lord of Scrivelhaye, of Tamworth tower and town," held a grant
of the lands of the Abbey of Polesworth on condition of doing battle in single
combat against all knightly enemies of his king.'

Getting back to the present (1860) the report continued:

> The new Police Act has been the death of pugilism. Its greatest professors
> now lead a hole-and corner life while training, or issue forth their challenges
> in mysterious terms. From this rapid downfall it has been just now for a time
> arrested by the first attempt to carry off the Champion's belt into another
> country—and, of course, that country was America. There is no disguising
> the fact that this challenge has led to an amount of attention being bestowed
> upon the prize ring which it has never received before; and, much as all
> decent people disliked the idea of two fine men meeting to beat each other
> half to death, it was nevertheless devoutly wished that, as somebody was to
> be beaten, it might be the American.

The fight lasted 2hr 20min. Sayers' right arm was broken in the sixth round, but
towards the end Heenan was practically blind.

In the 38th round Heenan got Sayers' head under his left arm and, supporting himself by the stake with his right, held his opponent bent down, as if he meant to strangle him. Sayers could no more free himself than if a mountain was on him. At last he got his left arm free, and gave Heenan two dreadful blows on the face, covering them both with the blood, but Heenan, without relaxing his hold, turned himself so as to get his antagonist's neck over the rope, and then leant on it with all his force. Sayers rapidly turned black in the face, and would have strangled on the spot but that the rules of the ring provide for what would otherwise be fatal contingencies, and both the umpires called simultaneously to cut the ropes. This was done at once, and both men fell heavily to the ground, Sayers nearly half strangled. The police now made a determined effort to interfere, which those present seemed equally determined to prevent, and the ropes of the ring having been cut the enclosure itself was inundated by a dense crowd, which scarcely left the combatants six square feet to fight in . . . At length the police forced their way to where they were fighting, in a space not much larger than an ordinary dining-table, and the referee ordered them at once to discontinue . . . Sayers' right arm was helpless, his mouth and nose were dreadfully beaten, and the side of his head and forehead much punished. Heenan was almost unrecognizable as a human being, so dreadful had been his punishment about the face and neck. Yet he was still as strong on his legs, apparently, as ever, thanks to his perfect training, and, after leaving the field of battle, he ran as nimbly as any of the spectators and leaped over two small hedges.

The result was declared a draw and a riot broke out amongst the 10,000 spectators. The Queensberry Rules were drafted five years later.

One leftover from the old days that remains to this day is the expectation that English boxers be 'natural gentleman'. The heroes of 'the Fancy' were presented, to a public increasingly eager for moral uplift and suspicious of their world of betting and blood, as models of kindliness and good manners, to suggest that the sport inculcated such respectable virtues as well as the more traditional English ones of 'bottom' and fair play. For example, Isaac Perrins, who lost to a paragon of politeness, Richard Humphries, 'the Gentleman Boxer', led his local church choir, and died as a result of helping to put out a fire in a neighbour's house. In our own age there are boxers like Frank Bruno and Henry Cooper, who come across as fundamentally decent blokes. Their raw courage and ringcraft do not rule out a genial and reflective satisfaction in their trade. Henry Cooper, in conversation with Dudley Doust in the *Sunday Times* (1977):

> The real thrill in boxing is when you hit the other geezer on the whiskers and you see that look in his eyes, that blank, dead look. Some people say, 'Watch the legs, the knees.' That's rubbish. The eyes tell you everything and in a split second you know he's gone and he'll never get up and it's marvellous . . . I look back at me life and I always say whatever I done I would do it again. I don't think I made any big mistakes. I think we done it right.

In the days when Cooper might have won the world championship he once floored the then Cassius Clay with his fabled left hook, ' 'Enery's 'Ammer'. After their second fight together, which was stopped in the sixth round, Clay went to Cooper's dressing room to say how sorry he was about going for the cut on Cooper's face. Cooper responded, cheerful in defeat, 'It was a pity. We was really enjoying ourselves. But I'd had done the same to you if I could.'

# HUNTSMEN AND OTHER ANIMALS

It is a disturbing paradox that a people who cannot abide cruelty to animals should hunt and shoot them with such unholy and prodigious zeal, unmatched by any other nation. For many Englishmen, even today, a good day's sport involves an indispensable contribution from the animal kingdom. Naturally the animals are loved and protected, admired and even respected, but only if they fulfil their role in what must be for them puzzling and dangerous rituals. The horse that falls at Becher's Brook, the salmon or trout brought to land, the pheasant tumbling helplessly from its flight, and Reynard himself, torn to pieces by the hounds, are all dearly loved by the English.

For one thing, this is how they keep their bloodstock and aristocracy in good fettle, ready for battle. Indeed, fox hunting, a uniquely English tradition of galloping wildly over the peaceful shires of England, seems to have translated directly onto the battlefields as the Charge of the Light Brigade. This uniquely English deployment of cavalry against a battery of cannon was precipitated by two keen fox-hunting men, Lord Cardigan and Captain Nolan. It was a fatal confusion of war with sport, noted by a French officer overlooking the carnage, Maréchal Bosquet: '*C'est magnifique, mais ce n'est pas la guerre.*'

Fox hunting developed into an excuse for reckless riding, bad language and a Byronic lifestyle—womanizing, fisticuffs with the lower orders, and the rest of it. Drinking, too: 'Fox hunters who have all day long tried to break their necks, join at night in a second attempt on their lives by drinking' (Bernard de Mandeville, *The Fable of the Bees*, 1722). It hardly seems possible to rescue the sport from the charge of encouraging an attitude of imbecilic irresponsibility. Anthony Trollope, however, had no trouble yoking it to the noblest traditions of English life (*English Sports and Pastimes*, 1868):

> We have all heard how the Emperor [Napoleon III] hunts the deer at Fontainebleau, and some of us have witnessed the stately ceremony. But there is in it not the slightest resemblance to English hunting. There is no competition; no liberty; no danger;—and no equality. The reason why this should be so—why hunting should not exist elsewhere as it does here in England—is easy to find; much easier than any reason why any custom so strange, so opposed to all common rules as to property, should have

*Lord Darlington's Hunt.* Lord Darlington of Raby (1766–1842) hunted a vast country in Yorkshire. A combination of sporting animals and countryside is very much the Englishman's taste in art.

domesticated itself among ourselves. We are to the manner born; and till we think of it and dwell upon it, the thing does not seem strange to us; but foreigners cannot be made to understand that all the world, any one who chooses to put himself on horseback, let him be a lord or a tinker, should have permission to ride where he will, over enclosed fields, across growing crops, crushing down cherished fences, and treating the land as though it were his own—as long as hounds are running; that this should be done without any payment of any kind exacted from the enjoyer of the sport, that the poorest man may join in it without question asked, and that it should be carried on indifferently over land owned by men who are friends to the practice, and over that owned by its bitterest enemies;—that, in fact, the habit is so strong that the owner of the land, with all the law to back him, with his right to the soil as perfect and as exclusive as that of a lady to her drawing-room, cannot in effect save himself from an invasion of a hundred or a hundred and fifty horsemen, let him struggle to save himself as he may.

Naturally, the English took their passions with them when they went abroad. It did not do to appear tractable to circumstances. Bad for morale. For want of fox, they chased hyena, dingo, kangaroo and pig—in fact, anything that would give them a 'good run'. Making do could sometimes go to bizarre lengths: Raymond Carr in his *English Fox Hunting* (1976) notes:

> When there was no animal to hunt, Englishmen in exile hunted paper. The Shanghai Paper Hunt was founded in the 1860s to pursue a human 'fox' in a red cowl laying a trail of paper. It prided itself on its English traditions, including the Hunt Dinner at which 'the worthy and plucky Master resumed his seat amidst a thunder of applause and hunt cries'. It had its collection of atrocious ballads. Its master behaved in the accepted manner: 'Damn it sir, you'd ride over a bed of geraniums.' It had its troubles. Old paper trails confused the hunt. The natives were 'extremely disagreeable' when fields charged over intensely cultivated land and set traps for the riders. The solution, as in the home version of such troubles, was to pay compensation and build bridges over irrigation channels. It was all very English.

Other sporting institutions were much more easily provided for in almost any part of the Empire. The enduring monuments of the British Empire remain cricket grounds and racecourses. Lord Cromer, in his *Political and Literary Essays* (1908–16), recalled:

> When I arrived in Cairo less than a year after the battle of Tel-el-Kebir had been fought (1882) every department of the administration was in a state of the utmost confusion. Nevertheless a race-course had already been laid out and a grandstand erected. A golf-course followed after a short interval.

Jan Morris, in *Pax Britannica* (1968), noted another example of the English arriving in a strange spot and setting up race meetings as other people might set up an altar and makeshift church to ward off local dark forces: 'When Queen Victoria sent four envoys from the Royal Horse Guards to visit Lobengula in his kraal, almost the first thing they did was to arrange a race meeting, including the Zambezi Handicap and the Bulawayo Plate.'

The Mecca for all these meetings was, of course, Ascot. The French Socialist, Flora Tristan, described in her *London Journal* what was already by 1840 a sporting institution:

> In England the races are great occasions which have all the character of a solemn ceremony in the eyes of the spectators. Ascot races are held in the last three days of May, and for the people of London and its environs they are what the august rites of Holy Week in Rome represent for Catholics, or the last three days of carnival for Parisians . . .
>
> Ascot is about thirty miles from London, and as the first race usually starts at midday, patrons must set out at four, five, or six o'clock in the morning to arrive in time. There is only one road, so between dawn and noon or early afternoon, more than three thousand vehicles of every description pass along it . . . but what I found quite admirable was that despite the difficulties of the route and the number of vehicles on it, the most perfect order was maintained every moment of the journey . . .

It must be admitted that the English have a special genius for managing horses; besides, they are accustomed to respect the order of precedence when they are out in force, and observe it with the precision of a Prussian regiment on parade. This discipline, which is found in no other people, is due to the system of government, for in this country everything is managed on the hierarchical principle . . . everybody knows his place . . .

The author was disgusted with the evils of English horsebreeding, gambling, gluttony and drunkenness at Ascot. Also, 'The English climate makes any country outing, if not impossible, at least a very painful experience . . .'

But look! The horses are off—six abreast! On every side voices are raised in exclamation: 'Oh! What a speedy racer! Prodigious rapidity indeed! Astonishing! Astonishing! Wonderful! Wonderful!'

Five races were run, with either eight, six, four or two horses, but the excitement was short-lived: a few minutes at the most, and the race was over.

At last, when it was almost six o'clock, the vehicles started on the way home. I thought there would be the most frightful confusion, but not at all. everything was done with the same discipline as in the morning; the police had the carriages of the nobility harnessed first, and if they judged any coachman too drunk to drive, he was removed from his seat and replaced. Drunk and incapable passengers were put inside the coaches, while any who were only half-drunk were settled on top between two sober companions so that they would not fall, and off they went in such a cloud of dust that they were soon lost to sight.

We arrived back in London at one o'clock in the morning, it was bitterly cold, the fog was thick and the damp penetrating; we were all chilled to the bone.

It was quite pitiful to see all the ladies who had set out in the morning so fresh and elegant returning covered with dust, dirty and completely unrecognizable.

In England this kind of outing is called a pleasure jaunt.

Of course, no discussion of English blood sports would be complete without a mention of the most famous and succinct description of all—and this from an Irishman, Oscar Wilde:

The English country gentleman galloping after a fox—the unspeakable in full pursuit of the uneatable.

*A Woman of No Importance*, 1893

'. . . a farcical pomp of war, parade of religion and Bustle with very little business, in
short poverty slavery and Insolence (with an affectation of politeness) . . .'
Hogarth's view of abroad may have been coloured by the fact that
he was arrested while making drawings for this picture of Calais Gate.

# CHAPTER TEN

## ·

# THE ENGLISHMAN ABROAD

> I travelled among unknown men
> In lands beyond the sea;
> Nor, England! did I know till then
> What love I bore to thee.
>
> William Wordsworth, 'I Travelled Among Unknown Men'

'Never go abroad.' was the advice of the fifth Earl of Cadogan; 'It's a dreadful place.' George V went abroad 'and it was horrid'. Heedless of this counsel from their betters, the English insist on finding out for themselves. How else could they confirm their worst suspicions of foreigners?

Richard Ford, in his *Handbook for Travellers in Spain* (1855) advised the Englishman to put England out of his mind:

> How few there, or indeed anywhere on the Continent, sympathize with our wants and habits, or understand our love of truth and cold water; our simple manly tastes; our contempt for outward show compared to real comfort; our love of exercise, adventure, and alternate quiet, and all that can only be learnt at our public schools.

Yes, as the white cliffs of Dover recede into the fog, the essential Englishman girds his loins for the struggle ahead. There will be rapacious inn-keepers and their cuisine which, whether insipid or over-spiced, can never be anything other than foreign. The natives will be surly, garrulous, servile, villainous and irremediably foreign. Transport services will be unreliable, uncomfortable, filthy (in a way that only foreigners know how to arrange) and foreign. The ultimate ordeal, will be the ancient monuments, the sublime cathedrals, the museums stuffed negligently with masterpieces—all entrusted by an undiscerning Providence to a sadly decayed race, and all to be endured appreciatively, according to the precise and unerring recommendations of Dr Baedeker. And he was foreign, too.

The tourist trade was invented by the English to take this travail out of

"She say you so long coming she let your room to other peoples and you will have to wait at the Airporto, till they are departo."

Cartoonist Karl Giles summarizes the English experience abroad in 1987.
Six hundred years previously, Chaucer had made the same point:

'Thou shalt make castels then in Spayne,
And dreme of joye, but al in vayne'

travel. In 1841 Thomas Cook had a brainwave: 'About midway between Harborough and Leicester, a thought flashed through my brain—what a glorious thing it would be if the newly developed power of steam railways and locomotion could be made subservient to the promotion of Temperance.' With this idea of 'Temperance Excursions' was born Cook's Tours. It would have pained Thomas Cook had he been able to foresee that his virtuous enterprise would allow the English tourist to become feared throughout Europe for drunken, violent behaviour.

For the first time, Europe was invaded by the English middle classes. Under the bustling command of Thomas Cook, who fortified his charges with solid English food, they were cocooned from the cupidity, the untrustworthiness and the generally lax moral tone that threatened the English traveller. There was no lotus-eating on a Cook's tour, though. The judicious handbooks of John Murray and Karl Baedeker set out a heavy menu of art and scenery to be consumed in the shortest possible time. There was an awful lot of it to be got through, and the Victorians were busy people.

# THE GRAND TOUR

By contrast, Arthur Young, in 1789, unfettered by Baedeker, was able to appreciate the château of Chambord in his own down-to-earth way. As he put it in his *Travels in France*, 'I could not help thinking that if the King of France ever formed the idea of establishing one complete and perfect farm under the turnip culture of England, here is the place for it . . .' Unfortunately, by 1789 it was a little late for Louis XVI to be thinking of turnip farms.

For a couple of hundred years the Englishman had gone abroad to take home anything nice that was not nailed down; any new and interesting idea that might be useful was likewise brought home. By the eighteenth century this had become a large-scale exercise in cultural looting and espionage, carried out by most of the English upper classes behind a smokescreen of eccentric and licentious antics. Manuscripts and marbles were bought for a song, military men looked at fortifications . . . and farmers looked at French châteaux straight from fairyland and thought of turnips. Nor did Arthur Young feel obliged to respond with much enthusiasm to Venice – 'not a theatre for the feelings of a farmer' he pronounced.

It was a long time before many people would admit that they were going abroad strictly for pleasure. You went perhaps for your health or, more certainly, for your education. Advanced travellers were called explorers.

But, at any one time, there were always a few Englishmen who lived abroad in order to lead a scandalous lifestyle, their wealth buying them, if not acceptance, then at least a local acquiescence. Sexual reprobates like Byron and stark atheists like Shelley helped to fix an extravagant image of the English 'Milord' or 'Godam' in the minds of the Europeans. Shelley, though, in a letter to Leigh Hunt, placed Byron's delinquency firmly (if quite unjustly) at the door of the degenerate Italian people: 'Young women of rank actually eat – you will never guess what – garlick! Our poor friend Lord Byron is quite corrupted by living among these people, and, in fact, is going on in a way not worthy of him.'

Shelley himself was able to remain uncorrupted, sustaining his own faith in godless humanity against the romantic Christian sophistry that was attempting to arrogate the awesome beauty of the Alps to a divine landscape architect. According to Edward Trelawny, 'A clergyman wrote in the visitors' book at the Mer de Glace, Chamouni, something to the effect: "No one can view this sublime scene, and deny the existence of God", under which Shelley, using a Greek phrase, wrote, "P. B. Shelley, Atheist", thereby proclaiming his opinion to all the world.' Running into Wordsworth at Lausanne, Trelawny remarked the effervescent conversation of this dour northerner:

> Our icy islanders thaw rapidly when they have drifted into warmer latitudes: broken loose from its anti-social system, mystic casts, coteries, sets and

sects, they lay aside their purse-proud, tuft-hunting, and toadying ways, and are very apt to run riot in the enjoyment of all their senses.

Actually, many gentlemen on the Grand Tour, armed with their letters of introduction, tuft-hunted as never before. James Boswell, admittedly a Scot, took a revolting delight in hob-nobbing with the extravagantly titled continental noblesse. In Corsica, however, where Napoleon would shortly be born, Boswell's charm conquered a more rough-hewn audience, playing Scots tunes on his German flute:

> The Corsicans were charmed . . . My good friends insisted also to have an English song from me. I endeavoured to please them in this too, and was very lucky in that which occurred to me. I sung them 'Hearts of Oak are our ships, Hearts of Oak are our men'. I translated it into Italian for them, and never did I see men so delighted with a song as the Corsicans were with Hearts of Oak. 'Cuore di querco,' cried they, 'bravo Inglese.' It was quite a joyous riot. I fancied myself to be a recruiting sea-officer. I fancied my chorus of Corsicans aboard the British fleet.
>
> *Journal of a Tour to Corsica*, 1768

There is no doubt that the Grand Tour supplied a very broad and practical finish to a young man's education, and ideally made him adaptable, cultivated and diplomatic. However, the English have always accepted the risks of a practical education, and the letters of Lord Chesterfield to his son in 1749–50 suggest that English football supporters abroad are following a tradition that goes back a long way:

> I am informed there are now many English at the Academy in Turin; and I fear those are just so many dangers for you to encounter. Who they are I do not know, but I well know the general ill-conduct, the indecent behaviour, and the illiberal views of my young countrymen abroad; especially where they are in numbers together . . . There are degrees in vices as well as virtues; and I must do my countrymen the justice to say they generally take their vices in the lowest degree . . . Their pleasures of the table end in beastly drunkenness . . they either quarrel among themselves, or sally forth, to commit some riot in the streets and are taken up by the watch . . . Thus they return home more petulant, but not more informed than when they left it; and show, as they think, their improvement, by affectedly both speaking and dressing in broken French.

# *STYLE*

Dimly aware that refinement was not exactly their strong suit, the English, from the sixteenth century onwards, raided the French and Italian bastions of Classical learning, of culture, and of all that was 'soigné'. Pretty soon—such is the

English passion for doing the 'right thing'—a gentleman would not think much of himself if he had not shipped home some antique statuary, introduced *le dernier cri* in interior design into the family home, and developed an un-English interest in his wardrobe. Even the intractable Dr Johnson, visiting Paris for the first time at the age of 66, 'abandoned the black stockings, brown coat and plain shirt he customarily wore in London and appeared in white stockings, a new hat and a French-made wig of handsome construction'.

It can work the other way around, of course. Inveterately unfashionable himself, the Englishman is the cause of fashion in others. Every so often, the French wonder if they cannot do something with the sartorial mess to be seen striding confidently down the Promenade des Anglais, and so proceed to sport 'le look anglais' with sickening panache.

'Le look anglais' is, naturally, not allowable in English society. Lord Harris, attempting to awaken fashionable interest in his own local product, once risked a Harris-tweed suit at Ascot. While his rank got him into the royal enclosure, Edward VII was not impressed: 'Hullo Harris. Goin' rattin'?'

The English may allow the French and Italians their laurels in matters of taste, but they tend to be uneasy in the presence of excellence—whether intellectual, artistic or sartorial. De Saussure noted this tribal philistinism in a letter of 1730:

> I daresay it would interest you to hear of the style and the way Englishmen usually dress. They do not trouble themselves about dress, but leave that to their womenfolk. When the people see a well-dressed person in the streets, especially if he is wearing a braided coat, a plume in his hat, or his hair tied in a bow, he will, without doubt, be called 'French dog' twenty times perhaps before he reaches his destination. This name is the more common, and evidently, according to popular idea the greatest and most forcible insult that can be given to any man, and it is applied indifferently to all foreigners, French or otherwise.

At length publishers for the tourist trade realized that the last thing an English-man wants is to talk like a Frenchman: 'A Gentleman of Quality' provided guidance in his 1894 book *French for the English*:

> 'Why is there no marmalade available?' is better understood in the form 'Quelle marmalade non?' 'Bring marmalade' may be simply rendered as 'Marmalade demandez' always remembering that the z is silent as in 'deman-*day*'. The little English joke about jam may be easily translated if one wishes to amuse the proprietor: 'Hier, marmalade; demain, marmalade; mais jamais marmalade de jour.' Such little pleasantries are often appreciated.

With such a command of 'franglais' one may rest easy in the assurance that one will not be taken for a Frenchman. Lord Chesterfield threw off this particular embarrassment with sarcastic ease:

> I shall not give my opinion of the French, because many a Frenchman has paid me the highest compliment they think that they can pay to anyone, which is, 'Sir, you are just like one of us.' I shall only tell you that I am insolent; I talk a great deal; I am very loud and peremptory; I sing and dance as I go along and lastly I spend a monstrous deal of money in [wig] powder.

To go abroad puts one in the genial position of being able to make telling comparisons. Smollett (*Travels through France and Italy*, 1766), revolted at the condition of the 'temple of Cloacina' at his inn at Nîmes (the proprietress had provided a seat for the ease of her English visitors, but the French guests preferred not to use it), concluded: 'This is a degree of beastliness which would appear detestable even in the capital of North Britain.'

Hygiene did not, however, go further than was proper. Cleanliness came a poor second after decency. The first action of a recent British ambassador to Paris was to have all the bidets in the Embassy removed. The shocking thing about the French is that a seemingly insanitary people should have a bidet in every home: clearly they have an obsessive regard for their undercarriage. Mind you, the more esoteric aspects of an English gentleman's education, traditionally (at least from Victoria's reign) completed in Paris, benefited from a quick check-up afterwards by the family doctor; then the Englishman would be ready for the pure love of a good woman. And he would know what to look for; as Lord Curzon admonished his second wife, 'Ladies never move.'

For more refined appetites, France could provide a terrible gastronomic discovery. In an 1835 letter to Richard York, Sydney Smith told how he arrived at Dessein's hotel in Calais:

> To compare it with any hotel in England is a violation of common-sense in breakfasting and dining. Such butter was never spread in England, no English hen could lay such eggs, no English servant could brew such coffee. The waiter and the chambermaid were as well bred as Lord and Lady Carlisle . . . It fills me with despair and remorse to think how badly I have been fed—and how my time has been misspent and waisted [*sic*] . . .

One's heart goes out to the victim of the contempt of Prince Francesco Caracciolo (1752–1799), as expressed in a report to Ferdinand I:

> I encountered a small fat Englishman on my way here. Though I led him along paths of music, philosophy, art and history he diverged continually to the subject that pleased him most: that of food. How very extraordinary for a nation that seems to know nothing about the arts of the table except to produce vast quantities of roast beef and turtle soup, to be interested so

exclusively in that of which they understand nothing. And the same with religion: they have sixty religions and no sauce.

Caracciolo ended his life at the end of a rope, on the orders of Nelson.

# TRAVELLERS

Released from the necessity of having to write their own guidebooks, the English gentry went abroad increasingly for diversion. A pack of hounds had long been established at Rome. Switzerland, on the other hand, was hardly hunting country. Dispatched to the Alps to gaze at the scenery and fill their lungs with crisp mountain air, Englishmen decided that the best thing they could do with all that scenery was to ski down it—or, better still, hurtle down it on a toboggan at about 100mph. The artlessly puerile spirit that founded the British Alpine Club in 1857 (some years before the Swiss and the Austrians founded theirs) and the alarming Cresta Run (probably as close as most Englishmen in the Alps come to a religious experience unless they are given to Shelleyan ecstasies) is difficult to recapture. But it seems that, even today, Britain is the only country in the world whose sporting representatives have been known to borrow hi-tech equipment

English tourists in the Alps *c*1870. The Victorian gentleman was a family man. Even an expedition up a glacier could not guarantee him a quiet day with his alpenstock and a taciturn Swiss guide.

from their competitors and then put in boisterously amateur performances for their country.

Whether as sportsmen or as explorers, the English, though in this case we mean perhaps largely the Scots, seemed to get everywhere. In his *Diary of the Besieged Resident in Paris* (1871) Henry Labouchere remarked that 'The French have a notion that, go where you may, to the top of a pyramid or to the top of Mont Blanc, you are sure to meet an Englishman reading a newspaper'.

A curious corroboration of this vision of exploring the lonely heights of the world and always finding that an Englishman has got there first and made himself at home is met with in Peter Fleming's account in *News from Tartary* (1936) of crossing the Mintaka Pass from China at 15,600 feet: ' . . . the track was inexplicably decorated with a fragment of *The Times* newspaper, and I took this for a good omen . . .'

There is a rich mine of eccentricity to be mined among the English travellers and explorers—not so much with the organized expeditions perhaps, like those of James Cook, the great navigator of the Pacific, who quite simply set the standards of humane competence at sea, but rather with those of the lone adventurers. There is certainly something peculiarly English in their eccentricity.

In one of his letters Horace Walpole offered a theory:

> The most remarkable thing I have observed since I came abroad, is that there are no people so obviously mad as the English . . . In England tempers vary so excessively, that almost everyone's faults are peculiar to himself. I take this diversity to proceed partly from our climate, partly from our government. The first is changeable, and makes us queer; the latter permits our queernesses to operate as they please.

## OUTSIDERS

Joseph Wolff was extremely fortunate to be able to retire at last to Somerset, which he did in 1845. Born a German Jew, he converted to Catholicism—in which faith he resolved to become Pope Hildebrandus I and abolish celibacy and the worship of the saints—but found, after his expulsion from the Catholic Church, that his true spiritual home was in the broad bosom of the Church of England.

Beloved by his adopted compatriots, he became an utterly heroic and incompetent missionary. In 1821, robbed on the road from Gaza, he was rescued by a certain Major Mackworth. He was subjected to the *bastinado* in Baghdad in 1824, when Colonel George Keppel came to his aid. In 1825, prostrate with typhus on the road from Tiflis, he was picked up by Colonel Sir James Russel. Shipwrecked on the shores of Cephalonia in 1827, he was greeted by the governor, Colonel Charles Napier, with the words, 'I know your sister-in-law, Lady Catherine Long, very well. She is one of the prettiest women I ever saw.' In 1832, staggering stark naked across the Hindu Kush towards Kabul, Wolff could hardly pray for those guardian-angel British officers to save him another time. Yet, that very night, Lieutenant Alexander Burnes arrived as the vanguard of the ill-fated British presence in that city.

Consequently, when in 1843 Wolff learnt of two British officers held hostage by the frightful Amir of Bukhara, he set off alone to rescue them, armed only with bibles, silver watches and three dozen copies of *Robinson Crusoe* in Arabic. It was Wolff's last, most futile and provocative trip. The two officers were long dead and Wolff very nearly joined them. But the gesture was appreciated, and his quixotic venture had the sort of moral effect throughout Central Asia that the British knew how to value.

A cleric of a different stamp, as offensive as Wolff was harmless, was Bishop Hervey, Earl of Bristol, who spent the large part of his ministry on the European continent collecting art, and who was described by one English observer as 'an Atheist, though a Bishop, constantly talking blasphemy, or indecently at least'. Hervey told Goethe that '*Werther* is a completely immoral damnable book'. But, as Goethe said of him, 'It was sometimes his whim to be offensive, but if one treated him equally offensively he would become perfectly amenable.'

Even Hervey's friends had to make allowances. He visited Lady Hamilton (this was pre-Nelson) and the two of them were joined by a lady of some notoriety in Neapolitan society. Hervey got up to leave, saying: 'It is permitted for a bishop to visit one sinner, but quite unfitting that he should be seen in a brothel.'

Englishmen have always had trouble with religious processions abroad. Not wanting to prostrate themselves in the mud or be assaulted for not doing so, they were best advised to be inconspicuous and discreet. It was quite unnecessary for Bishop Hervey, vexed as he may have been by the procession of Corpus Christi passing beneath his window at Siena when he was trying to eat his dinner, to seize a tureen of hot pasta and throw the contents into the middle of the sacred group. He had to move very quickly, for an old man, to make his escape to Padua.

On the other hand, it may be that the bishop was surreptitiously a kind man. A surprise visitor to his house in Naples reported:

> A decent elderly woman came in to pay her respects and asked him how he did. 'Like a Bishop', says he, and pointing to a pile of stuff—'look here,' says he, 'this is for you' . . . she burst into tears, and began kissing his hand, saying she was not worthy to kiss his hand, and would like to kiss his foot. 'No,' says he, 'I am no Pope, tho' I am a Bishop. I am a heretic and must be damned you know?'

He was imprisoned for a while by the French for espionage; in the true manner of an eighteenth-century Englishman he reported everything he saw, and was not prepared for a more cautious—not to say paranoid—age in the wake of the Revolution. Hervey eventually died in 1803.

His monument in his diocese of Derry was subscribed to by both the Roman Catholic bishop and the Dissenting minister. Maybe this was in recognition of his humanity, or maybe it was merely that they appreciated that their own pastoral missions showed up rather well by comparison with his—it is hard to say. But an Irish girl, Catherine Wilmot, who saw Hervey in Rome a few months before his death did not see a man preparing to meet his Maker: 'The last time I saw him he was sitting in his carriage between two Italian women, dress'd in white Bed-gown and Night-cap like a witch and giving himself the airs of an Adonis.'

In 1817 Charles Waterton, the naturalist, arrived in Rome on a pilgrimage. Here he fell in with an old school chum, a certain Captain Jones. The necessity to celebrate their schooldays overcoming their reverence for the great monuments of their faith (they had both been at Stonyhurst), the two of them climbed the dome of St Peter's and left their gloves on top of the lightning conductor. Warming to their work, they proceeded to take on the Castello di Sant' Angelo, each posing on one leg on the head of the guardian angel. No Roman steeplejack being found who was prepared to do the job, Waterton very gallantly pacified his spiritual headmaster by going up again to fetch down the gloves.

As a taxidermist, Waterton liked to capture animals alive. In South America he wrestled with boa-constrictors, in true *Boy's Own* fashion using his braces to tie up their jaws. To get a specimen of a cayman he had to ride the beast as it plunged for freedom: 'Should it be asked', he wrote in his *Wanderings in South America* (1823), 'how I managed to keep my seat, I would answer, I hunted some years with Lord Darlington's fox hounds . . .'

He returned home to his estate in Yorkshire, where, flapping a pair of crude wings, he dove off a farm building. Deciding to take his study of aviation no further, he returned to taxidermy. At the same time that Charles Darwin was preparing to outrage the religious Establishment with the idea that they were close relatives of the great apes, Waterton was remodelling a series of specimens of South American primates to make them look like the great heresiarchs of the Protestant Reformation.

# *EXPLORERS OF THE NILE*

In 1857 the Royal Geographical Society, subsidizing that great epic of nineteenth-century exploration, the quest for the source of the Nile, made an odd choice of joint leaders, Sir Richard Burton and John Speke. Speke, a big-game hunter and teetotaller—unreflective, sanctimonious, and a veteran of the Sikh wars, the very model of a Victorian public-school man—had already had a difficult time with Burton on an expedition to Somaliland. Burton, satanic and fascinating, was the model of a villain from some Victorian melodrama. His fond and unperceptive father had intended him for the Church. Instead Burton had gone to India, where Charles Napier, with a sure instinct for finding the man for the job, had appointed him to investigate the homosexual brothels of Karachi. Burton immediately found his vocation; subsequently he was to win a general notoriety as a connoisseur and translator of oriental 'curiosa'.

Speke averted his eyes when confronted with stark naked savages; Burton was more likely to pull out his ruler. Together, however, they discovered in 1858 Lake Tanganyika. Then, leaving Burton to rest for a while, Speke came across Lake Victoria; this, to Burton's disgust, Speke declared (on very flimsy evidence) to be the source of the White Nile. In 1860 the Royal Geographical Society commissioned Speke to go back to Africa and confirm his discovery. This time he was accompanied by a more upright and straightforward—if not so clever—colleague, James Grant, a veteran of the Indian Mutiny. 'The Nile is settled,' Speke cabled home firmly.

Burton, meanwhile, ignored on his return to England, went on to pursue his distasteful anthropological researches in West Africa; among other concerns, he was eager to get hold of gorilla's brains, said to be a powerful aphrodisiac.

Five years after their expedition together, Burton and Speke were invited to sort out their differences about the source of the Nile in a public debate arranged by the Royal Geographical Society. They met briefly the day before, without a word, and Speke went out and accidentally shot himself. The sort of man who would take on the devil himself in a stand-up fight might well crumble at the prospect of confronting Mephistopheles in a lecture hall.

Clearly, African explorers were not what they had been. But worse was yet to come. When David Livingstone, seen from a considerable distance by the British public as a saintly hero, was appointed to clear up this business of the Nile once and for all, and when Henry Stanley was commissioned by an American newspaper to rescue him, the stage was set for Britain's most outrageous double-act in darkest Africa. Stanley was subsequently to clear up the mystery of the Nile with typical ruthless, no-expense-spared American efficiency. But, when he ran to earth the great living national treasure, Livingstone, he realized that the solemnity of the occasion required him to conduct himself as an Englishman would. He approached with the unruffled courtesy of a gentleman meeting someone off a train. In an agony of self-consciousness he walked deliberately up to Livingstone, took off his hat, and said:

> 'Dr Livingstone, I presume?'
> 'Yes,' said he, with a kind smile, lifting his cap slightly.

The British public really appreciated this absurdly bathetic tableau. The Royal Geographical Society, however, was unmoved. One distinguished Fellow of the Society, Clements Markham, dismissed Livingstone as 'not an accomplished traveller', while Stanley was simply 'a howling cad': 'Damn public estimation, the fellow has done no geography!'

# THE SOUTH POLE

Just as Africa was the proper sphere for enterprising British army officers, so Polar exploration was the preserve of the Royal Navy. The Elizabethan Martin Frobisher and the Victorian John Franklin—who with all his men, died amid the frozen seas of the Arctic in 1845—were engaged in the same centuries old project: trying to find the Northwest Passage. Captain Robert Scott and his rival Ernest Shackleton explored the southern ice-cap in the wake of Captain James Cook and James Ross.

Shackleton was a plausible Irishman. On the voyage of the *Discovery* under Scott in 1901–4 he had brought with him a make-up box, conjuring tricks and the works of Browning. It was only to be expected that he might be tricky and underhand enough to steal Scott's thunder by making his own assault on the South Pole in 1908 from Scott's Antarctic base. Getting to within 100 miles of it, he galvanized Scott to make his own, doomed, attempt.

Shackleton thoroughly enjoyed being honoured, fêted and knighted. Robert Scott, however, would be knighted only posthumously—he was anyway ill-at-ease in the limelight. Nor would he be the first to reach the South Pole. The Norwegian Roald Amundsen, thoroughly professional, well equipped, lucky and sharp, if not sneaky, did that as soon as he knew that Scott was on his way. What Scott did achieve was to record his gallant failure, and the fortitude of his party, manifestly unfavoured by the gods, in such a way as to make mere success a small and picayune thing by comparison.

The chivalric attitude had been instilled into Scott's first expedition by Sir Clements Markham, who had insisted on each officer and scientist taking with him his own flag and motto, designed by Markham himself, to be attached to their sledges in what he assured them was the grand tradition of English polar exploration. Scott's motto was the old watchword of the Royal Navy, 'Ready, Aye Ready'. Edward Wilson, who was to die with Scott on the journey back from the Pole, was given, as his 'strange device', *Le Bon Temps Viendra*. (Markham was a godfather to Scott's son. The other godfather was J. M. Barrie, which was why the boy was called Peter.)

Another piece of cultural equipment burdening Scott was a disinclination to submit animals, particularly dogs, to the ruthless exploitation and privations that polar expeditions required. He justified his decision not to rely on dogs by suggesting that it was not quite playing the game.

The gallant Captain Scott tried to emphasize austerely that his
expedition was a scientific rather than a sporting one: 'Any attempt to
race must have wrecked my plan, besides which it doesn't appear the
sort of thing one is out for.'

Scott and his four companions, having arrived at the South Pole and found
they had been beaten to it, died on the long walk home in the ordinary way of
polar explorers – of frost-bite and scurvy and starvation. But Scott's diary and
letters, which he dutifully composed while he led his dying men to the limits of
their strength, ensured the immortality of the expedition members in the nation's
consciousness, imbued as they were with Scott's knowledge of the code and
conduct of the English gentleman in a tight spot. It fell to the 'soldier', Captain
Lawrence Oates, to show how a British officer goes to his death. His memorial
inscription read: 'Hereabouts died a very gallant gentleman, Captain L. E. G.
Oates of the Inniskilling Dragoons. In March 1912, returning from the Pole, he
walked willingly to his death in a blizzard to try to save his comrades, beset by
hardship'.

There is nothing particularly English about gallantry, but the way in which
it is expressed may be. Oates's last words were a laconic masterpiece of good
taste: 'I am just going outside, and may be some time.' Scott wrote: 'Though we
tried to dissuade him, we knew it was the act of a brave man and an English
gentleman.' Stephen Gwynne, in his book *Captain Scott* (1929), wrote of Scott that

> His supreme achievement is that he touched the imagination of his country
> as no other man has done during the course of this century . . . He imposed

*195*

upon the public his own set of values—yet not as his own, but as the standard by which England should measure the worth of action . . . To the very end when we can look into his mind, we find him constantly at watch on himself, for ever keeping himself up to the mark—never content to let himself rest or slacken.

## A FEW TIPS

To the Englishman the exercise of practical ingenuity and boy-scout resourcefulness is one of the chief attractions of travelling. There is nothing a hard-bitten traveller likes better than to offer the fruits of his experience to those who follow:

> A frank, joking, but determined manner, joined with an air of showing more faith in the natives than you really feel, is the best. It is observed that a sea-captain generally succeeds in making an excellent impression on savages: they thoroughly appreciate common sense, truth, and uprightness; and are not half such fools as strangers usually account them.
>
> Sir Francis Galton, *The Art of Travel*, 1867

In short, the manner that the Englishman generally adopts as soon as he steps off the boat at Calais will serve pretty well wherever he goes.

> In the matter of language it is always best to go to a little more trouble and learn the exact equivalent if possible. 'I am an Englishman and require instant attention to the damage done to my solar topee' is far better than any equivocation that may be meant well but will gain little respect.
>
> *Guide to the Native Languages of Africa*,
> 'A Gentleman of Experience', 1890

> With the single exception of the best brands of champagne, the writer is unable to recommend, beside pure whisky and brandy, any other form of alcoholic beverage for use in the tropics. Beer and porter, especially the stronger kinds, provoke liver derangements and claret of good quality can rarely be obtained by the traveller.
>
> Freshfield, Wharton and Dobson, *Hints to Travellers*, 1889

One SAS major offered advice on how to survive in Borneo: 'Get some jungle boots, good thick trousers and strong shirts. You won't want to nancy about in shorts once the first leech has had a go at you, believe me.' Another expert gave a few tips on social survival in Borneo: 'Oh yes—take *lots* of postcards of the Queen, preferably on horseback, and showing all four legs, because they think she's all of a piece.' (Redmond O'Hanlan, *Into the Heart of Borneo*, 1984.)

In *Eōthen* (1844), Alexander Kinglake provided an illuminating version of an interview with the Pasha at Belgrade, showing the difficulty of interpreting between the essential Englishman and the essential Turk—between the magniloquence that is vital to the Turk and the plain speaking that is vital to the Englishman:

**DRAGOMAN** (to the Pasha): His Lordship, this Englishman, Lord of London, scorner of Ireland, Suppressor of France, has quitted his governments, and left his enemies to breathe for a moment, and has crossed the broad waters in strict disguise, with a small but eternally faithful retinue of followers, in order that he might look upon the bright countenance of the Pasha among Pashas—the Pasha of the everlasting Pashalik of Karagholookoldour.

**TRAVELLER** (to his dragoman): What on earth have you been saying about London? The Pasha will be taking me for a mere cockney. Have not I told you *always* to say, that I am from a branch of the family of Mudcombe Park, and that I am to be a magistrate for the county of Bedfordshire, only I've not qualified, and that I should have been a Deputy-Lieutenant, if it had not been for the extraordinary conduct of Lord Mountpromise, and that I was a candidate for Goldborough at the last election, and that I should have won easy, if my committee had not been bought. I wish to heaven that if you *do* say anything about me, you'd tell the simple truth.

**DRAGOMAN**: [is silent]

**PASHA**: What says the friendly Lord of London? Is there aught that I can grant him within the pashalik of Karagholookoldour?

**DRAGOMAN** (growing sulky and literal): This friendly Englishman—this branch of Mudcombe—this head-purveyor of Goldborough—this possible policeman of Bedfordshire is recounting his achievements, and the number of his titles.

**PASHA**: The end of his honours is more distant than the ends of the Earth, and the catalogue of his glorious deeds is brighter than the firmament of Heaven!

*Chairing the Member* engraving after Hogarth. A print of the last of four
canvases satirizing the farce of an English election. Liberty included
the liberty to buy and sell votes, and to intimidate people so that they
could stand up to your intimidation like Englishmen. The English
constitution at this time was the envy of Europe.

# CHAPTER ELEVEN

———— • ————

# THE ENGLISHMAN'S LIBERTY

B ritish slaves were known in Rome to be unreliable, surly and of particularly poor quality. Tacitus wrote in *Agricola*: 'The Britons themselves submit to levies, tribute and the tasks laid upon them by the government, if they are not treated oppressively. Oppression they cannot bear, being reduced far enough to give obedience, but not yet far enough to be slaves.'

The idea of liberty may be vitally important to the English, but they are little interested in abstract formulations of class oppression. Talleyrand, in 1792, had almost given up on the English: 'The truth is that the mass of the nation is generally indifferent to those political discussions that cause so much stir among us.'

Raising the revolutionary consciousness of the English working man is indeed uphill work. In *Venice Preserv'd* (1682) Thomas Otway suggested that English liberty stands upon a modest enough platform:

> Give but an Englishman his whore and ease,
> Beef and a sea-coal fire, he's yours for ever.

One might add, give him a patch in which to grow prize leeks, allow him his pigeons and ferrets, his flower shows and his dog shows, his bingo, his matchbox tops and his wine societies, his darts, his snooker, his bowls and his golf—in short, what Matthew Arnold called 'an Englishman's heaven-born privilege of doing as he likes' (*Culture and Anarchy*, 1869). If, on top of all that, you don't empower anyone in a uniform to stop him in an English street and ask him for his identity papers, he will consider himself a free man.

## *THE CONSTITUTION*

Suspicious of both the government of the day and state interference—not that they have a 'state' that one can put one's finger on—the English retain an

*199*

extraordinary trust in the power of their constitution to meet their needs. It can do this because no one can say what it is—not exactly, anyway. 'It's an unwritten constitution,' say the English loftily. This at least makes it extremely flexible. A. J. P. Taylor offered a rule-of-thumb guide: 'In our flexible system any practice is constitutional which is tolerated by contemporaries.'

The Houses of Parliament look suitably immemorial and vaguely medieval, despite having been built in 1834. Correspondingly, according to Walter Bagehot in his *The English Constitution* (1867), England became in 1832 a 'disguised Republic'; while remaining to all appearances a 'constitutional monarchy', except that what he called the 'dignified' and the 'efficient' parts of government were separated without people really noticing: 'The characteristic merit of the English Constitution is, that its dignified parts are very complicated and somewhat imposing, very old and rather venerable; while its efficient part, at least when in great and critical action, is decidedly simple and rather modern.' Bagehot is sometimes impatient with a lot of the useless flab that this elderly gentlemen has to carry:

> According to our system the Chancellor of the Exchequer is the enemy of the Exchequer; a whole series of enactments try to protect it from him. Until a few months ago there was a very lucrative sinecure called the 'Comptrollership of the Exchequer', designed to guard the Exchequer against the Chancellor; and the last holder, Lord Mounteagle, used to say he was the pivot of the English Constitution . . .

For all this weight of tradition, though, the constitution very often operates more nimbly than many a foreign set of government machinery, however trimly and explicitly laid out.

War leaders are something of a speciality with the English. No sooner does disaster strike their gallant but minute little army than Lloyd George or Winston Churchill is drummed into office to take charge. (Bagehot cited the case of Palmerston, called in in place of Lord Liverpool during the crisis of the Crimean War. As it was said at the time, 'We turned out the Quaker, and put in the pugilist.')

This is where the vagueness about the constitution becomes a genuine advantage: the English can appoint a dictator like Churchill to get things done, and his authoritarian style will be untrammelled by any strict limits to his powers. Trust, though, is the key. The English actually believe that their liberties are implicitly guaranteed, not only by the Bill of Rights of 1688 but simply by breathing the air of England:

> Slaves cannot breathe in England; if their lungs
> Receive our air, that moment they are free . . .

Thus wrote Cowper in 'The Task' in 1784, ignoring the fact that the British slave trade was not abolished until 1807—and the last slave not emancipated until 1834.

The liberties of the English are rooted in history, experience, precedent and tradition, rather than being founded upon some set of principles designed by well meaning people—who might, for example, consider that the right to bear arms should be a fundamental liberty. But there is a problem: Magna Carta and Habeas Corpus are no talisman against an unscrupulous prime minister, because as far as safeguarding English liberties goes they are not worth the parchment they are inscribed on.

What Stephen Langton did when he cornered King John on 15 June 1215 was to set up a battle standard for posterity, and to make Runnymede a place of pilgrimage for American lawyers: 'No free man shall be taken or imprisoned or dispossessed or exiled or in any way destroyed, nor will we go unto him . . . except by the lawful judgement of his peers or the law of the land.' Nowadays, of course, the principles agreed at Runnymede are usually pre-empted by those of the European Court of Human rights, where Britannia—with the shifty, weasally demeanour of the constant offender—is so embarrassingly often found in the dock.

The English do not like to throw things away. One just never knows when they might come in useful. One may tell the time by one's digital watch, but meanwhile the old grandfather clock keeps ticking away, still vaguely reliable and profoundly impressive. Bagehot identified the Crown and the House of Lords as the 'dignified' parts of the constitution. Today, even the House of Commons and the Cabinet are largely bits of machinery that keep ticking away, while the real business is carried on in 'smoke-filled rooms', or indeed by the prime minister alone.

Rowdy schoolboy behaviour, 'unparliamentary' language, and occasional physical violence are, however, the sure signs that the democratic process is still alive and kicking in the House of Commons. A German visitor in 1827, although appalled by 'the want of decorum' in the Lower House, nevertheless concluded: 'When I question myself as to the total impression of this day, I must confess that it was at once elevating and melancholy; the former when I fancied myself an Englishman, the latter when I felt that I was a German' (A German Prince, *A Tour in Germany, Holland and England in the Years 1826, 1827 and 1828*, 1832).

# THE LAW

As Bagehot pointed out, 'of all nations in the world the English are perhaps the least a nation of philosophers'. They distrust hard and fast principles and political systems. The result is that, as G. K. Chesterton put it in an article in the *Daily News* in 1905, 'The English law . . . is uncommonly like an impressionistic picture of a rainy day. The Code Napoleon is like a coloured photograph of Rome'—which gives a very rough idea of the difference between Roman and common law.

The Anglo-Saxons were ruled by loyalty and custom. The king would clarify these customs by taking the advice of his wisest subjects. And the Anglo-Saxon mentality retains a stubborn instinct for right and wrong. Kipling's Saxon, as seen through the eyes of his imagined Norman Baron (who seems to be more than the ignorant delinquent that almost every other Norman baron was), reflects the picture that the English like to have of their rude beginnings—rough-hewn but already pregnant with the majesty of British justice:

> The Saxon is not like us Normans. His manners are not so polite.
> But he never means anything serious till he talks about justice and right,
> When he stands like an ox in the furrow with his sullen set eyes on your own,
> And grumbles, 'This isn't fair dealing,' my son, leave the Saxon alone.

'Norman and Saxon'

Norman kings established a common law that overruled feudal jurisdiction, a common law rooted in custom and past cases rather than in fixed and fundamental principles laid down by a lawgiver. In the twelfth century, under the common law, one could not be imprisoned for an undefined offence, one had the right to know who one's accusers were, and one could not be interrogated without trial, which meant that one had a right to silence. In a barbarous age, these principles of the Englishman's liberty were as miraculous an achievement as the greatest Gothic cathedrals. And there are few Englishmen who would not sooner see Westminster Abbey reduced to a heap of rubble than allow the basic principles of British justice—those principles that have won the freedom of the individual throughout the world—to be limited, clipped away, prorogued or hedged about to fulfil the national security needs of a paranoiac and dishonourable executive. Exactly this happened during the wars with Revolutionary France, when Habeas Corpus was suspended and Wordsworth and Coleridge, on their long rambles in the Lake District, were followed by government spies on the suspicion that they were agents not only of revolutionary poetry but also of Revolutionary France.

For six or seven hundred years every individual in England has been supposedly free and equal before the law, and has been considered innocent until proved guilty by a jury of twelve good men and true—the celebrated but delicate 'Golden Thread' that runs through the English legal system. It is the pride of the common law that it is no respecter of persons. Indeed, according to Sir Thomas Elyot in *The Boke of the Governour* (1531), on one occasion the son and heir of Henry IV, Prince Hal, was committed for contempt. His father was delighted to have 'a judge, who feareth nat to ministre justice, and also a sonne who can suffre semblably and obey justice'.

Edward Coke, as Chief Justice of the Court of Common Pleas under James I, probably sailed the majesty of the law as close to the royal wind as anyone. James I, like his unfortunate son, never mastered the great English art of fudging issues and letting sleeping dogs lie. The only King of England in 1000 years to write a book (though George III—known as 'Farmer George'—contributed to the *Agricultural Magazine* under the name Robinson), James wanted everything out on the table where he could see it. In November 1608 he met the Judges of the realm to graciously assure them that he, as king, would always protect the common law. Coke, to his eternal credit, took a deep breath and pointed out the flaw in this kindly gesture: 'The common law protecteth the king,' he said mildly. James, spluttering with rage, called him a traitor, and Coke was obliged to administer the final insult to his bookish sovereign by remarking that his majesty was not learned in the laws of his realm of England. But ever the diplomat and seeing that James appeared to be about to have a fit, he grovelled for pardon.

The king, seeing that his chief minister, Robert Cecil, had joined Coke on all fours, demanded: 'What hast thou to do to intreat for him?'

'In regard he hath married my nearest kinswoman,' Cecil fudged magnificently.

## THE CROWN

The English learnt very early on to distinguish between the Crown and the person of the monarch, so that a sort of loyalty to the office could be maintained while disposing of an unsuitable incumbent. The loyalty has remained a potent unifying force ever since. As we have seen, the concept of the state has no precise meaning for the English, and so instead they have the Crown. Over the Crown there still hovers the idea of a relationship, whereas the idea of the state is somehow alien and totalitarian: as Bagehot insisted, 'our freedom is the result of centuries of resistance, more or less legal, or more or less illegal, more or less audacious or more or less timid, to the executive government . . . We look on State action, not as our own action, but as alien action.'

The war-cry of the Peasants' revolt was 'King and Commons', that of the Roundheads, 'King and Parliament'. In our own day the wives of striking miners have appealed with petitions to the Queen. The Crown still commands a higher loyalty than the government in office. As their attempts to interfere with government became increasingly ignored, the royal family learnt to offer guidance in modes, morals and mores instead. But, retaining as it does the vestiges of ancient prerogatives, the monarchy can be a powerful focus for popular opinion when a long-standing executive and a centralized bureaucracy lose touch with human needs, realities and rights.

In the seventeenth century, Lord Halifax had already recognized that the monarchy was about as necessary as the fairy on the top of the Christmas tree: 'Monarchy is liked by the people for the bells and the tinsel, the outward pomp and gilding, and there must be milk for babes, since the greatest part of mankind are, and ever will be, included in that list . . .'

The idea is to engage the national emotions in great occasions like a royal wedding (what Bagehot calls 'the brilliant edition of a universal fact') where they can do no harm, while a few sensible if unattractive people actually govern the country – 'the last people in the world to whom, if they were drawn up in a row, an immense nation would ever give an exclusive preference' (Bagehot again). The English tend even now to be suspicious of an obviously imposing politician. Certainly an English politician should think carefully before capping his teeth, straightening his nose or dying his hair: the English public, not born yesterday, wants to see faults and weaknesses. If a politician's image is too studied, he is trying to set himself up as an icon. The monarchy is the only national icon the English will generally put up with.

And there is nothing deferential in their worship of it. In his *England* (1970) Nikos Kazantzakis, the author of *Zorba the Greek*, recalled an incident from about 1940:

> The train arrived. The King appeared, smiling, slender, slightly weary. All the Englishmen thundered and waved their arms and opened their mouths to sing. Some sang the royal anthem, others sang gay, simple little tunes. And a few of them chanted psalms from the Gospels. There was no slavish uniformity here. Everyone was expressing his joy, but freely, in his own separate way. In England the masses manage to save their independence and individual dignity from getting completely drowned. They are no herd, dully and monolithically following a slogan. They know how to take the same slogan and adapt it to a completely different entity. They bestow a nuance of freedom upon necessity, and they chant religious hymns or gay songs or national anthems, each group with its own spirit, to welcome back their King.

Edmund Burke's view – and it is perhaps the rationale or even the rationalization for the British constitution – is that society cannot be forcibly wrenched into perfect order. In 1660 the English completed their great experiment. They had found the only period in their history when they had been without a monarch interesting but uncomfortable. They hadn't been able to *relax*. There had been a lot of enthusiastic moral interference in their lives, some bizarre legislation (such as adultery being punishable by death, although there is no evidence that any jury was prepared to give a verdict of guilty in such a case), a plague of batty religious ideas aired, and a lot of soldiers about – in fact, they had experienced a military dictatorship. Since this was England, it had not been as bad as it might sound. But the restoration of the monarchy was like returning to a roaring log fire after a brisk and invigorating walk on a rather foul day.

Lord Clarendon addressed Parliament in September 1660:

> The King is a suitor to you . . . that you will join with him in restoring the whole nation to its primitive temper and integrity, its old good manners, its old good humour and its old good nature; good nature a virtue so peculiar to you, that it can be translated into no other language, hardly practised by any other people . . .

The old Establishment was back, and everyone could put their feet up. There would be no unpleasantness. Of course, the Stuarts would in due course have to go—mulishly Papist—and William the Dutchman would prove disappointing. Charles II had been disgusted to see William of Orange go to bed on his wedding night dressed in woollen drawers—hardly the attitude one looks for in someone who is supposed to be founding a dynasty. The German family, though, proved almost ideal, took to the job like a duck to water and, barring the occasional wobble, have stuck at it ever since.

Turning a constitutional monarchy into a parliamentary democracy over a period of 300 years without a major constitutional crisis was the very considerable achievement of the great English Establishment.

## THE ESTABLISHMENT

The ruling class has been allowed a long innings. The main reason for this is their acceptance of the principle of primogeniture, established by law in 1295. Concentrating landed wealth and aristocratic titles in a few hands, it cruelly thrust younger sons out into the world to do something useful. Thus in England the governing class has never conformed to an aristocracy, or caste. Unlike anywhere else, the younger sons of noblemen are commoners—or, rather, gentlemen.

This wonderfully affirming title, the richest prize in English social life, and in general awarded by those below one in the social scale ('he's a real gent') and denied by those above ('he is not a gentleman'), is an open class. The middle classes are pacified by the promise that they have only to make enough money in order themselves, within a generation, to be accepted as gentlemen equal in rank, if not in 'connections', with the surplus offspring of the greatest houses in the land. Thus the ruling class is continually flushed through with new blood —and, more importantly, new money. The nobility has never been much concerned with 'blood' as such; indeed, upstart heiresses have been welcomed with delight as daughters-in-law.

People wonder what exactly makes a gentleman, how a gentleman should behave, and so on. Actually it's chillingly simple. If one was born into a bit of money and brought up as an Englishman, then one is a gentleman. The idea is that, having made a lot of money, one is in a position to take up power, but first one has to submit to the notion that money isn't everything. Now that money is generally accepted to be fairly nearly everything, the concept of the gentleman is almost obsolete. (As late as the 1960s, however, cricket pavilions had different changing rooms for 'gentlemen', who had initials and, at the end of their names, 'Esq.', and 'players', who didn't. Thus an unreliable middle-order bat or an erratic off-spinner might be 'J. E. Smith Esq.' on the scorecard, while the star player might be, and probably would be, just plain 'Smith'.)

Essentially, then, being a gentleman meant that one didn't do things for money, although exceptions might be made if one did things for sufficiently large sums of money. This is one of the reasons that England is a country of amateurs, of voluntary societies, of charitable organizations, of local worthies running local affairs. And local worthies have been running local affairs since Anglo-Saxon times. Even when a succession of strong and nasty Norman Kings imposed a centralized government, no bureaucracy built up. From the fourteenth century, local worthies acted as unpaid JPs: this amateur, semi-feudal administration of the law is a peculiarly English institution.

Hilaire Belloc's 'The Justice of the Peace' gives us a sardonic look at this curious official:

> Distinguish carefully between these two,
>     This thing is yours, that other thing is mine.
> You have a shirt, a brimless hat, a shoe
>     And half a coat. I am the Lord benign
> Of fifty hundred acres of fat land
> To which I have a right. You understand?
>
> I have a right because I have, because,
>     Because I have—because I have a right.
> Now be quite calm and good, obey the laws,
>     Remember your low station, do not fight
> Against the goad, you know, it pricks
> Whenever the uncleanly demos kicks.
>
> I do not envy you your hat, your shoe.
>     Why should you envy me my small estate?
> It's fearfully illogical in you
>     To fight with economic force and fate.
> Moreover, I have got the upper hand,
> And mean to keep it. Do you understand?

Mrs Hemans' celebrated eulogy of the country seats of the English ruling classes

'The Homes of England', made one important point: they were 'home'. The country squire belonged to his domain as much as it belonged to him:

> The stately homes of England,
> How beautiful they stand . . .

But Noel Coward completed the verse with a steely aside of his own:

> To prove the upper classes
> Have still the upper hand.

The rule of the Lord of the Manor, and other feudal survivals, were eventually challenged by democratic voices, particularly from the growing centres of population. In a pamphlet issued in 1837 Richard Cobden revealed: 'A late parliamentary candidate for the borough of Salford held the high office of ale taster; and the Manchester Directory for 1833 records that our richest banker, an individual whose princely fortune would entitle him to a dukedom in any other country in Europe, held the responsible post of *muzzler of mastiff dogs and bitches* . . .' Recalling the Peterloo massacre of 16 August 1819, in which a political rally was dispersed with the loss of 11 lives, Cobden urged Mancunians to

> INCORPORATE YOUR BOROUGH! And thenceforth . . . (no) Tory squire or parson will ever come into your town at the head of a dozen magisterial bumpkins, first to let loose a troop of fox hunters, disguised as yeomanry cavalry, to try the metal of their swords upon helpless women and children, and afterwards to return public thanks to the officers and men for their extreme forbearance on the occasion!

This feudal irruption into the politically aware world of nineteenth-century Manchester was the sort of mistake the ruling class so rarely made. To the question, 'What shall we come to in this country? Shall we lose our property?' the Duke of Wellington replied: 'Yes, we shall not have a commotion, we shall not have blood, but we shall be plundered by forms of law.' As he surveyed the sea of newly elected MPs from the peers' gallery after the Reform Bill of 1832, he avowed, 'I have never seen so many bad hats in my life.' On the same occasion Lord Bathurst muttered, more portentously, 'Ichabod, for the glory is departed.' Which seems to have been overdoing it a bit until we realize that, for all the march of history, in many places in England time had stood still. The local squires 'owned' the votes of their tenants; they even effectively owned their opinions. This was the reality beneath the hazy graciousness of benevolent paternalism, milady visiting the poor and the sick, the devoted forelock-pulling, and the peasants all gathering in the great hall to drink enthusiastic toasts to their lord and master. It was nearly all genuine, though—genuine loyalty and genuine benevolence. John Stuart Mill wrote in a letter to Giuseppe Mazzini:

> The English of all ranks and classes, are at bottom, in all their feelings, aristocrats . . . the very idea of equality is strange and offensive to them. They do not dislike to have many people above them as long as they have some below them . . .

In short, English liberty includes the liberty to look down your nose at the Jones's and to get in with the local squire. Thackeray encapsulated it in *Vanity Fair* (1847–8): 'Whenever he met a great man, he grovelled before him as only a free-born Englishman can do.'

# *TORY DEMOCRACY AND THE MANDARINS*

As early as 1835 Disraeli made the extraordinary claim that 'the Tory party in this country is the national party; it is the really democratic party of England'. So that was all right then. No need for anything silly like a revolution. The aristocracy in England, unlike anywhere else, kept the middle classes from taking power by not resisting. This political judo is described by Palmerston: 'Separate by reasonable concessions the moderate from the exaggerated, content the former by fair concessions and get them to assist in resisting the insatiable demands of the latter.'

The Primrose League, founded by Lord Randolph Churchill, was an early version of the Young Conservatives. It provided an opportunity for people of the most modest social background to hobnob with the upper classes and meet persons of the opposite sex. No wonder Marx was disappointed. 'But what is a "Tory Democracy"?' Wilfred Scawen Blunt once privately asked Randolph Churchill. 'To tell the truth I don't know myself what "Tory Democracy" is,' Lord Randolph replied, 'but I believe it is principally opportunism.'

Harold Macmillan described the rapid adjustments that were made to enable a man who was quite clearly the antithesis of a gentleman to take the office for which he was otherwise so well equipped:

> Shortly before Disraeli became Leader of the Party, the old Duke [of Portland]'s sons, Lord George Bentinck and Lord Henry Bentinck, came to him and said: 'Father, there is only one man who can lead the Tory Party—and he is a fancy little Jew.' 'But is he a country gentleman?' asked the Duke. 'No,' they said, 'he is a fancy little Jew.' 'Only a country gentleman can lead the Tory Party,' said the Duke. 'We'll make him one,' said the sons.

And they did. They provided him with an estate, on loan.

In 1923 the Establishment did not panic when the Tories failed to secure an overall majority. It courteously held the door open for the Labour party, in coalition with the Liberals, to lead a government for the first time. George VI muttered a resumé of the Establishment's reasons for sanguinity after Labour's landslide victory in 1945: 'Thank God for the Civil Service.'

Appointed head of Edward Heath's 'Think Tank' in 1970, Victor Rothschild was suddenly initiated into the secret of British politics: 'I never realized the country was run by two men whom I've never heard of.' The Civil Service is the last-ditch defence of the Establishment. From here, armed with red tape, bland, sceptical and sly, it will no doubt continue to fight until the bitter end. It is a typically foggy institution in which reforms, particularly of itself, can get completely lost. People were worried in the nineteenth century that the introduction of competitive examinations to replace appointment by patronage would bring all sorts of chaps into the Civil Service who were just not quite right. 'There are places in life which can hardly be well filled except by "Gentlemen",' wrote Anthony Trollope plaintively in his autobiography. He need not have worried. The Civil Service looks after the Establishment by all sorts of concealed manoeuvres and is certainly not to be penetrated by anything so ephemeral as a democratically elected government.

The mandarins are fastidiously contemptuous of the politicians who stride down their corridors reeking of vulgar political battles. Sir Alexander Cadogan, Permanent Under-Secretary of State for Foreign Affairs 1938–46, confided to his diary,

> Silly bladders! Self-advertising, irresponsible nincompoops. How I *hate* Members of Parliament. they embody everything that my training has taught me to eschew — ambition, prejudice, dishonesty, self-seeking, light-hearted irresponsibility, black-hearted mendacity.

However, a few words in White's or the Reform, and another plank in the government's election platform gives way. It is all hugely reassuring. Part of the style is to be sweetly naive and amateurish: in December 1948 a Washington radio station asked various foreign diplomats what they would like for Christmas.

'Peace throughout the world,' said the French ambassador.

'Freedom for all people enslaved by imperialism,' was the reply sent in by the Russian ambassador.

Then came the answer of the British ambassador, Sir Oliver Franks: 'Well, it's very kind of you to ask. I'd quite like a box of crystallized fruit.'

## FRESH GALES OF ASSERTING LIBERTY

In *England in the Eighteenth Century* (1844) Friedrich Engels reported: 'The English have no common interests . . . only out of individual interests do they act together as a whole. In other words, only England has social history. Only in England have individuals as such, without consciously advocating general principles, promoted the advance of the nation.'

The English have an honourable history of Bolshevik-style behaviour, however. As early as 1381, the threat of a poll tax was enough to stir the working classes into revolt. Revolutionary theory was provided by the immortal John Ball, an excommunicated priest: 'My good people, things cannot go well in England, nor ever shall, till everything be made common, and there are neither villeins nor gentlemen, but we shall all be united together, and the lords shall be no greater masters than ourselves' (Froissart's *Chronicle*).

Unfortunately, the excellent fighting talk was not matched by the calibre of negotiator the rebels chose. Wat Tyler of Maidstone had the diplomatic touch of a tavern brawler. It was a hot day in June when Richard II rode out to meet the rebel army at Smithfield, armed with nothing except a willingness to offer any number of empty promises.

Wat Tyler struts across the chronicles of his brief glory, cocky and unawed, a dog determined to make the most of his day. Idly flourishing a dagger in one hand, he shook the king's hand and assured him that 'we shall be good companions'. King Richard readily agreed to the complete dismantling of the Establishment, 'that all men should be free and of one condition'. It was at this point that Tyler's manners let him down badly. He called for a flagon of water and 'rinsed his mouth in a very rude and disgusting fashion before the King's face. And then he made them bring him a jug of beer, and drank a great draught . . .' The situation deteriorated. Insults were exchanged with members of the king's retinue, weapons were produced, and the pride of Maidstone fell half-dead from his wounds—and with him died England's sole opportunity to experience a proletarian revolution.

The worrying thing about the Peasants' Revolt from the point of view of the class struggle is not that the peasants were so easily taken in by the king's 'common touch' but that, in their rampage through London, they killed not only authority figures like the Archbishop of Canterbury but also any foreigners, at least anyone who could not pronounce 'bread and cheese' to their satisfaction.

Xenophobia is so useful to the preservation of the status quo that it was incorporated in a nowadays suppressed verse of the National Anthem:

O Lord our God arise
Scatter her enemies,
And make them fall:
Confound their politics,
Frustrate their knavish tricks,
On thee our hopes we fix,
God save us all.

During the great naval mutiny at Spithead and the Nore in 1797, Henry Long wrote to the Admiralty from HMS *Champion*, at once undeferential and matey: 'Damn my eyes if I understand your lingo . . . but in short give us our Due at once and no more at it, till we go in search of the Rascals the Enemies of our Country.' It did not seem to occur to the mutineers that they might have more in common with French revolutionaries than with the lordly stuffed shirts at the Admiralty. But, to be fair, it should be said that in 1940 the British Establishment had more to lose from democracy than from the fascism against which they united the country. Very few of them put class interests before national liberty.

Dissent, even rebellion, has long been recognized not as a threat but as essential to keep the constitution fresh and rosy. Lord Halifax, in his political credo, *The Character of a Trimmer*, wrote in 1699:

> Our Government is like our climate. There are winds which are sometimes loud and unquiet, and yet with all the trouble they give us, we owe great part of our health unto them; they clear the air, which else would be like a standing pool, and instead of refreshment would be a disease unto us. There may be fresh gales of asserting liberty, without turning into such storms or hurricanes, as that the state should run any hazard of being cast away by them.

John Bull was invented in 1712, along with Nicholas Frog (the Dutch), Lewis Baboon (Louis XIV) and others, by John Arbuthnot in a series of satirical pamphlets. John Bull was a 'boon companion, loving his bottle and his diversion', but very 'apt to quarrel with his best friends, especially if they pretend to govern him'.

The men whose toast had landed butter-side-up at the Restoration dismissed the Republican experiment as an interesting idea doomed to failure: 'the 'rules of commonwealth are too hard for the Bulk of Mankind to come up to', wrote Lord Halifax. Oliver Cromwell, powered by a burning religious inspiration had tried to sustain a very English revolution. There was nothing delicate or polite or Victorian about the English Puritans. 'I beseech you in the bowels of Christ, consider that ye may be mistaken,' Cromwell once roundly advised some stubborn Scots Presbyterians. He was as plain and forthright in his person. He instructed the man who painted his portrait, 'Mr Lely, I desire you would use all your skill to paint my picture truly like me, and not flatter me at all; but remark all these roughnesses, pimples, warts and everything, otherwise I will never pay a farthing for it.' His features seemed set in a mould of integrity. 'If you prove false, I will never trust a fellow with a big nose again,' said his colleague, Sir Arthur Haslerig.

Cromwell was described once as appearing in the House of Commons wearing a cheap and not very clean suit, with specks of blood on the collar—thus launching the now traditional alliance between English Republicanism and artless tailoring. Charles James Fox, originally an enormously wealthy dandy, took to wearing in the House of Commons an old blue frock-coat that he fancied made him look like a veteran American revolutionary. Nowadays Labour Party leaders feel obliged to attend state banquets in lounge suits—which is acceptable enough, because these things can be smoothed over. Where they make their mistake is to dress down for a public ceremony. When Michael Foot appeared on Remembrance Day at the Cenotaph in a donkey jacket, one wag from his own party said, 'I knew we were going to lose the next election when Michael changed his tailor to Millett's.'

No ideologist—not, as he said, 'wedded or glued to forms of government'—Cromwell took the stopper off the Englishman's political consciousness by the simple process of removing the monarchy. As a Puritan, he disdained magic and totems. Calling the troops in to eject the Rump Parliament in 1653, he looked at the mace on the table of the House of Commons and said: 'What shall we do with this bauble? Here, take it away.' But, as a realist, even Cromwell had to start fudging in the end. Walking once with Bulstrode Whitelocke in St James's Park, he suggested that the English preferred a government 'with something of monarchical in it'.

Otherwise they would never agree on anything. And, amid the intellectual bedlam of the time, the heirs of Tyler had found a truer and more measured voice in Gerard Winstanley, the spokesman of the 'Diggers', who very straightforwardly acted upon his belief in human community. It was an ideal of freedom that would have had every landowner in the country wondering if he would not, after all, prefer a government 'with something of a monarchical in it': In his *A Watch-Word to the City of London* (1649) he wrote: '. . . I took my spade and went and broke the ground upon George Hill in Surrey, thereby declaring freedom to the Creation, and that the earth must be set free from entanglements of lords and landlords . . .' His biblical posture was rudely interrupted by a Mr Drake, who arrested him for trespass, but Winstanley went on to address the victors of the Civil War: '. . . now the common enemy is gone, you are all like men in a mist, seeking for freedom, and know not where nor what it is: and those of the richer sort of you that see it are ashamed and afraid to own it . . . For freedom is the man that will turn the world upside down, therefore no wonder he hath enemies.'

Milton, England's first great Republican, believed passionately that the English people should not need to be told what they might read and what they might not read:

> . . . And though all the winds of doctrine were let loose to play upon the earth, so Truth be in the field, we do injuriously, by licensing and prohibiting, to misdoubt her strength. Let her and Falsehood grapple; who ever knew Truth put to the worse, in a free and open encounter?
>
> *Areopagitica*

Cromwell likewise spoke for freedom of conscience. To the dogmatic Scots Presbyterians he complained,

> Your pretended fear lest error should come in, is like the man who would keep all wine out of the country, lest men should be drunk. It will be found an unjust and unwise jealousy to deprive a man of his natural liberty upon a supposition he may abuse it.

Cromwell was caustic, too, about a human tendency that continually needs to be exposed: 'This hath been one of the vanities of our contest . . . Every man saith, "O give me liberty", but give it him and . . . he will not yield it to anybody else.' The freedoms demanded by the Puritans would not be lost, even if Dr Johnson's interpretation of them would be dubiously cavalier: 'In short, Sir, I have got no further than this: every man has a right to utter what he thinks truth, and every other man has a right to knock him down for it.'

The Puritans drew the line at plays and maypoles, of course, but William Congreve, the Restoration playwright, in a 1695 letter to John Dennis, saw a natural association of English liberty and English humour:

> I look upon Humour to be almost of English growth; at least, it does not seem to have found such encrease on any other soil. And what appears to me to be the reason of it, is the great freedom, privilege and liberty which the common people of England enjoy. Any man that has a humour is under no restraint, or fear of giving it vent; They have a proverb among them, which, may be, will shew the bent and genius of the people as well as a longer discourse: 'he that will have a May-Pole, shall have a May-Pole.'

Voltaire paid the common tribute of Anglophiles: 'It is a country where men think freely and nobly, without the restraint of any servile fear. If I followed my inclinations, I would settle here with the sole intention of learning how to think.'

The freedom to give vent to one's opinions, even if merely on a soap box at Hyde Park Corner, provides a channel whereby the Establishment can keep in touch with what people are and are not prepared to put up with. As Disraeli said, 'The English have not committed fewer blunders than others, but being free to criticize their rulers according to individual conscience, have shown themselves as a people more sensible of their errors.'

While Thomas Paine was introducing to the world *The Rights of Man* (1791–2), based on his involvement with the French and American revolutions, a cheerful shapeless figure, Charles James Fox, was introducing his countrymen to some idea of their duty; to the idea, with the impeachment of Warren Hastings, that there might be some moral responsibility attendant upon wealth, power and Empire—that, indeed, the ideal of liberty might be higher than that of patriotism.

Although born to aristocratic privilege, Fox resolutely took the part of French revolutionaries, American freedom-fighters and the Irish, and he saw to it that the British share of the African slave trade was abolished.

As a child he had been utterly spoilt: a champion of the underdog he might be, but he disposed of astronomical sums of money in aristocratic vices. He used to bet heavily and unsuccessfully on horses from his own stable, complaining, 'My horses can run very fast—but they do not like to tire themselves.' Eventually his friends passed a hat round a wide circle of his admirers and came up with enough to provide him with £3000 a year. Offering charity to the great man seemed a ticklish proposition: 'How will he take it?' they worried. But someone who knew him well reassured them: 'Quarterly, I suppose.'

An unlikely hero of the people his profligacy at the gaming tables was matched by his ardour and application in the Commons. His achievement was to establish opposition as part of the constitution, thus bedding in the Englishman's determination to hear both sides of a matter, and indeed making it axiomatic that there is always another side to hear. However, he would never have called himself 'His Majesty's Loyal Opposition' because one of his very few enemies was the king, George IV. He was struck off the Privy Council for toasting: 'Our sovereign Lord, the People.'

## SOBER-SUITED FREEDOM

It is the land that free men till,
That sober-suited Freedom chose,
The land where, girt with friends or foes
A man may speak the thing he will;

A land of settled government,
A land of just and old renown,
Where freedom slowly broadens down
From precedent to precedent . . .

Tennyson, 'You Ask Me Why'

There is some truth in this uninspiring image of English freedom as a sensible, respectable and respectful fellow, easing his belt out notch by notch as his rights are slowly fed to him. But Tennyson was writing in the nineteenth century; everything was working out in some inevitable way for the best, as if by some unseen machinery. All one had to do was be patient, positive and benevolent. In a letter to Thomas Hughes, Charles Kingsley summarized the attitude:

Do the work that's nearest,
Though it's dull at whiles,
Helping when we meet them,
Lame dogs over stiles.

The freedom of the working man has been anything but sober-suited in the past. There were gin riots in 1736 over the freedom to drink gin at a reasonable price. There were the Gordon riots of 1780 – a sort of popular pogrom against Roman Catholics (wealthy ones, anyway) – and put down with swift and sanguinary vigour. Besides 'No popery!' there was the perennial cry, 'No wooden shoes!'; the English working classes were adamant that they would not be reduced to the penury of French peasants and have to wear such foot wear. And in 1820 the mob found itself deeply concerned about George IV's marital situation with regard to Princess Caroline.

In the wake of the French Revolution there were those who wondered if it might not be worthwhile getting one going in England. A broadsheet confiscated in 1793 explained:

> My friends, you are oppressed, you know it. Lord Buckingham who died the other day had thirty thousand pounds yearly for setting his arse in the House of Lords and doing nothing. Liberty calls aloud, ye who will hear her voice, may you be free and happy. He who doe not, let him starve and be DAMNED.
>
> NB Be resolute and you shall be happy. He who wishes well to the cause of Liberty let him repair to Chapel Field at Five O'clock this afternoon, to begin a Glorious Revolution.

The most characteristic riots of the eighteenth century were those for 'Wilkes and Liberty' in the 1760s. An ugly devil, and a member of the notorious Hell-Fire Club, John Wilkes was in 1763 tried and acquitted of seditious libel against the king, George III, in the 45th issue of his weekly, *The North Briton*; '45' became a powerful political slogan. Also in 1763 Wilkes was responsible for a porno-graphic and blasphemous parody of Alexander Pope's *Essay on Man* (1733–4), called *An Essay on Woman*, which purported to come from the pen of the Bishop of Gloucester, Dr William Warburton. Eighteenth-century society was not easily outraged, but as Mrs Harris, wife of the English scholar and statesman James Harris, wrote to her son, the future Earl of Malmesbury, 'His blasphemy with regard to our Saviour is enough to shock even those who never think of religion.'

Irresistibly successful at the polls in his constituency of Brentford, no sooner would Wilkes take his place in the House than his colleagues would pack him off to prison. His public popularity was thereby if anything increased. In prison he was sent 45 pounds of tea and 45 pounds of cheese; 45 hogsheads of tobacco arrived from America. In Brentford 45 chimney-sweeps ceremoniously consumed 45 pounds of beef, 45 pounds of ham, 45 pounds of bread and drank 45 pots of beer. Wilkes' features were found everywhere, even leering from commemorative pottery. His release from prison in 1770 was celebrated in Northampton by 45 couples dancing 'Wilkes's Wriggle'. Thereafter he became associated with all sorts of issues and industrial disputes unconnected with the question of Parliamentary privilege – 'Wilkes and Coalheavers Forever!' He eventually rehabilitated himself and became Lord Mayor of London. In June 1780 he was to be found having rioters shot as they attempted to storm the Bank of England.

There was nothing sober-suited about the Luddites of 1811–12, who smashed the new textile machinery that was taking men's livelihood away. A document found at Chesterfield market shows that they felt less than feudally about their masters:

> I ham going to inform you that there is Six Thousand men coming to you in Apral and then We will go and Blow Parlement house up and Blow up all afour hus labring Peple Cant Stand it No longer dam all Such Roges as England governes but Never mind Ned lud when general nody and his harmy Comes We Will soon bring about the greate Revelution then all these greate mens heads gose of.

More worrying was this letter, left in a colliery manager's house which had been broken into during a riot in 1831, expressing the sober realization and gentle determination of a Durham miner:

> I was at yor hoose last neet and meyd mysel very comfortable. Ye hay nee family and yor just won man on the colliery, I see ye hev a greet lot of rooms and big cellars and plenty wine and beer in them which I got ma share on. Noo I naw some at wor colliery that has three or fower lads and lasses and they live in won room not half as gude as yor cellar. I dont pretend to naw very much but I naw there shudnt be that much difference. The only place we can gan to o the week ends is the yel hoose and heve a pint. I dinna pretend to be a profit, but I naw this, and lots of ma marrers na's te, that were not tret as we owt to be, and a great filosopher says, to get noledge is to naw yer ignerent. But weve just begun to find that oot, and ye maisters and owners may luk oot, for yor not gan to get se much o yor way, wer gan to hev some o wors now . . .

But, while the revolutions of 1848 were toppling governments abroad, the English working classes were slowly building up independent trades unions. Chartism, a genuinely working-class movement with the slogan 'Peacefully if we can, forcibly if we must', proclaimed a dogged loyalty to the constitution. One Wiltshire Chartist stated his political objectives as 'plenty of roast beef, plum pudding and strong beer by working three hours a day'.

In 1889, in the wake of a successful dockyard workers' strike, Jim Connell, one of the dockers, wrote a hymn, *The Red Flag*, which is solemnly, if a little sheepishly, sung whenever two or three members of the Labour Party are gathered together:

> The people's flag is deepest red;
> It shrouded oft our martyred dead;
> And ere their limbs grew stiff or cold
> Their heart's blood dyed its every fold.

Portrait of John Wilkes. Wilkes' popularity was a gentle reminder that 'the power of King, Lords, and Commons, is not an arbitrary power. They are the trustees, not the owners, of the estate.' (Dedication to The Letters of Junius, 1772.)

Keir Hardie (Spy cartoon), who wore a deerstalker hat to his first day in Parliament, not the mythical cloth cap. It was in fact his yellow check trousers which were remarked on.

*Then raise the scarlet banner high*
*Within its shade we'll live and die.*
*Though cowards flinch and traitors sneer,*
*We'll keep the Red Flag flying here.*

It waved about our infant might
When all ahead seemed dark as night;
It witnessed many a deed and vow—
We must not change its colour now.

> It well recalls the triumphs past;
> It gives the hope of peace at last.
> The banner bright, the symbol plain
> Of human right and human gain.
>
> With heads uncovered swear we all
> To bear it onward till we fall.
> Come dungeon dark or gallows grim,
> This song shall be our parting hymn.

Marx's colleague Engels felt, however, that the English couldn't be rushed. In the introduction to *Socialism: Utopian and Scientific* (1892) he wrote:

> . . . But for all that the English working class is moving . . . It moves, like all things in England, with a slow and measured step . . . And if the patience of the movement is not up to the impatience of some people, let them not forget that it is the working class which keeps alive the finest qualities of the English character, and that, if a step in advance is once gained in England, it is, as a rule, never lost afterwards.

As Engels was writing this, Robert Tressell was creating his classic of British socialism, *The Ragged Trousered Philanthropists*, posthumously published in 1914: '. . . if it were possible to construct huge gasometers and to draw together and compress within them the whole of the atmosphere, it would have been done long ago, and we should have been compelled to work for them in order to get money to buy air to breathe . . .' Again around the same time, in 1892, the founder of the Parliamentary Labour Party and the first working-class MP, Keir Hardie, was triumphantly taking his place in the House of Commons. A Scotsman and an ex-miner, he was provided, by History at least, with a cloth cap, although Bernard Shaw would call him 'the damnedest natural aristocrat in the House of Commons'. At last, it seemed, sober-suited freedom had come into his own. But looking around him, as Aneurin Bevan, in *In Place of Fear* (1952), later described the experience of entering Parliament,

> . . . his first impression is that he is in church. The vaulted roofs and stained-glass windows, the rows of statues of great statesmen of the past . . . Here he is, a tribune of the people, coming to make his voice heard in the seats of power. Instead, it seems he is expected to worship; and the most conservative of all religions—ancestor worship.

There is a well authenticated anecdote confirming this impression of ecclesiastical—even feudal—authority that lingers over the Mother of Parliaments and showing that the whole tenor of British constitutional institutions is well designed to produce a knee-jerk response of homage and fealty. A Tory MP, Neil Marten, was showing a group of his constituents round the Houses of Parliament when Lord Hailsham hove into view in full rig as Lord Chancellor of the Realm. 'Neil!' cried Hailsham, and they did at once, all of them.

# THE INDEPENDENT ENGLISHMAN

In an essay, 'The Bravery of the English Common Soldier', Dr Johnson pondered one of life's mysteries, the common Englishman's notion that he is 'born without a master':

> The equality of English privileges, the impartiality of our laws, the freedom of our tenures, and the prosperity of our trade, dispose us very little to reverence of superiors. It is not to any great esteem of the officers that the English soldier is indebted for his spirit in the hour of battle, for perhaps it does not often happen that he thinks much better of his leader than of himself . . . he was born without a master, and looks not on any man, however dignified by lace or titles, as deriving from nature any claims to his respect, or inheriting any qualities superior to his own.
>
> There are some, perhaps, who would imagine that every Englishman fights better than the subjects of absolute governments because he has more to defend. But what has the English more than the French soldier? Property they are both commonly without. Liberty is, to the lowest rank of every nation, little more than the choice of working or starving, and this choice is, I suppose, equally allowed in every country. The English soldier seldom has his head very full of the constitution, nor has there been, for more than a century, any war that put the property or liberty of a single Englishman in danger.

The curious fact remains that Englishmen need not necessarily take seriously a lot of things that other Englishmen hold sacred, like the empire, the Battle of Britain, Boy Scouts, the C. of E., Dr Livingstone, Nelson, Churchill and playing the game—but as for Liberty,

> It is not to be thought of that the Flood
> Of British freedom, which, to the open sea
> Of the world's praise, from dark antiquity
> Hath flowed, 'with pomp of waters unwithstood',
> Roused though it be full often to a mood
> Which spurns the check of salutary bands,
> That this most famous stream in bogs and sands
> Should perish; and to evil and to good
> Be lost for ever. In our halls is hung
> Armoury of the invincible Knights of old:
> We must be free or die, who speak the tongue
> That Shakespeare spake; the faith and morals hold
> Which Milton held.—In every thing we are sprung
> Of Earth's first blood, have titles manifold.

> Wordsworth, 'It is Not to be Thought Of,'

# ACKNOWLEDGEMENTS

*The publishers are grateful to the following for permission to reprint copyright material*

**W. H. Allen** Adrian Mitchell 'Celia, Celia' from *The Picador Book of Erotic Verse* **The Architectural Press** Nikolaus Pevsner *The Englishness of English Art* 1956 © The Estate of Sir Nikolaus Pevsner **Edward Arnold** E. M. Forster *Two Cheers for Democracy* 1951 (USA © Harcourt Brace Jovanovich) **Athena** G. Damis Nikos *Kazantzakis England* 1970 **Jonathan Cape** John Keegan *The Face of Battle* 1976 Philip Mason *The Men Who Ruled India* 1963 (Reprinted by permission of Anthony Shiel Associates) **Cassell** John Laffin *Tommy Atkins* 1966 **The Daily Express** J. B. Morton ('Beachcomber') 'By The Way' column **Duckworth** Hilaire Belloc *Complete Verse* 1954 **Faber and Faber** Jan Morris* *Farewell to Trumpets* 1978 **Hamish Hamilton** Nancy Mitford* *The Pursuit of Love* 1945 **Heinemann** Bob Cooper *A Song For Every Season* 1971 **Hodder and Stoughton** Geoffrey Moorhouse *To the Frontier* 1984 **Hogarth Press** Nirad Chaudhuri *Autobiography of an Unknown Indian* 1987 **Hutchinson** John Chandos *Boys Together* 1984 **The Independent** Peter Dunne report 16 January 1989 **Herbert Jenkins** P. G. Wodehouse *Right Ho, Jeeves* 1934 *Thank You, Jeeves* 1934 **Macdonald** Alan Wykes* *Abroad* 1973 **Macmillan** (London and Basingstoke) A. G. Macdonell *England Their England* 1933 (USA © St Martin's Press Inc. NY) Osbert Sitwell *Left Hand Right Hand* 1945 **Methuen** Noel Coward *The Lyrics of Noel Coward* 1983 Brian Gardner *Churchill in his Time* 1968 **Midas Books** (Tunbridge Wells) Sydney Greenwood 'Stoker Greenwood's Navy' 1983 **John Murray** John Betjeman 'The Olympic Girl' from *Collected Poems* 1958 **Oxford University Press** Lord Berners** *First Childhood and Far from The Madding War* NE 1983 **Putnam** Bruce Lockhart *The Marines Were There* 1950 **Routledge** Dennis Kincaid *British Social Life in India* 1937 **Salamander Press** Redmond O'Hanlon *Into the Heart of Borneo* 1984 **The Sun** quote from Clive Lloyd **The Sunday Times** Dudley Doust report 5 June 1977 **Quartet Books** Aneurin Bevan *In Place of Fear* NE 1979 George Hutchinson *The Last Edwardian at No. 10* 1980 **Sidgwick & Jackson** David Miller *England's Last Glory* 1986 **The Times** World Cup victory report 1966 Gerald Davies report 12 February 1989 **Viking Penguin** Jan Morris* *Pax Britannica* NE 1979 **Weidenfeld & Nicolson** Raymond Carr *English Fox Hunting* 1976 **Yale University Press** Mark Girouard *The Return to Camelot* 1981.

\* *Reprinted by permission of the Peters Fraser & Dunlop Group Ltd.* \*\* *Reprinted by permission of Oxford University Press.*

*Every effort has been made to trace the owners of copyright but the publishers apologize to any owners whose rights have been unwittingly infringed.*

PICTURE CREDITS

Reproduced by permission of the Cecil Beaton Estate *back cover*; Reproduced by permission of the Trustees of the British Museum 158, 176; E.T. Archive *front cover*, 170; Express Newspapers 184; Hulton Deutsch Collection 26, 173, 189; Mansell Collection 9, 25, 124, 217 (right); National Gallery, London *frontispiece*, 68; National Maritime Museum, London 50, 63; National Maritime Museum, London/Photo Bridgeman Art Library 59; National Portrait Gallery, London 34, 54, 88, 96, 142, 162, 217 (left); The Parker Gallery/Photo E.T. Archive 122; Popperfoto 195; Reproduced by permission of *Punch* 32; Reproduced by kind permission of The Queen's Regiment 28; Tate Gallery, London 6, 73, 77, 146, 179, 182; Tate Gallery London/Photo Bridgeman Art Library 136; Reproduced by courtesy of the Board of Trustees of The Victoria & Albert Museum 20, 38, 80, 101.

# INDEX

*Page numbers in italics refer to illustration captions.*